THE DUBLIN-BELFAST DEVELOPMENT CORRIDOR:
IRELAND'S MEGA-CITY REGION?

T0326309

The Dublin-Belfast Development Corridor: Ireland's Mega-City Region?

Edited by John Yarwood
Former Director, Urban Institute, Ireland

Foreword by Sir Peter Hall
University College, London

Routledge
Taylor & Francis Group

LONDON AND NEW YORK

First published 2006 by Ashgate Publishing

2 Park Square, Milton Park, Abingdon, Oxon OX14 4RN
711 Third Avenue, New York, NY 10017, USA

Routledge is an imprint of the Taylor & Francis Group, an informa business

First issued in paperback 2016

British Library Cataloguing in Publication Data

The Dublin-Belfast development corridor: Ireland's mega-city region? – (Urban and regional planning and development series)
   1.Regional planning – Ireland – Congresses 2.City planning
   – Ireland – Dublin – Congresses 3. City planning – Northern
   Ireland – Belfast – Congresses 4.Dublin (Ireland) –
   Economic conditions – 21st century – Congresses 5.Belfast
   (Northern Ireland) – Economic conditions – 21st century –
   Congresses
   I.Yarwood, John R.
   307.1'2'09415

Library of Congress Cataloging-in-Publication Data

The Dublin-Belfast development corridor: Ireland's mega-city region? / edited by John Yarwood.
      p. cm -- (Urban and regional planning and development series)
   Includes index.
   ISBN 0-7546-4702-1
   1. Regional planning – Ireland. 2. Regional planning – Northern Ireland. 3. Regional planning – Ireland – Dublin Metropolitan Area. 4. Regional planning – Northern Ireland – Belfast Metropolitan Area. 5. City planning – Ireland – Dublin Metropolitan Area. 6. City planning – Northern Ireland – Belfast Metropolitan Area. 7. Economic development. I. Yarwood, John R. II. Series: Urban and regional planning and development.

   HT395.I73D73 2006
   307.1'209417--dc22   2006006429

ISBN 978-0-7546-4702-7 (hbk)
ISBN 978-1-138-26249-2 (pbk)

Contents

List of Figures

List of Tables

About the Authors

Derek Birrell

Derek Birrell is Professor of Social Administration and is currently Head of the School of Policy Studies at the University of Ulster. He has carried out research and published widely on the topics of local government, policy making, devolution, voluntary sector and housing policy. He has carried out a number of studies on aspects of cross-border cooperation in Ireland including collaboration in health, housing, personal social services and the voluntary and community sector. In 2000 he completed a major study on cross border cooperation in local government funded by the Centre for Cross-Border Studies in Armagh.

Niall Cussen

Mr Niall Cussen is a Senior Planning Adviser with the Spatial Planning Section and Heritage and Planning Division of the Department of the Environment Heritage and Local Government. Since January 2000, Mr Cussen has been a key member of the team that prepared the National Spatial Strategy. Since the Governments adoption and launch of the strategy in November 2002, Mr Cussen has been closely involved in its implementation through interactions with Government Departments and Agencies as well as Regional and Local Authorities.

Educated at the National University of Ireland Maynooth and University College Dublin, where he graduated with a Masters degree in Regional and Urban Planning in 1989 and a former president of the Irish Planning Institute, Mr Cussen has worked as a planner for over 15 years in a broad range of urban and rural contexts in both forward planning and development management as well as at local and national levels. The experience above has included working in authorities as diverse as counties such as Clare and Meath, Dublin City, An Bord Pleanala giving Mr Cussen a unique insight into the Irish Planning System.

Menelaos Gkartzios

Menelaos Gkartzios is a is a graduate of the Agricultural University of Athens and University College Dublin with degrees in Agricultural Economics and Rural Development and Environmental Resource Management. He is currently a Researcher in Urban Institute Ireland and Department of Planning and Environmental Policy, University College Dublin. His research interests include rural housing and consumer preferences, counter urbanisation trends, rural development and urban-rural relationships. Menelaos is currently undertaking research on metropolitan decentralisation in the Dublin city-region, which is funded by the Higher Education Authority through Urban Institute Ireland.

Philip Geoghegan

Philip Geoghegan is Senior Lecturer in the MSc Urban Design Programme in UCD School of Architecture, Landscape and Civil Engineering. He is also Principal of iCON Architecture and Urban Design, which has recently won the Irish Planning Institute Award for Conservation in Planning, and was previously commended in the European Conservation Awards for the publication, 'Building Sensitively in Ireland's Landscape'. He is currently acting as vice-chairman of the Europa Nostra/European Union Awards for Conservation, which is an annual award scheme attracting over 250 entries throughout Europe. He is a partner in a reseach programme between the Universities of Oulu, Finland, UCD, and the Technical University of Budapest, in a common research entitled *Heritage at Risk, Europe's Disappearing Villages*.

Jim Hetherington

Jim Hetherington is a Principal Planner in the Department for Regional Development, Northern Ireland. He had over 25 years experience of land use development control and development plan preparation in the public sector before joining the team that prepared the first UK spatial plan. Currently he has responsibility to lead in monitoring and managing the implementation of the Regional Development Strategy for Northern Ireland, interregional cooperation in spatial planning, developing key stakeholder involvement and collaborative working with academic institutions. He has a strong interest in promoting spatial planning education and skill transfer by practioners.

Brian Kelly

Brian Kelly is a graduate of the University of Ulster at Coleraine and Queens University of Belfast, from which he respectively holds the degrees of Bachelor of Environmental Science and Master of Town & Country Planning. His Masters thesis investigated Border Networking as a means of superseding polycentric development, with the aim of devising a strategy for transnational peripheral regions - for which he received the Hawker Siddeley Prize from the University's Faculty of Engineering. He is now employed by a leading independent planning consultancy in the United Kingdom. Other professional interests include the evolving science of comprehensive development, including the preparation of *Concept Masterplans* and *Design Concept Statements*.

Malachy McEldowney

Malachy McEldowney is Professor of Town and Country Planning at the School of Environmental Planning in Queen's University of Belfast and was Head of School between 1993–2002. He worked as an architect in Belfast and London and was a professional town planner in Leicester between 1973–79. He joined Queen's University from De Montford University in 1981. He was Visiting Professor to the School of Architecture and Urban Planning in the University of Kansas in 1984 and to the University of Niteroi, Rio de

Janeiro, in 1988. His research interests incorporate urban design and conservation, but in the past few years have focused on public participation in planning, including a key role in the public consultation programmes for the Regional Development Strategy for Northern Ireland and the Belfast Metropolitan Area Plan. He has published widely in the above subject areas and last year was editor and contributor to the four-volume EU COST research series on Outskirts of European Cities.

Niamh Moore
Dr Niamh Moore is a Lecturer in the Department of Geography, University College Dublin. She teaches contemporary and historical urban geography; social geography; and the geographical implications of globalisation processes. Niamh's main research interests are in urban regeneration, particularly of former industrial sites, and urban heritage and sustainability. She is a Research Associate of the Urban Institute Ireland and is Co-convenor of its Housing, Land and Sustainable Communities Research Cluster.

Michael Murray
Michael Murray is Reader in Spatial Planning in the School of Planning, Architecture and Civil Engineering at Queen's University, Belfast. He holds a PhD in Planning from Queen's University and is a Member of the Irish Planning Institute and the Royal Town Planning Institute. His research interests include rural planning and development, participatory governance, and strategic spatial planning on all of which he has published widely.

Brendan Murtagh
Dr Brendan Murtagh is a Reader in Environmental Planning at Queens University and chartered town planner with extensive experience in urban regeneration in Northern Ireland. Dr Murtagh has researched and written extensively on urban and regional development policy and is a member of the *Best Practice Panel* of the British Urban Regeneration Association (BURA). He has recently worked with the Department for Social Development on the Neighbourhood Renewal Strategy, *People and Place*, in Northern Ireland and on the EU URBAN Community Initiative in Belfast and Derry/Londonderry.

Derry O'Connell
Derry O'Connell, an architect and town planner, lectures at the School of Geography, Planning and Environmental Policy, University College Dublin. He has worked with local authorities in Dublin and with The National Building Agency where he headed the Urban Design Unit, preparing regeneration plans for many Irish towns. His current research concentrates on the operational structure of small towns in Europe. He has lived and worked in both the Republic of Ireland and Northern Ireland.

Chris Paris

Chris Paris holds degrees in Geography (BA Hons., Soton), Town & Regional Planning (MPhil., Glasgow) and Urban Research (PhD 'Social theory and housing policy', ANU). Chris has been Professor of Housing Studies at the University of Ulster since September 1992, having previously spent 6 years at the University of Canberra, where he was Director of the Australian Centre for Local Government Studies between 1986 and 1989. Chris is a member of the Centre for Research on Property and Planning, in the University of Ulster's School of the Built Environment, and a member of the 5-rated Built Environment RAE unit of assessment. He is a corporate member of the Planning Institute of Australia and an associate of the Urban Institute of Ireland. He is an Honorary Professor at the Centre of Urban Planning and Environmental Management at the University of Hong Kong and Adjunct Professor in Social Science and Planning at RMIT University, Melbourne.

Chris has over 30 years experience in universities in the UK, Ireland and Australia. He has over a hundred publications in scholarly and professional journals, as well as authorship of many books and research monographs. His most recent book *Housing in Northern Ireland and comparisons with the Republic of Ireland* was published in December 2001 in the Chartered Institute of Housing 'Policy and Practice' series. He has recently completed research, funded by the Northern Ireland Housing Executive, on demographic change and housing need in Northern Ireland. His ongoing research and writing includes housing and urban-regional change in Ireland, collaboration in research on affordable housing in Australia, and developing comparative research on second homes across borders.

John Prosser

John Prosser was appointed to the Faculty at the University of Colorado in 1966 and currently Professor of Architecture and Urban Design. John Prosser is also a former Dean of the College as well as a Director of the Urban Design programme for 15 years. He created the original environmental impact assessment course in 1970, taught it for 10 years and managed numerous EIA's from a few hectares up to 240 square kilometres. John has maintained a private practice since 1969 and has worked in many western states on large-scale city, airport, campus, research, corporate, business, retail and neighbourhood projects. For many years John has been a member of six national, states, city and private design review boards. He graduated from Kansas University in 1955 with BSc in Architecture later with MArch degree from Carnegie Mellon University in 1961. Between his studies he became a pilot in USAF SAC command. John is listed in *Who's Who in the World, in America* and *Among America's Teachers*. Over 20 years he has been a member of the Urban Land Institute while serving on both the Community Development and Affordable Housing Councils. His wife, Ann is a psychologist, they together have five children and divide their time living in Denver and Donegal.

Declan Redmond

Dr Declan Redmond is a lecturer in the Department of Regional and Urban Planning at University College Dublin. He is Programme Director of the Master of Regional and Urban Planning degree and teaches modules on housing and planning, planning methodologies, environmental assessment and property development. His principal research interests revolve around housing and planning. He has undertaken doctoral work on regeneration and tenant participation and is currently involved in projects investigating housing affordability; the role of private residents associations in the planning system; and the participation of disadvantaged communities in the planning system. He is a Research Associate of Urban Institute Ireland and is involved in the Housing, Land and Sustainable Communities research cluster. He is also a research associate of the Centre for Urban and Regional Studies at Trinity College Dublin and is a board member of Cluid Housing Association.

Mark Scott

Dr Mark Scott is Director of Research and Lecturer in the Department of Regional and Urban Planning, University College Dublin, where he lectures in Rural Planning and Management and Public Policy and Governance. His main research interests include urban and rural development and territorial governance, and ongoing research projects include examining spatial policy in rural Ireland, participatory processes and public policy, and transport and urban planning. Mark is a Research Associate of the Urban Institute Ireland and is co-convenor of its Housing, Land and Sustainable Communities Research Cluster.

Martin Sokol

Dr. Martin Sokol joined Urban Institute Ireland, University College Dublin, as a Post-doctoral Research Fellow in January 2003. His main research interests include the issue of the 'knowledge-driven economy' and its implications for cities and regions in Europe. He has been involved in a number of research projects including POLYNET, a major European project on geography of advanced producer services and the sustainable management of European Polycentric Mega-City Regions. Martin is a graduate of the University of Bratislava (Slovakia) in Architecture and Town Planning. He gained a Master's Degree in Town and Regional Planning from the University of Grenoble (France) and holds a doctorate from the University of Newcastle upon Tyne (England, UK) on regional development. He is currently a Lecturer in Geography at Queen Mary, University of London.

Chris van Egeraat

Van Egeraat is a research fellow at the Department of Geography/National Institute for Regional and Spatial Analysis, National University of Ireland (NUI) Maynooth. He holds a doctorate degree from Dublin City University Business School. Van Egeraat has been employed as a research officer at the Economic and Social Research Institute, the former Centre for Local and Regional Development at NUI

Maynooth, Dublin City University Business School and Urban Institute Ireland, University College Dublin. On a contract basis he has been involved in various research projects, including: The European Observatory for SMEs; Enterprise Ireland Sector Competitiveness Project and the Interreg 3 North European Trade Axis (NETA) project. His research work and publications focus on the subject of global production networks and regional development. Van Egeraat is a member of the Committee of the Regional Studies Association Irish Branch and functions as the Royal Irish Academy contact person for the Geography of the Information Society Commission of the International Geographical Union. Email:cvane@nuim.ie

Jim Walsh
Professor Jim Walsh, D.Litt., is Vice President for Innovation and Strategic Initiatives at NUI Maynooth where he was Head of the Department of Geography between 1995 and 2005. A founding member of the National Institute for Regional and Spatial Analysis (NIRSA) and the International Centre for Local and Regional Development (ICLRD) he has published extensively on a wide variety of topics related to regional and rural development and spatial planning. Recent books include *Regional Planning and Development* (2000), Ashgate Publishing (co-edited with D. Shaw and P. Roberts) and *Partnerships for Effective Local Development* (2004), ULB (co-edited with J. Meldon). He has been appointed to several national fora including the National Economic and Social Council, and the Expert Advisory Group for the National Spatial Strategy. At present he is the representative for Ireland in the European Spatial Planning Observation Network (2002–2006). He is a strong advocate of strategic spatial planning throughout the island of Ireland.

John Yarwood
Dr Yarwood was born in 1946. He holds a Batchelor of Architecture from Edinburgh University and both a Masters degree in Urban and Regional Planning and a Doctorate from Sheffield University. His career began in English local government, and he was Head of Architecture at Telford Development Corporation from 1978 to 1984. He was Head of Urban Renewal department for the Government of Bahrain, and then worked in consultancy in eastern Europe and the Middle East. He worked as an internal consultant for the World Bank in China and elsewhere, and was then Director of Reconstruction in the European Union Administration of Mostar from 2004 to 2007. His book 'Rebuilding Mostar' was published by Liverpool University Press. He then led the preparation of the Cork Area Strategic Plan. He contributed to the Greater Dublin Area Regional Planning Guidelines, before joining the Urban Institute Ireland. After leaving UCD in 2004, he returned to consultancy, working in Dubai, Aden and currently Albania. He has taught at MIT, Rutgers, IHS, Glasgow School of Art and elsewhere. He was elected to be a Fellow of the Royal Asiatic Society, and in 1998 was appointed MBE. His current position is that of International Planning Consultant.

Foreword
By Sir Peter Hall

The Dublin-Belfast Corridor could be like Thurber's Unicorn in the Garden: a mythical beast. But students of Thurber might remember the ending of that tale, so politically incorrect that nowadays no one would publish it: the husband saw the beast, his wife insisted it was mythical and tried to get him declared insane, but he managed to turn the tables and saw her taken away to the booby hatch. Thurber's moral was: 'Don't count your boobies before they are hatched'. You might say that this is also the point of this book.

The reason is that the distinguished contributions, most co-authored by contributors from the two halves of the Irish border, manage to establish pretty definitively that the Dublin-Belfast corridor is a myth. Developed in the wake of the Good Friday agreement, it has been a useful device in bringing together both academics and policy-makers from the Republic and the Province in pursuit of a common objective – to such a degree that it became the theme of a major conference in 2003, from which this book has resulted. And there was every reason to promote the concept, because – as even the most casual visitor will know – the corridor has long been singularly under-developed. Its transport infrastructure was until recently perhaps the poorest connecting any two major cities in the whole of western Europe. That, it could be argued, was the result of the extraordinary 30-year-history of the Troubles north of the border, which had inhibited investment and almost stopped development in Northern Ireland generally and in Belfast in particular. With this totally artificial constraint removed, it could confidently be asserted, the corridor would rapidly assume its rightful role alongside other transnational European examples like Paris-Brussels, Brussels-Amsterdam or Amsterdam-Cologne.

There was an additional reason for this enthusiasm: European policy, enshrined in the 1999 final version of the European Spatial Development Perspective, officially promoted the idea of polycentric urban development. True, the major thrust of that policy was at the European scale, promoting development outside the central European pentagon bounded by London, Paris, Milan, Munich and Hamburg. But the concept could apply equally at regional level, to promote the development of polycentric mega-city-regions which would help promote more sustainable development around overheated and congested core cities like London or Dublin. Polynet, a major EU-funded project which provided the basis for several chapters, aimed specifically to study such regions; the Dublin-Belfast corridor logically became one of eight regional case studies in North West Europe.

But, as the essays show, there is little evidence of the emergence of a corridor, or of polycentric development more generally, as yet. Dublin is beginning to spread out into a ring of satellite towns which as yet are mainly dormitories but which planners hope to develop as real counter-magnets. Yet if anything growth is stronger west of Dublin, along the highways to Galway and Limerick, than along the new motorway towards Belfast. There is not much evidence, so far, of border effects between the adjacent towns of Dundalk and Newry, despite official efforts to promote cooperation – most notably, through the new connecting motorway across the border which is under construction as this book goes to press.

That might change in the longer run. John Yarwood, in a thoughtful concluding essay, posits that within twenty years new infrastructure, notably a high-speed train connecting the two major cities, could transform geographical space, promoting the growth of such border places. That may well prove to be the case: spatial impacts, whether of political changes or new investments, take decades to work themselves out.

Peter Hall
Bartlett School of Planning
University College London

Preface

Urban Institute Ireland plays many roles, but a key one is advancing our understanding of city regions and their functioning from a variety of perspectives. Dublin and Belfast dominate the urban landscape in the island of Ireland, and understanding their interaction and the potentials in this regard is clearly an important issue. Space between them is shrinking as transport infrastructure continues to shorten travel times. By late 2007, it should be possible to drive all the way on divided highway between the two, and there are now eight trains a day each way, with a travel time of just over two hours. Although in demographic and economic terms they are dominant in Ireland, internationally they are only medium sized cities. An idea that has intrigued many over the years is whether they together could provide the critical mass to better compete on the world stage, benefiting not only themselves, but the island as a whole. The concept also raises the role and collaborative potential for smaller adjacent urban areas along the corridor, namely Newry in Northern Ireland, and Dundalk in the Republic of Ireland. Their challenge is to ensure that they benefit from the dynamism of Belfast and Dublin, rather than finding that their potential is drained by the centrifugal forces that grow ever stronger at both ends of the corridor.

Rivalry is good when it drives new ideas and innovations. It is bad when it results in the world being viewed as a zero sum game – whatever is good for Belfast must be bad for Dublin and vice versa. Creating sufficient understanding about potentials and perspectives so that we can find mutually beneficial collaborative space that transcends cultural clichés, historic enmities, and differing political systems, currencies, economic and social policies, is what this book is about. Cities and the societies and institutions that run them are complex organisms not easily moved to make radical choices. This book is designed to help move the debate forward.

I am pleased that Urban Institute Ireland took a leading role in bringing these ideas to the table. In this context, I am especially grateful to John Yarwood, then director of UII, for providing the leadership to make the conference happen, and subsequently to stay the course and engage in the tedious chivvying of recalcitrant authors to bring promise to reality in the form of this book.

Frank J. Convery, Director
Urban Institute Ireland
www.urbaninstitute.net

Acknowledgements

Obviously my main gratitude must go to those authors who contributed chapters to this book, but there also were a lot of others who played vital roles in its preparation.

The 2003 conference in Newry was chaired by Bill Morrison, and he did a superb job, authoritative but relaxed and witty. He was also a leading light on the committee which planned the conference. The main liaison with the two government departments occurred through Niall Cussen in Dublin and Jim Hetherington in Belfast. Also Newry and Mourne council played a strong role, with enthusiastic support never lacking. I should particularly mention Gerry McGivern, their Development Director. Several people gave quite a lot of time to the design-brainstorm sessions which prepared the hypothetical regional plan for the corridor. The members of this group included Professor Bill Morrison, (former City Architect and Planning Officer for Belfast), Sean O'Laoire, (a consultant architect-planner from Dublin), Henk van der Kamp, (Head of the Planning Department, Dublin Institute of Technology), Dr William Hynes, (of the Planning Department at UCD), and Professor Malachy McEldowney, (of the Planning Department at Queen's University Belfast, all of whom made a great contribution). The task of organising the conference was taken on by Brenda O'Hanlon, Harriet Duffin and Jane Governey. That it was such a success is largely due to their professionalism and hard work.

Turning now to the Greater Dublin Area Regional Planning Guidelines (RPG,) the involvement of Urban Institute Ireland arose from an invitation from Jack Sheehan and Conall MacAongusa of Atkins Ireland. They led the efforts of the overall team, with skill and energy. Particular acknowledgements are due to Bernard Feeney (of Goodbody Economic Consultants), for his work on the topic of economic development, and to David Jordan for his work on demography. Some important parts of this book are based on their outstanding contributions to the Guidelines. We should also thank Mary Darley, the team leader on behalf of the client, for her guidance and support.

The POLYNET project, 'The Sustainable Management of Polycentric Mega-City Regions in North Western Europe' included an Irish team comprising Martin Sokol, Chris van Egeraat and myself. We are grateful to all the participants from the other universities, but most especially to the Institute of Community Studies, London (now The Young Foundation). This was the lead team, and I must mention especially Sir Peter Hall, Kathy Pain and Nick Green. Much of the thinking in this book arises directly from their vision. The Global and World Cities (GaWC) Study Group and Network at Loughborough University also played a key role in the analytical work of this research project. Particular thanks should go to Professor

Peter Taylor, the Co-Director, as well as David Evans, David Walker and Dr Michael Hoyler, all of whom made a vital contribution to the methodology.

Also, I am grateful to Gearoid O'Riain and Aiden Power for help on both graphics and the mathematics associated with the POLYNET work. The Dublin Transportation Office, and particularly John Henry, the Director, Mick McAree and Eoin Farrell, were also immensely helpful, and much of that has also found its way into the book. Regarding both POLYNET and the RPG, I must thank Dr Andrew MacLaran (of Trinity College) for his contribution to our debate. He led a number of seminars and gave several deeply impressive lectures at the Urban Institute Ireland about aspects of contemporary change in the structure of Greater Dublin.

Finally, of course, I must pay tribute to the Urban Institute Ireland itself, based at University College Dublin. Maeve McAleer, the Administrator, performed all those duties of support which enabled the conference, the consultancy and the research project to proceed smoothly, and she did it with dedication and skill. Additionally, I am grateful to Brendan O'Donoghue, the Chairman of the Institute and to Professor Frank Convery as well as Professors Anngret Simms and Loughlin Keely, for their cheerful support and avuncular advice when it was much needed.

Obviously, there have been many other people contributing directly and indirectly to this book. I am probably omitting to mention the names of many who deserve mention, and I must now beg forgiveness for this. Also, it has inevitably fallen to my editorial lot to engage in synthesis and linkage of separate contributions. This is a risky job, fraught with possible misunderstandings. Therefore I must express my admiration for the separate contributions from so many sources, but also take the blame where I have been guilty of misinterpretation.

Thanks are due to the Ordnance Survey Ireland for permission to reproduce some of their maps in this publication (Permit no: 8059).

John Yarwood

Chapter 1

Overview and Summary

John R. Yarwood

Former Director, Urban Institute, Ireland

Preamble

This is an amazingly interesting and hopeful time to live and work in Ireland. There are several reasons for thinking this. The political problems in the north are clearly easing, whatever upsets and doubts arise on the way. The Republic in particular has had an astonishing economic efflorescence, and indeed the combination of political calm and the boom of the neighbouring economy have brought benefits to the quality of life in the north. This is manifest in the good, quotidian relations between north and south within the professional, business and academic life of the island. The unthinkable has become quite normal territory for speculation, and mental barriers or narrow institutional loyalties seem well on the way to disappearing.

I remember Peter Hall saying to us some time ago that the Dublin Belfast Corridor would have come into existence long ago, were the sectarian and political divide not so far entrenched, because the economic logic was otherwise invincible. The picture of this divide might resemble the friction which builds up between tectonic plates and then releases itself in a sudden change. If so, there might in future be an unexpected explosion of energy which drives the corridor forward in unexpected ways.

Certainly many people talk as if an economic corridor did already exist or was coming into existence, but as this book indicates, there is precious little concrete evidence of it. Others suggest, (quite reasonably in my view), that anyway it has enormous potential, which is waiting to be released and realized. If there were a vision of the emerging corridor as it is at this moment in history, then it might be a vision of car-commuters driving south to jobs in Dublin, past those streaming north to jobs in Belfast, but this could not be viewed as any form of success.

What do I mean by 'potential'? Here we have two medium-sized or large European cities, one of which has enjoyed an astonishing economic boom, with ports, airports and several good universities, which are linked by an express rail service and by a motorway (most of the way). Between and around these cities are large areas of open countryside, with several small towns, most of which are suburban dormitories in function, (more or less). One of the cities, (at least), is suffering grievously from the results of over concentration of business in its core area allied to car-dependency. The creation of a polycentric region (with efficient internal movement plus the spatial integration of movement with activity), would maximize the scale of markets and improve the spatial balance between workplaces and residences, thus reducing the demand for movement. Perhaps because this answer is so obvious, several contributors argue here that the concept is accepted and that it is built into the strategic and local plans which have already been adopted.

But frankly, I doubt this. For sure, it is on the agenda, but there are few, if any signs of serious commitments at high level and no programme of coordinated action. There is no corridor plan or even the prolegomena for a plan. This book is, (so far as I know), the first such attempt. Why is there little firm progress?

I suspect the truth may be that the Irish do not like to expose grandiose plans, because their instincts lead them to focus on the local, and to allow the big picture to emerge gradually from the automatic coalescing of numerous local visions. This modest, ruralist style gives the country much of its undoubted charm. There will be some missed opportunities, perhaps.

The benefits foregone might be twofold. Firstly, we could enhance the competitiveness of the island in the international marketplace for business locations by increasing the scale of markets accessible regionally and internationally. Secondly, by adopting a more rational settlement and movement pattern, we could ameliorate many of the existing structural difficulties. The journey-to-work distances could be cut if the spatial pattern of jobs were brought closer to that of residences, and the extreme car-dependency were reduced by improving public transport patronage. This would involve the creation of multi-modal movement integrated into activity corridors. More compact settlement forms would protect the countryside in general and water resources in particular.

Introductory Remarks

This book is a collection of essays around the twin topics of the Dublin-Belfast Development Corridor and the associated challenge of cross-border development. The essays span a range of disciplines, including economics, geography, regional studies and urban planning. The authors include academics and senior policy-makers in various sectors.

The Corridor is quite a popular idea and it has been often mentioned in recent years, although more in rhetoric than solid research. See *Figure 1.1 General Location Map of Corridor*. One suspects it remains in the realm of wishful thinking. Indeed, in their contributions to this volume, Chris van Egeraat, Professor Chris Paris and John Yarwood present evidence which by implication questions whether it exists on the ground at all. Some contributors to this volume write as if the idea was an accepted part of official policy, but my impression is a contrary one.

Nevertheless, it is Ireland's only chance to create a polycentric mega-city region on a scale large enough to compete with major urban clusters of continental Europe. It might even be argued that the continuing prosperity of the island depends upon its adoption, (although it has been commented that such a corridor would have emerged already on the ground were it not for the political difficulties associated with a split jurisdiction).

At the very beginning, we should say briefly and simply what the term 'corridor' is taken to mean. A corridor is a linear form which an agglomeration of settlements may take. It could be based on a linear infrastructure system, or an economy which is integrated spatially in a linear structure. The corridor concept may involve linking together several towns or cities, (existing, expanded or new), by various modes of movement and communication so that markets (for labour and skills, suppliers and customers, land and property) are created on a larger scale at a lower movement time/cost than would be the case if the settlements were broadly autonomous. The individuality of the constituent towns could be maintained, however, and 'sprawl' could be strictly avoided. Each town might develop its unique economy and cultural attributes, which would then function in a manner complementary to those of the others, so that the whole system released synergy beyond the scale of the separate parts. An internally balanced and self-sustaining land use and activity pattern within each urban centre is thought to be possible. This is implied by the term 'polycentric', of course. There are reasons to believe that emerging business behaviour and consequent criteria for investment will favour regions having such attributes, and a nation having such a region is likely to be more competitive than those which do not. In such a mega-city region, workers will have access to a greater number and variety of jobs; consumers will have access to superior cultural and commercial facilities; and businesses will likewise have access to larger numbers of employees, skills and training facilities, as well as larger, more competitive markets for both supply and demand for goods, services, land and buildings.

The idea has been frequently mentioned in debate and research about development studies internationally. It is a key theme for the European Union. Curiously, however, in Ireland, it has never been the subject of focused study until now. It is certainly a key idea, and the policy community in Ireland should address its potential more seriously than hitherto.

Corridors Across International Borders

The Dublin-Belfast Corridor is, of course, divided by the only international land border which Britain or the Irish Republic have. There are few other potential or actual development corridors in Europe which are thus divided. One might think of Bratislava/Vienna or Bayonne/San Sebastien. Copenhagen/Malmo is linked by the Oresund bridge, but lacks an actual land border. However, it is probably fair to say that the Dublin/Belfast case is the most significant in Europe, not least because it is very highly politicized. In the discussion below, I am indebted to Patsy Healy for her helpful observations, which are particularly germane to the Irish case.

Building new kinds of cross-border relations has been a major theme in recent European Union regional and spatial development policy. This is in part a consequence of the search for greater economic integration between the national economies of the European Union. It has been supported by the focus on major transnational infrastructure projects. But it is also a consequence of changing economic, social and cultural geographies as the geopolitics of Europe as a whole has shifted, leading to the EU 'enlargement' project. There is now a substantial experience of the consequences of shifts in border geographies and of institutional mechanisms designed to foster particular kinds of improvements in cross-border relations.

There appear to be two dimensions to this experience. The first is the complex nature of the relations and cultural associations which weave across and around political and administrative borders. Borders may cut across previously well-connected areas, or areas which once were perceived as integrated places. Or they may mark deep cleavages in economic and social relations and cultural identities. In most cases, borders are marked and crossed by a diversity of economic and social relations, each with their own spatial patterning and particular way of recognising (or ignoring) a border. This implies that any deliberate initiative in 'border crossing' is entering a complex economic and social terrain which will be re-ordered in some way or other by the initiative. Consequently, it is desirable that a rich understanding is obtained of the nature of the multiple relations and identities in which a border has meaning and impact in order to assess how these will be affected by any initiative.

The second dimension concerns the processes through which initiatives in building sensitive and knowledgeable cross-border relations might evolve. Such initiatives are about creating new institutional capacities, incorporating knowledge resources (intellectual capital), relational resources (social capital) and mobilisation capacity (political capital). Those seeking to take initiatives in building the institutional capacity to promote new kinds of cross-border relations need to make careful choices about how to focus attention (through knowledge and concept development? network building? creating 'arenas'?); who to involve, how and when; and how to develop some legitimacy, authority and acceptability for their actions, both within the immediate area and in the wider constituencies likely to be affected by what they do.

Sources of the Book

The material in the book arises from three principal sources, with which the Urban Institute Ireland (UII) has been intimately involved since January 2003.

- Conference: the Harvard Graduate School of Design-Irish Universities Urban Planning Conference of September 11th–12th 2003, held in Newry City, Northern Ireland, on the subject *The Dublin-Belfast Corridor 2025.*
- Consultancy: the *Greater Dublin Area Regional Planning Guidelines* for the constituent Regional Authorities, submitted and approved in December 2003.
- Research: the Irish contribution to the EU funded INTERREG IIIB project *The Sustainable Management of Polycentric Mega-City Regions in North West Europe,* involving a consortium of eight universities (known as POLYNET), under the overall direction of Sir Peter Hall.

The UII was invited to join the consultancy team, which also included Atkins Ireland, Goodbody Economic Consultants, and Tom Philips Associates. The universities contributing to the POLYNET project were the Sorbonne (Ile de France), Amsterdam (Delta Metropolis), Free University of Brussels (Central Belgium), Heidelberg (Rhein-Main), Dortmund (Rhein-Ruhr), Zurich (Central Switzerland) and the Institute of Community Studies (Southeast England), in addition to the Urban Institute Ireland (Dublin-Belfast). The Global and World Cities (GaWC) consortium based at Loughborough University assisted all the partners with the analysis.

Summary of the Book's Contents

We begin with a literature review by Martin Sokol: (Chapter 2). It expounds some of the main concepts which underpin the substance of this book, including the knowledge economy, the learning region, the world city and the polycentric region. Particular reference is made to the work of Saskia Sassen and the GaWC group at Loughborough university. Some aspects of associated theoretical positions, such as the proposition that knowledge drives economic development, are critically appraised. Finally, Sokol reports the recent efforts in Dublin to stimulate the emergence of a knowledge economy. However, he suggests that Dublin as a city may be too small to succeed in the long term, and proposes that the Dublin-Belfast Corridor might be a way to create a viable critical mass.

After this international review of the academic literature, we move to focus upon practice in Ireland and specifically upon the east coast. The next chapter concerns the two spatial strategies, one for the Republic, (the 'National Spatial Strategy' or NSS,) and the other for Northern Ireland, (the 'Regional Development Strategy' or RDS, also called 'Shaping Our Future'). The general intention is, of course, to place our specific topic in the context of current spatial development policy in Ireland as a whole. The authors are Niall Cussen, Senior Planning Advisor, Department of Environment, Heritage and Local Government, Dublin, and Jim Hetherington, Principal Officer, Department for Regional Development, Belfast. The authors stress the importance of developing strong self-supporting economies in major towns such as Drogheda, Dundalk and Newry, in order to prevent the corridor becoming a commuter belt for the two cities. The need to place the corridor in the framework of balanced development of the island as whole is important, so that the west coast and other remoter areas are not weakened. Finally, the approach to implementation is stressed, and the challenge of 'embedding' the strategy in all aspects of governance is discussed, as well as the role of the private sector.

I asked Professor Jim Walsh, (a prominent geographer and Chairman of the National Institute for Regional and Spatial Analysis), and Dr Michael Murray, (of Queen's University Belfast) to write a critical appraisal of these two official policy documents, and this is Chapter 4. Walsh and Murray make several critical reflections upon both the NSS and the RDS, including the need to link them together, and the need to turn a static concept into a dynamic framework for sustainable change. They make a plea for a strong rural role to be understood, and urban dominance to be avoided. The role of the corridor in the context of the entire island, particularly its less developed parts, is expounded.

At the time when the Urban Institute Ireland was organising the conference on the corridor, we were also starting work on the research project concerning the management of polycentric mega-city regions. The UII was part of a multi-national team, led by Peter Hall and referred to as POLYNET. Several contributions to this book are based on work undertaken for the POLYNET project, including Chapter 5 on the regional structure.

This includes data on the spatial distribution of resident population and economic activity, indicating the serious spatial imbalance between them, and discussing its implications. It also presents data on commuting flows. It considers the regional structure, by devising the rank-size order of settlements, the degree of self-containment, and the statistical measure of functional and special polycentricity. The conclusion is that the Dublin region is mono-centric to a degree unusual in North West Europe.

The Irish planning system, of which the National Spatial Strategy is part, includes 'Regional Planning Guidelines' documents to be prepared by Regional Authorities for their regions. The purpose of an RPG document is to apply the National Strategy to a region in sufficient detail to allow the constituent Planning Authorities, (namely the counties within the region), to prepare the County Development Plans. In the case of Dublin, however, the Mid-East region and the Dublin region are required by statute to prepare a single document known as 'The Regional Planning Guidelines for the Greater Dublin Area', or RPG-GDA. This document, which Urban Institute Ireland helped to prepare, is discussed in Chapter 6.

The data-analysis and policy formulation work is summarized, and the concrete proposals are described. These include the designation of 'satellite towns' around Dublin, with the aim of generating economic expansion there, and improving the spatial balance of residence and work, as well also as improving the integration of development and activity into multi-modal movement corridors. The relationship to the philosophy of polycentric regional development is discussed, as also is the relationship of the guidelines' concept to the corridor.

This review of the context of the corridor began at the large (national) scale and is working down to the local (county/district) scale. It concludes therefore with an account of the current development plans for local areas within the corridor. In the Republic, the plans are the responsibility of the county councils, but Northern Ireland has a different system, and plans are prepared by the district offices of the Department of the Environment, Northern Ireland. In order to present a comprehensive coverage, senior academics from both Dublin and Belfast, namely Professor Malachy MacEldowney and Derry O'Connell, collaborated to prepare Chapter 7.

The local plans considered include those for Meath, Louth, Antrim, Larne, Craigavon and Lisburn. The authors surveyed the attitudes and aspirations of the local planners, and debated these with them. A mixed picture emerges, with considerable interest in, and awareness of the corridor in evidence.

However, it seems clear that a corridor strategy (and the planning necessary to bring it into existence) cannot arise by 'sticking together' a number of adjacent local plans. On the contrary, the first task is to conceive the totality of the corridor concept, and then embed the concept within each constituent locality. This principle is taken up again in the final chapter of the book, when we try to imagine what a corridor plan might look like.

This concludes the first part of the book. Moving on now to the second part, we present seven chapters, each of which focuses upon one sectoral topic. The topics are transportation, service firm connections, land management, urban design, housing, planning and institutions.

Chapter 8 considers the role of transportation in the development and functioning of corridors. The main author is Professor John Prosser, (Department of Architecture and Urban Design, University of Colorado), who was a Visiting Fellow, Urban Institute Ireland. He gives a US perspective to his observations on emerging Irish practice.

Prosser points out that Ireland is currently more car-dependant than the US. He refers to the 'New Urbanism movement and the principles of "Transit Oriented Development' in the US. He reviews the planning work of the Dublin Transportation Office, and considers their work in the field of coordinating public transport and urban structure, including the IFPLUTS planning approach. The principles espoused by the Cork Area Strategic Plan are mentioned, (envisaging a polycentric growth corridor based around a re-opened railway line).

Chapter 9, by Drs van Egeraat and Sokol, is on the subject of connectedness of advanced producer service firms, which we researched as part of our POLYNET work.

The notion of an economic corridor suggests the existence of linkages of some sort between the constituent urban nodes. Research tends to analyse commuter flow data to investigate the existence of economic corridors. Other linkages, notably those involving the flow of resources, goods, services and information are believed to be important, but are seldom analysed in detail, due to the lack of readily available statistics. Chapter 9 aims to address this gap, (in the context of the Dublin-Belfast Corridor). Using data gathered as part of this comparative international research project into polycentric urban regions (POLYNET, Interreg IIIb) this chapter provides a quantitative analysis of intra-firm information flows in advanced producer services sectors.

The authors start with a brief introduction of the study region (mainly the segment of the Dublin-Belfast corridor from Wicklow to Dundalk, although they present some data on the linkages with Newry and Belfast as well) including a history of the development of business services. They then describe two central concepts – 'economic corridor' and 'polycentricity' – and the way these are related. Subsequently they outline the methodology used to analyse service business connections. This involved an investigation of the intra-firm office networks of over 180 multi-locational service firms with offices in the region. Individual offices were coded on the basis of the importance of their functionality in various regional and global urban centres. The resulting matrix was used to calculate the relative situation of centres in the urban network as well as to derive a measure of connectivity (on the regional to the global scale), which was used as a proxy for service-sector information and knowledge flows between urban centres. The next section presents the results. The conclusion is used to discuss the conceptual relevance of the Dublin-Belfast corridor in the light of the connectivity data.

The subsequent chapters tackle other planning themes, beginning with land management and in particular land *delivery* as a vital means to achieve polycentric urban form. This chapter, by Drs Mark Scott, Declan Redmond, Niamh Moore and Menelaos Gkartzios, focusses on three interrelated challenges at a range of spatial scales: firstly, the potential of urban brown field lands for inner-urban consolidation is assessed using a number of criteria, including cost, liability, legislative and environmental issues. This is followed by a discussion relating to edge of city expansion. Thirdly, the relationship between key development nodes in the corridor region and smaller settlements and rural areas is examined. The chapter concludes by highlighting the challenges facing policy-makers in attempting to secure the optimum polycentric urban development of the corridor, including the timing and cost of land delivery, planning procedures and political processes, as well as consumer and lifestyle choice.

Chapter 11 concerns urban design and local environmental quality, pointing out the importance of accommodating the corridor development to the existing historic urban forms and the landscape character. Several short case-studies of small settlements, each with unique historic characteristics, are described, (such as Whitetown, Carlingford, Baltray/Queensborough, Collon and Termonfeckin). The danger is that the process of corridor development might be insensitive to small details, and could perpetrate much damage on the ground. The chapter observes that recent development has been so insensitive that one is justified in having such fears, and it concludes by proposing several helpful principles.

In the corridor conference at Newry in 2003, we had a wonderful talk on 'Cross-Border Trade and the "Digital Island" Programme'. This was given by Aidan Gough, Director of Strategy and Policy, Inter*Trade*Ireland. Unfortunately it has proved impossible for Aidan to make a contribution to this book, but those with a serious interest in this dimension of the corridor should certainly be aware of the work of Inter*Trade*Ireland, and perhaps consult their website. Their remit is the development of cross-border trade and an all-island economy, focusing particularly on the exploitation of digital technology by businesses across the island. Seven project areas are being pursued, such as cross-border telecoms infrastructure, all-island common tariffs, and seamless internet-based services. Inter*Trade*Ireland's operating environment is an island economy straddling two political jurisdictions. Included within its legislative remit is the exchange of information on trade, business development and related matters, (and specifically in the areas of telecommunications, information technology and electronic business). The 'Digital Island' concept has been put forward by Inter*Trade*Ireland, the Department of Enterprise, Trade and Employment in the Republic of Ireland and the Department of Enterprise, Trade and Investment in Northern Ireland as a policy-level framework aimed at seeking the fullest exploitation of the digital technologies by businesses across the island.

The next three chapters concern housing, planning and institutions. Chapter 12, by Professor Chris Paris, explores dimensions of change in the border region, primarily in terms of housing development and population movement, set within the context of an overview of the housing and planning systems in the two jurisdictions. The chapter reviews previous research on housing in the border counties and introduces new census analysis and interview data. This is put into a wider context of changing planning regimes and urban systems within the two jurisdictions, especially the Regional Development Strategy in Northern Ireland and the National Spatial Strategy in the Republic.

Research by Paris and Robson argued that the image of the border region changed during the 1990s: *from* one of a heavily militarized and depressed region experiencing structural economic and social problems, *to* an increasingly de-militarized region with growing prosperity, experiencing rapid growth in private sector housing investment. There were strong signs of increasing cross-border urban development, in both the Dublin-Belfast corridor and in the northwest where Derry was clearly generating 'overspill' development into Co. Donegal. This analysis was put into a context of wider changes within the two jurisdictions, including widespread metropolitan de-concentration, private sector housing booms and re-structuring of social housing systems. The study concluded by arguing that there was both continuity and change within the border region with increasing market inter-relations between the two jurisdictions but continued differences in terms of legal and administrative structures.

Paris and Robson have examined recent census and other housing data in both jurisdictions and attempted to assess whether there has been any distinctive population concentration in the Dublin-Belfast corridor. They also conducted further interviews with planning officials in the border region, mainly during June 2003, to identify whether there have been any significant changes since the earlier study was carried out during 1999–2000, especially in terms of housing and related developments. This chapter presents the first cut analysis of that more recent work.

The census analysis indicates very strong population growth in *all* areas of Dublin's emerging outer commuter belt, with no distinctive concentration in the Dublin-Belfast corridor. Likewise, emerging spatial population trends in Northern Ireland do not indicate any strong Belfast-Dublin component. Paris argues that changes in both jurisdictions show metropolitan de-concentration *generally* from Dublin and Belfast with no particular emphasis on the corridor. This raises the question: 'what corridor?' The interviews with planning officials highlighted the widespread incidence of new housing development throughout the border region, once again calling into question whether there is anything particularly distinctive about the Dublin-Belfast corridor. Planning officials noted extremely high volumes of work and saw few significant barriers to cross-border housing development. It is noted, in passing, that areas of high second home development stand out as having *high* levels of new house building but relatively *low* levels of recorded population increase: especially in north and west Donegal.

The chapter concludes with some preliminary answers to questions about the corridor and also reflects on the capacity of the two planning systems to respond in a 'joined up' way.

The next chapter, by Murtagh and Kelly, examines the topic of planning in cross-border areas of Ireland, including the applicability of the European Spatial Development Perspective, (ESDP.) It makes a conceptual connection between the ESDP and the National Spatial Strategy in the Republic of Ireland and the Regional Development Strategy in Northern Ireland. However, the chapter argues that the utility of the ESDP outside national growth corridors, such as Dublin-Belfast, is limited. Using experience in the North West, it suggests that the city region offers a more locally relevant way to understand cross-border spatial dynamics in peripheral areas. The chapter concludes by drawing out the implication for multi-scalar governance, infrastructure and regional planning in Ireland.

The chapter by Professor Derek Birrell, concerns the institutional arrangements which have emerged to deliver cross-border initiatives. They seem to have an *ad hoc* quality, and the reason for this may be the political distance between the two sides in the North, which makes them reluctant to envisage profound, permanent arrangements at this time. Perhaps it is more sensible to continue to practice and slowly refine ostensibly *ad hoc* approaches.

Cross border co-operation between local authorities has increased substantially in the last twenty years. The major impetus for the growth of co-operation came from two sources, namely local political initiatives and EU funding initiatives.

Another influence has been those facilitating mechanisms, (mainly NGOs), which have aimed to foster and develop cross border co-operation, (particularly the Local Authority Linkages Programme of Co-operation Ireland). Cross border co-operation in local government has to be set in the context of some significant differences between the two jurisdictions in terms of structure, functions, forms of governance and politics.

Five different forms of cross-border linkages can be identified: one-to-one linkages between councils; local government cross border networks; linkages between councils and another public body; partnerships involving local authorities; and transnational local authority linkages.

The main focuses of cross border projects have tended to be economic development, tourism, community services and urban and rural development. The most developed models of co-operation are three cross border networks. The networks known as North West Region, East Border Region and Irish Central Border Area (ICBAN) have adopted a regional border corridor approach with an emphasis on infrastructural and economic development. A number of different models of managing cross-border cooperation have emerged. The achievements here must also be seen in the context of overcoming a number of political, attitudinal, structural and practice barriers to cooperation.

In the final chapter of the book offers a visionary perspective. We have attempted to synthesize key conclusions or insights from earlier chapters, and to present them (in an imaginative but concrete manner) as planning proposals about an eastern seaboard development corridor. It has been evident that few people, if any, have a concrete (let alone an agreed) picture of what the Dublin-Belfast Corridor might look like. The organisers of the 2003 conference therefore decided to produce a hypothetical physical plan as a reference point for debate. This chapter arose from a series of design-debates or 'charettes' led by the author. A plan is presented. It is not to be taken as a well-researched and debated proposition such as a consultant might bring forward. Its aim is to intrigue and inspire, and to stir debate. In particular, the message is that a corridor plan will not emerge by 'sticking together' numerous local plans, but, on the contrary, a vision for the entire corridor should inform the plans for all the constituent segments.

In the first part, several key principles or policies are described, and their application in reality, on the ground, is made clear. These include the creation of a multi-modal movement system, with linkages between modes, (e.g. train and car,) at interchange points, (where stations, bus stops and car parks are closely integrated). These would be the nodal places of maximum accessibility, where existing settlements as well as key future investment zones are located. Proactive delivery of serviced land, is the second principle. The third principle is the sensitive accommodation of development to local landscapes. The principles of polycentric spatial structuring within the corridor concept are debated.

The second part presents the physical plan. The plan incorporates the structure of the Greater Dublin Area Regional Planning Guidelines; (as described in an earlier chapter). A long-term structure for the Greater Belfast Metropolitan Area, consistent with the corridor concept, arose from the 'charette', and is also mooted here. The chapter concludes with some general observations about the implementation issues.

Conclusion

The book aims to put the corridor idea more firmly on the public agenda. Most people will be aware that it is controversial in two spatial dimensions: north-south and east-west. Oddly enough, the latter may be the most enduring argument. In other words, the north and south of this island may find it possible to cooperate in the creation of a corridor because both north and south could reap a handsome dividend. On the other hand, the rural west may bury their north/south differences in order to rescue their remote regions from a shared economic decline. It does seem likely, however, that the continuously increasing prosperity of an eastern corridor will drive success in the west of the island, whilst a policy which restrained such prosperity in order to 'save' the west, will inadvertently curtail the key drivers of the west's economy.

This book may seem to contain a contradiction. On the one hand, most of the contributors take it for granted that the corridor is an inevitable and desirable idea, or even that it exists already, or is in the process of coming about. On the other hand, Yarwood (in Chapter 5), Van Egeraat and Sokol (in Chapter 9) and Paris (in Chapter 12) argue that it is not in existence at this time, and they present the evidence for that assertion. The corridor exists, it would seem, as an aspiration in the minds of many. Is it any more than that? But beyond this, the question is whether it should become an objective of public policy.

Certainly this book poses more questions than it prescribes answers. But the aim, in any case, is to stimulate continuing study and debate around the corridor theme. In Ireland, this has not been as focused or as lively as it should have been. The two official spatial strategy documents do not, in my opinion, address the topic head on, (although the senior political figures and expert civil servants on both sides of the border are well aware of the issues and willing to converse on the matter). It would be good if they gave a more proactive push, since the formation of a well planned and managed corridor might offer the best chance for competitive success in international place-marketing and hence increasing investment, employment and prosperity.

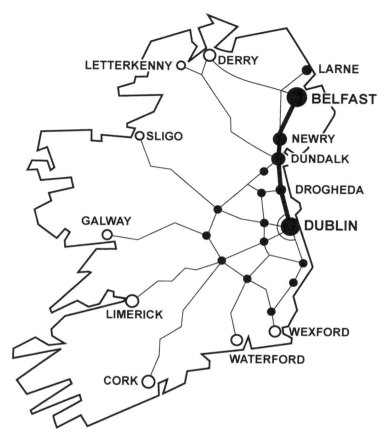

Figure 1.1 General Location Map of Corridor

Chapter 2

City-Regions in the Global Knowledge Economy

Martin Sokol

Research Fellow, Urban Institute, Ireland

Introduction

In recent decades, the world's economic system has been undergoing dramatic changes. Many commentators point to two major trends: the advancement of *globalisation* and the increasing *knowledge-intensity* of economic processes. Simultaneous effects of these two trends have led to a suggestion that we witness a transformation towards a 'global knowledge economy'. This chapter considers the implications this 'global knowledge economy' may have for city-regions. In doing so, the chapter first introduces some key concepts associated with the process of globalisation, focusing on the work of Saskia Sassen on 'global cities', the 'world city network' concept developed by the Globalisation and World Cities Study Group and Network (GaWC) and the notion of 'global city-regions' elaborated by Peter Hall. It then moves on to offer a critical debate on the concepts that see the emergence of knowledge-based cities and regions as an inevitable and welcome corollary to the 'global knowledge economy' (while specifically addressing the concept of the 'learning region'). The chapter concludes by considering the relevance and the implications and this debate for Dublin and the Dublin-Belfast corridor.

Global Cities and City-Regions

With the perceived advances of globalisation, terms such as 'global cities' and 'global city-regions' have been gaining prominence in both academic and policy discourses. This is notwithstanding the fact that the meanings of 'global' on the one hand and of the 'city-region' on the other hand, have been open to alternative or even diverging interpretations. Simultaneously, and perhaps not surprisingly, the notions of the 'global city' and/or 'global city-region' have been subject to a continuing debate (see Scott, 2001). Several key concepts dealing with the implications of globalisation for city-regions have emerged from this debate.

One of the most respected concepts is that of the 'global city' developed by Saskia Sassen (2001a). Sassen has pointed at the emergence of global cities as important nodes of economic organisation in the current phase of economic development, which is marked *inter alia* by the ascendancy of information technologies, an increase in the mobility and liquidity of capital, privatisation, deregulation, the opening up of national economies to foreign firms, and the growing participation of national economic actors in global markets (see also Sassen, 2001b). Reviewing the impact of globalisation and the global spread of ICTs, Sassen has argued that the following key processes work to reinforce the position of certain cities on the global economic stage.

According to Sassen, geographical dispersal and simultaneous integration of economic activities of global firms highlights the importance of their strategic central corporate functions (management, coordination, servicing, financing). However, these centralized functions become so complex that corporations outsource them to specialized information-intensive firms (accounting, legal, public relations, programming, telecommunications, and so on). Importantly, Sassen argues, these specialized firms are subject to agglomeration economies that cannot be replaced in electronic space. Consequently, these firms heavily concentrate in a limited number of leading global cities that are in turn becoming 'production sites for the leading information industries of our time' (Sassen, 2001b, p.83). Sassen also noted that in order to ensure seamless service for global corporations, specialized service firm are themselves becoming global through alliances and worldwide networks of offices (Sassen, 2001a, 2001b).

This latter point has been further developed by the Globalisation and World Cities Study Group and Network (GaWC) based at Loughborough University. Building on Sassen's work, GaWC researchers have taken advanced producer service firms as key economic agents, but focused on their inter-city networks. In other words, they emphasized *relational* aspects of global cities, meaning the way global cities are interconnected with each other (and with the rest of the global economy) through intensive information flows of service firms. Therefore, instead of identifying global cities through their various *attributes*, leading cities are identified on the basis of mutual *relationship* between them (see Taylor, 1997, p.324–325, *inter alia;* see Hall, 2001 p.61, for a review). This way, 'world cities' are seen as being 'interlocked' by service firms into a worldwide world city network (see also Taylor et al., 2002).

These ideas have been complemented by Sir Peter Hall who has argued that if global 'cities' are defined in terms of their *external* information exchanges, then global 'city-regions' should be defined in terms of corresponding *internal* linkages (Hall, 2001 p.72). Hall has suggested these internal linkages reflect an extremely complex and sophisticated internal geography. This geography is 'quintessentially polycentric' (ibid., p.73) as many functions (back offices, logistical management, new-style headquarters, media centres, and so on) relocate over time to decentralized locations (ibid., p.74) amid increasing specialization. Elsewhere, Hall (1999) has referred to these global city-regions as 'mega-cities', 'mega-city regions', large-scale 'networked urban regions' or 'multi-core metropolis'. A *functional* definition of such city-regional structure would imply that its constituent parts display linkages in terms of commuting to work, education, shopping, entertainment and culture, and services (Hall, 1999 p.7). There is still a lot to be explored about this local mega-city regional structure. The international research project on Polycentric Mega-City Regions (POLYNET) initiated by Sir Peter Hall and Kathy Pain in 2004 (and referred to elsewhere in this book), has aimed at understanding functional 'linkages' and 'connectivity' within selected city-regions of North-West Europe, while focusing on information flows of advanced producer service firms (see also Chapter 9 by van Egeraat and Sokol in this volume).

Conceptualising City-Regions in the 'Knowledge-Based Economy'

In parallel to the above discussions on the implications of *globalisation* for cities and city-regions, a controversial debate has been taking place about the implications for city-regions of the emerging *knowledge economy*. Within such an economy, it has been argued, the key element of economic development is *knowledge* in its various forms, fundamentally reshaping the way economic processes work in the 'knowledge era'; (for example Lundvall and Johnson, 1994, Castells, 1996, Burton-Jones, 1999, Giddens, 2000, Leadbeater, 2000, Cooke, 2002, Rodrigues, 2002 and see also policy documents such as EC, 1996; EU, 2000 and OECD, 1997 *inter alia*).

There have been numerous attempts within economic geography, planning theory, industrial sociology and the social sciences in general to conceptualize the implications of the transformation towards the 'knowledge economy' for cities and regions. Concepts such as 'new industrial spaces' (Scott, 1988), 'technopoles' (Castells and Hall, 1994), 'post-industrial cities' (Savitch, 1988), 'post-industrial metropolises' (Graham and Marvin, 1996; Soja, 2000), 'informational cities' (Castells, 1989), 'learning regions' (Florida, 1995a; Morgan, 1997), 'intelligent cities' (Komninos, 2002), 'innovative cities' (Simmie, 2001) or 'knowledge-based cities' (Simmie and Lever, 2002; *inter alia*) have been devised to capture the nature of change at both the urban and regional level. Increasingly, academic literature sees 'city-regions' as being at the epicentre of this fundamental transformation of advanced economies and societies towards a new 'knowledge era'.

There are striking disagreements, however, about the nature of the 'knowledge economy' and its implications for cities and regions. A number of authors highlight the problematic nature of the 'knowledge era' concept, and the sharpening of social and spatial inequalities in particular (for example Castells, 1989, Sassen, 2001a, Graham and Marvin, 2001, Scott et al., 2001). Others seem to imply that the transformation towards 'knowledge city-regions' is not only inevitable but also desirable, conveying the hope that the old socio-spatial divisions and contradictions of industrial capitalism will give way to a more equal and spatially harmonious development as the emerging new global 'knowledge age' sets in.

Perhaps the most suggestive account of the latter approach has been offered by Richard Florida in his seminal article *towards the learning region* (Florida, 1995a). Florida asserts that we are witnessing an epochal transformation 'from mass production to a knowledge-based economy' (Florida, 1995a p.534). Within such a knowledge-based economy, 'knowledge and human intelligence will replace physical labour as the main source of value'; (ibid., p.535). Regions, in his view, represent 'a key element of the new age of global, knowledge-based capitalism' (ibid., p.528), or 'key economic units in the global economy' (ibid., p.531). For Florida, this reflects the fact that regions are 'becoming focal points for knowledge creation and learning in the new age of global, knowledge-intensive capitalism, as they in effect become *learning regions*' (ibid., p.257). These *learning regions*

> '...function as collectors and repositories of knowledge and ideas, and provide the underlying environment and infrastructure which facilitates the flow of knowledge, ideas and learning' (ibid., p.257).

Part of the environment or infrastructure of a 'learning region' is, to use Florida's terms, 'manufacturing infrastructure' (including networks of firms), 'human infrastructure' (knowledge workers), good physical and communication infrastructure, a capital allocation system and financial market and effective 'industrial governance'. The latter feature includes 'formal rules, regulations and standards' as well as 'informal patterns of behaviour between and among firms, and between firms and government organizations' that are 'attuned to the needs of knowledge-intensive organizations' (ibid., p.534).

Indeed, 'knowledge-intensive organisations' are at the very heart of the 'learning region' as portrayed by Florida. A model of such a 'knowledge-intensive organisation' is a transnational corporation implanted into the heart of the 'learning region' through foreign direct investment (FDI). It is integrated with the global marketplace and able to 'harness knowledge and intelligence at all points of the organization from the R&D laboratory to the factory floor' (ibid, p.534). In the knowledge-intensive factory, teams of R&D scientists, engineers and factory workers are becoming 'collective agents of innovation', while the lines between the factory and the laboratory 'blur' (ibid., p.259). Indeed,

> 'like a laboratory, the knowledge-intensive factory is an increasingly clean, technologically advanced and information-rich environment (where) workers perform their tasks in clean room environments, alongside robots and machines which conduct the physical aspects of the work' (ibid., p.529).

Ultimately, what Florida evokes here is a rather benign picture of city-regions of the 'new age of capitalism'. For Florida, this 'new age of capitalism' requires a 'new kind of region', which would be modelled around the principles of the knowledge-intensive firms. These are likely 'to blend the ability of Silicon Valley–style high-technology companies to spur individual genius and creativity, with strategies and techniques for continuous improvement and the 'collective mobilization of knowledge' (ibid., p.534). The 'learning region' must therefore 'develop *governance structures* which reflect and mimic those of knowledge–firms' (ibid., p.534; emphasis added), i.e. to embrace principles of knowledge creation and continuous learning (ibid., p.532).

Interestingly, for several authors, the 'learning region' paradigm represents a 'radical democratic agenda' as well (Amin and Thrift, 1999, p.308). Such an agenda would ensure that *economic efficiency* is combined with *social equity* through active participation (*via* 'associationist' structures) across economy, state and civil society. This would give a voice to previously excluded or marginalized groups of people (Amin and Thrift, 1999, p.306–308; see also Cooke and Morgan, 1998 for similar arguments). It is not surprising, then, that the prospect of both economically competitive *and* socially cohesive 'learning regions' has met with such extraordinary attention in policy circles (Lagendijk and Cornford, 2000). 'Learning regions' and similar concepts have quickly become examples of 'best practice' in local and regional development (Malecki, 2000, p.114) and have been enthusiastically embraced by policy-makers across the world as models for city-regional governance. However, it appears that the city-regional concepts based on learning, knowledge creation and localized capabilities, suffer serious shortcomings, to which we now turn.

Limitations of 'Knowledge-Based' Approaches

Indeed, the 'learning region' concept itself (and 'new economic geography'/'new regionalism' more widely), has been subject to serious criticisms (Hudson, 1999; Lovering, 1999, Markusen, 1999, Smith et al., 1999, Martin and Sunley, 2001, MacKinnon et al., 2002 inter alia). These criticisms highlight problems with the basic terms and definitions, (including the notions of region, knowledge, learning and institution), overall fuzzy conceptualisation, the lack of empirical evidence and, finally, limited policy relevance. This section aims to further this critique by addressing the issue of the 'knowledge-based' or 'knowledge-driven' economy itself. Two simple, but fundamental questions emerge here.

The first problematic issue is whether we are really experiencing a transition to a 'knowledge–based' or 'knowledge–driven' economy. This section supports the view that there is no convincing evidence that (even the most advanced) economies have actually moved beyond the (capitalist) market economy. Indeed, many 'knowledge economy' enthusiasts themselves acknowledged that despite the alleged 'radical' transformation, the economy remains capitalist (cf. Florida, 1995a; inter alia). If we acknowledge this, however, we must then question whether contemporary economies can be seen as *knowledge*-driven. Rather, it should be admitted that the capitalist market economy is, and always was, *profit-*

driven. Within such an economy, the final goal is not knowledge but profit. In fact, the importance of the market imperative for profit is likely to increase with the advance of neo-liberal globalisation. This is not to say that knowledge does not play an important role; indeed, knowledge can be a part of a profit-seeking process (and probably always was). But it is neither the only nor necessarily the most important part of the process. Indeed, the crucial evidence of the *growing* importance of knowledge for economic development is still missing. Therefore, the notion that we are witnessing a transition towards a 'knowledge-driven' economy cannot be taken for granted (see Sokol, 2003, 2004; for more details).

The second issue that needs to be examined (on a more abstract level) is whether an economy can be *knowledge*-driven at all. Indeed, the concepts that highlight *knowledge* as the main (if not the only) factor of economic growth need to be scrutinized. In other words, the very assumption that knowledge creates wealth (central to the 'knowledge–driven economy' thesis) should be seen in a critical light. Indeed, at best, such an assumption could be seen as an oversimplification that does not take into account the influence of other factors, such as, for example, power. At worst, such an assumption may be misleading as it overlooks the possibility of a reversed causality (that wealth creates knowledge). Acknowledging the existence of the reversed causality, of course, means turning the logic of the 'knowledge-driven economy' upside down. As a result, the picture of a simple, one-directional causal relationship between 'knowledge' and 'wealth' disintegrates, while a more complex (but perhaps more accurate) matrix emerges. This matrix would consider 'knowledge', 'wealth' and 'power' as being mutually linked through a web of complex, multidirectional, direct and indirect relations (Sokol, 2003, 2004; Sokol and Tomaney, 2001).

Such a situation places a question mark over the concepts that regard *knowledge* and *learning* as key explanatory factors of city-regional development. A fundamental question arises: are city-regions economically successful *because* they are knowledge-intensive, or are they knowledge-intensive as a consequence of the fact that they are economically successful? Such a dilemma can be resolved, at least on an abstract level, by acknowledging the possibility of the mutually reinforcing process between knowledge and wealth, i.e. through increasing returns from investment in the knowledge-base. However, a much more complicated picture emerges when such a possibility is considered at the urban/regional level. Indeed, placing the city-region back into the context of the wider political economy results in a much more complex picture of the flow of knowledge and wealth, with ambivalent implications for urban/regional prosperity. The acknowledgement of the circular and cumulative causation process between knowledge, wealth and power in a socio-economic system and its introduction into a spatial context, has further implications for an alternative conceptualisation of the space-economy (see Sokol, 2003). While the principles of the circular and cumulative causation process in the spatial context are well known (Myrdal, 1957; Kaldor, 1970), once these are complemented by the insertion of the categories of knowledge and power into the equation, we may see a disturbing picture of polarising space-economic processes (see also Sokol, 2004).

On one side of the process, one could imagine economically successful city-regions that have resources to invest in quality education and costly research and development (R&D) activities. Innovations emerging from such investment can be turned into profits and these re-invested back into the regional 'knowledge-base' and its infrastructure, resulting in 'cumulative learning' (cf. Maskell *et al.*, 1998, p.184; Landabaso, 2000, p.83), which attracts further investment and skilled workers and creates a possible 'virtuous circle' scenario (see also Malecki, 2002, p.931; Thwaites and Oakey, 1985, p.6). However, building on previous rounds of long-term investment, such agglomerations of high-value 'knowledge-sub-economies' (seen by some as 'knowledge cities' or 'learning regions') tend be found in the most-advanced countries (cf. Benko, 1991), often within or close to established economic 'hotspots' such as large metropolitan areas (see Castells and Hall, 1994; Castells, 1996, p.390; see also Simmie, 2001; Simmie, 2002a, 2002b, 2002c; Simmie et al., 2002).

On the adverse side of the circular and cumulative causation process, however, are less favoured areas, cities and regions that can be trapped in a 'vicious circle', stripped of both investment and talented 'knowledge workers'. Due to the adverse side of this 'cherry picking', such places are usually less endowed with modern communication infrastructure (Graham and Marvin, 1996, 2001) or emerge as 'off-line' (Robins and Gillespie, 1992) or 'switched-off' territories (Castells, 1996; see also Gillespie, 1991; Richardson and Gillespie, 2000; Gillespie et al., 2001).

Implications for Dublin and the Dublin-Belfast Corridor

At first sight, Dublin could be seen as a good example of a successful city-region in the 'knowledge age', in part belying the logic of the circular and cumulative causation. Indeed, the capital city of what was once a peripheral European economy, Dublin emerged as an engine of Ireland's rapid economic and employment growth in the 1990s. The city-region has enjoyed the benefits of an increasing interconnectedness with the global economy, and in particular from the global mobility of capital, successfully attracting a high volume of foreign direct investment. Significantly, much of the new economic activity has appeared in the 'new economy' and internationally traded services sectors, reaffirming the role of Dublin within the national, European and global economy (cf. Bannon et al., 2000; Morgenroth, 2001; *inter alia*) and underpinning a wider move towards the 'service economy' or 'information society' (cf. Bannon, 2004).

In parallel to these trends, there has been a proliferation of 'knowledge–based' discourses which have been gaining considerable ground in various strategy documents and policy initiatives. The Dublin Development Board has been attempting to turn Dublin into a 'learning city' and the Dublin Chamber of Commerce has been keen to support Dublin's transformation into a 'World Class e-City'. In parallel to these efforts, Dublin City Council has been developing (with significant difficulties) the 'Digital Hub', apparently seen by the Irish Government as one of the central elements in building a knowledge-driven economy in Ireland (see also IDA Ireland, 2003). Meanwhile, the Dublin Employment Pact has in recent years organized a series of high profile events aimed at examining Dublin's position in the global knowledge economy. Finally, in 2004, the Dublin Chamber of Commerce published its vision for the city *Imagine Dublin 2020* (Dublin Chamber of Commerce, 2004). One of the primary objectives of the vision is to encourage the emergence of Dublin as a 'knowledge city'. In part echoing Florida's idea of a 'learning region' (presented above) the document portrays an image of Dublin 2020 as

> a 'knowledge city' that generates, attracts and retains high quality skills. Nobody leaves the learning cycle, but everybody develops their personal, professional and civic abilities continuously ... education and learning is available to everybody. Creative and innovative thinking is a natural part of living in Dublin .... Well-developed physical infrastructure and a high quality living environment sustain merging of knowledge, society and commercial activities in Dublin' (ibid., p.2).

It is hard to refute such a positive vision for the city. Indeed, reflecting on the spectacular economic growth this city-region had experienced in the 1990s one might be tempted to label Dublin as an emerging 'post-industrial metropolis' or a 'knowledge-based city', playing an increasingly central role in national competitiveness and economic prosperity. This purported success, however, has not been achieved without creating its own contradictions within the Irish space–economy, especially in terms of regional economic imbalance (Bannon, 2004). Furthermore, within the city itself, the expected benefits of the 'new economy' have failed to materialize for many people and even for whole communities (Killen and MacLaran, 1999; Drudy and MacLaran, 2001; Moore, 2003; Punch et al., 2004; inter alia).

Dublin is thus presented with numerous challenges, of which simultaneously maintaining and strengthening competitiveness and cohesion is perhaps the key one. On the side of competitiveness, Dublin will face ever-increasing competition for investment coming from the global market place. Its ability to attract and retain high-value economic activities will be tested further. Dublin may be seen as an emerging 'global city' (see Taylor et al., 2002, p.100) but it is important to realize that Dublin, despite its dynamic growth, remains a rather small-scale 'node' within the 'world city network'. Meanwhile, the volume and quality of economic activities of individual cities will determine their position within an evolving 'world city network' (that is marked by new forms of hierarchy and subordination). It is possible that Dublin, as a 'global city' will find, preserve and develop a profitable 'niche' within the global division of labour, but it is also possible that it will have to endeavour to increase its relative size in order to attract activities of certain scale and scope. Here the question of the Dublin-Belfast corridor will become critical as it may provide an improved chance for creating the critical mass of a 'global mega-city region' necessary for anchoring an advanced 'knowledge economy'. To achieve this, innovative approaches and new holistic governance arrangements may be needed. At the same time, policy-makers will have to realize that the 'knowledge economy' alone will not guarantee social and spatial cohesion and that bold policy instruments will be needed to safeguard social peace and territorial justice at the local, city-regional and national levels.

References

Amin, A., and Thrift, N. (1999), Institutional issues for the European regions: from markets and plans to socioeconomics and powers of association. In Barnes, J. and M. Gertler (eds), *The New Industrial Geography: Regions, Regulation and Institutions*. 292–314 (London and New York: Routledge).

Bannon, M.J., Rhys Thomas, S. and Cassidy A. (2000) *The Role of Dublin in Europe* (Dublin, DOELG).

Bannon, M.J. (2004), 'Service Activity Concentration in Dublin and its Implications for National Urban Policy and the Regional Development of the Country'. Paper presented to the 'City-Regions: Economic Change, Technology and Knowledge Society' Research Group's Guest Lecture series, Urban Institute Ireland, University College Dublin, Dublin, 3 June 2004.

Benko, G. (1991), *Geographie des technopoles* (Paris: Masson).

Burton-Jones, A. (1999), *Knowledge Capitalism: Business, Work, and Learning in the New Economy* (Oxford: Oxford University Press).

Castells, M. (1989), *The informational city: information technology, economic restructuring and the urban-regional process* (Oxford: Blackwell).

———, *The Information Age: Economy, Society and Culture, Vol. I: The Rise of the Network Society* (Oxford: Blackwell).

Castells, M., and Hall, P. (1994), *Technopoles of the World: The Making of 21st Century Industrial Complexes* (London.: Routledge).

Cooke, P. (2002), *Knowledge Economies: Clusters, Learning and Cooperative Advantage* (London and New York: Routledge).

Cooke, P., and Morgan, K. (1998), *The associational economy: firms, regions, and innovation* (Oxford: Oxford University Press).

Drudy, P.J. and MacLaran, A. (.) (2001), *Dublin: Economic and Social Trends*, Volume 3 (Dublin, TCD/CURS).

Dublin Chamber of Commerce (2004), *Imagine Dublin 2020: Our Vision for the Future of the City* (Dublin: Dublin Chamber of Commerce).

European Commission (EC) (1996), *Living and working in the information society: People first (Green Paper),(COM(96) 389 final)* (Brussels: EC).

European Union (EU) (2000), *Extraordinary European Council* (Lisbon, 23 and 24 March 2000): *Presidency Conclusions*, available at: <http://europa.eu.int/council/off/conclu/mar2000/>; accessed on 10 June 2000. Brussels: European Council / European Union.

Florida, R. (1995a), Toward the learning region. *Futures.* 27(5): 527–536.

———, (1995b), *The industrial transformation of the Great Lakes Region.* In Cooke P. (ed.), *The Rise of the Rustbelt.* 162–176. (London: UCL Press).

Giddens, A. (2000), *The Third Way and its Critics* (Cambridge: Polity Press).

Gillespie, A. (1991), Advanced communications networks, territorial integration and local development. In Camagni R., *Innovation networks: spatial perspectives.* 214–229 (London and New York: Belhaven Press).

Gillespie, A., Richardson, R., and Cornford, J. (2001), Regional development and the new economy. *European Investment Bank Papers* 6(1): 109–132.

Graham, S., and Marvin, S. (1996), *Telecommunications and the City: Electronic Spaces, Urban Places* (London: Routledge).

———, (2001), *Splintering urbanism: networked infrastructures, technological mobilities and the urban condition* (London and New York: Routledge).

Hall, P. (2001), Global City-Regions in the Twenty-first Century. In Scott A.J. *Global City-Regions: Trends, Theory, Policy* 59–77 (Oxford: Oxford University Press).

———, (1999), Planning for the Mega-City: A New Eastern Asian Urban Form? In Brotchie, J.F., Batty, M., Blakely, E., Hall, P. and Newton, P., *Cities in Competition* pp.3–36 (Melbourne: Longman Australia).

Hudson, R. (1999), The learning economy, the learning firm and the learning region: A sympathetic critique of the limits to learning. *European Urban and Regional Studies* 6(1): 59–72.

IDA Ireland (2003), *Ireland, Knowledge is in our nature* (Dublin: IDA Ireland).

Kaldor, N. (1970), The case for regional policies. *Scottish Journal of Political Economy* 17: 337–345.

Killen, J. and MacLaran, A., (1999), *Dublin: Contemporary Trends and Issues for the Twenty-First Century.* Dublin: The Geographical Society of Ireland (Special Publication 11); The Centre for Urban and Regional Studies, Trinity College, Dublin.

Komninos, N. (2002), *Intelligent Cities: Innovation, Knowledge Systems and Digital Spaces* (London and New York: Spon Press).

Lagendijk, A. and Cornford, J. (2000), Regional institutions and knowledge – tracking new forms of regional development policy. *Geoforum* 31: 209–218.

Landabaso, M. (2000), Innovation and regional development policy. In Boekema, F., Morgan, K., Bakkers, S. and Rutten, R., *Knowledge, Innovation and Economic Growth: The Theory and Practice of Learning Regions* 73-94 (Cheltenham: Edward Elgar).

Leadbeater, C. (2000),. *Living on Thin Air: the New Economy* (London: Penguin).

Lovering, J. (1999), Theory led by policy? The Inadequacies of the 'New Regionalism' (illustrated from the case of Wales). *International Journal of Urban and Regional Research* 23(2): 379–396.

Lundvall, B.A., and Johnson, B. (1994), The Learning Economy. *Journal of Industrial Studies* 1(2): 23–42.

MacKinnon, D., Cumbers, A. and Chapman, K. (2002), Learning, innovation and regional development: a critical appraisal of recent debates. *Progress in Human Geography* 26(3): 293–311.

Malecki, E.J. (2000), Creating and sustaining competitiveness: Local knowledge and economic geography. In Bryson, J.R., Daniels, P.W., Henry, N. and Pollard J., *Knowledge, Space, Economy* 103–119 (London and New York: Routhledge).

———, (2002), Hard and soft networks for urban competitiveness. *Urban Studies* 39(5–6): 929–945.

Markusen, A. (1999), Fuzzy concepts, scanty evidence, policy distance: the case for rigour and policy relevance in critical regional studies. *Regional Studies* 33(9): 869–884.

Martin, R. and Sunley, P. (2001), Rethinking the 'economic' in economic geography: Broadening our vision of losing our focus? *Antipode* 33(2): 148–161.

Maskell, P., Eskelinen, H., Hannibalsson, I., Malmberg, A. and Vatne, E. (1998), *Competitiveness, localized learning and regional development: specialisation and prosperity in small open economies* (London and New York: Routledge).

Moore, N. (2003), 'Social polarization and policy responses in Dublin's inner city'. European Academy of the Urban Environment/Urban Institute Ireland Conference, Dublin and Belfast.

Morgan, K. (1997), The Learning Region: Institutions, Innovation and Regional Renewal. *Regional Studies* 31(5): 491–503.

Morgenroth, E. (2001), *Analysis of the Economic, Employment and Social Profile of the Greater Dublin Region*. Dublin: The Economic and Social Research Institute.

Myrdal, G. (1957), *Economic Theory and Under-Developed Regions* (London: Gerald Duckworth).

OECD (1997), *Global Information Infrastructure – Global Information Society* (Paris: OECD).

Punch, M., Redmond, D. and Kelly, S. (2004), 'Uneven development, city governance and urban change: unpacking the global-local nexus in Dublin's inner city', Paper for 'City Futures' – An International Conference on Globalism and Urban Change, Chicago, USA, 8–10 July.

Richardson, R. and Gillespie, A. (2000), The Economic Development of Peripheral Rural Areas in the Information Age. In Wilson, M.I. and Corey K.E., *Information Tectonics: Space, Place and Technology in an Electronic Age* 199–218 (New York: John Wiley & Sons, Chichester).

Robins, K. and Gillespie, A. (1992), Communication, organisation and territory. In Robins, K., *Understanding Information: Business, Technology and Geography* 145–164 (London: Belhaven).

Rodrigues, M.J. (2002), *The New Knowledge Economy in Europe: A Strategy for International Competitiveness and Social Cohesion* (Edward Elgar: Cheltenham, UK and Northampton, MA, USA).

Sassen, S. (2001a), *The Global City: New York, London, Tokyo (Second edition)*

(Princeton and Oxford: Princeton University Press).

———, (2001b), Global Cities and Global City-Regions: A Comparison. In Scott A.J., *Global City-Regions: Trends, Theory, Policy* 78–95 (Oxford: Oxford University Press).

Savitch, H. (1988), *Post-industrial cities: politics and planning in New York, Paris and London* (Princeton: Princeton University Press).

Scott, A.J. (1988), *New Industrial Spaces: Flexible Production Organisation and Regional Development in North America and Western Europe* (London: Pion).

———, (2001), *Global City-Regions: Trends, Theory, Policy* (Oxford: Oxford University Press).

Scott, A.J., Agnew, J., Soja E.W. and Storper, M. (2001), Global City-Regions. In Scott, A.J., *Global City-Regions: Trends, Theory, Policy*. 11–30 (Oxford: Oxford University Press).

Simmie, J., (2001), *Innovative cities* (London: Spon Press).

———, (2002a), Knowledge spillovers and reasons for the concentration of innovative SMEs. *Urban Studies* 39(5–6): 885–902.

———, (2002b), Trading places: competitive cities in the global economy. *European Planning Studies* 10(2): 201–215.

———, (2002c), Innovation, international trade and knowledge spillovers in the London Metropolitan Region. *Scienze Regionali* 1: 73–92.

———, and Lever, W.F. (2002), Introduction: The Knowledge-based City. *Urban Studies* 39(5–6): 855–857

Simmie, J., Sennett, J., Wood, P. and Hart, D. (2002), Innovation in Europe: a tale of networks, knowledge and trade in five cities. *Regional Studies* 36(1): 47–64.

Smith, A., Rainnie, A. and Dunford, M. (1999), Regional trajectories and uneven development in the 'New Europe': rethinking territorial success and inequality. *Working Paper 2–99, Regional Economic Performance, Governance and Cohesion in an Enlarged Europe, ESRC project, ESRC/University of Sussex, http://www.geog.sussex.ac.uk/research/changing–europe/workpapers.html, (accessed on 9 June 2000).*

Soja, E. W. (2000), Postmetropolis: Critical Studies of Cities and Regions (Oxford: Blackwell).

Sokol, M. (2003), *Regional Dimensions of the Knowledge Economy: Implications for the 'New Europe'.* Unpublished PhD Thesis. Centre for Urban and Regional Development Studies, University of Newcastle upon Tyne, England, UK.

———, (2004), 'The "Knowledge Economy": A Critical View'. In Cooke P. and Piccaluga A., *Regional Economies as Knowledge Laboratories* (Cheltenham: Edward Elgar) pp.216–231.

Sokol, M. and Tomaney, J. (2001), Regionalising the Knowledge Economy: What's the Point? In Maconochie, A. and Hardy, S., *Regionalising the Knowledge Economy (Conference Proceedings of the Regional Studies Association Annual Conference)* 108–110 (Seaford: RSA).

Taylor, P.J. (1997), Hierarchical Tendencies Amongst World Cities: A Global Research Proposal. *Cities* 14: 323–332.

Taylor, P.J., Walker, D.R.F. and Beaverstock, J.V. (2002), Firms and Their Global Service Networks. In Sassen, S., *Global Networks, Linked Cities* 93–115 (New York and London: Routledge).

Thwaites, A.T. and Oakey, R.P. (1985), Editorial introduction. In Thwaites, A.T. and Oakey R.P., *The Regional Economic Impact of Technological Change* 1–12 (London: Frances Pinter).

Chapter 3

Implementing the National Spatial Strategy and the Regional Development Strategy for Northern Ireland within the Dublin-Belfast Corridor

Niall Cussen
Senior Advisor, Department of Environment, Heritage and Local Government, Republic of Ireland

Jim Hetherington
Principal Planner, Dept. for Regional Development, Northern Ireland

Introduction

The spatial concept of a Dublin-Belfast corridor has been gaining increasing acceptance in recent years. Planning along the physical corridor between the two largest cities on the island of Ireland has traditionally been focused on various administrative and planning units of territory north and south of the Border rather than on a corridor, in economic or transport terms.

In the south, development plans in the late 1990s started to mention the concept of a Dublin Belfast corridor and the concept began to influence high level goals and aims of development plans such as the Fingal Development Plan of 1998 and the Meath County Development Plan of 2000.

By the time the Regional Development Strategy for Northern Ireland, 'Shaping our Future', and the National Spatial Strategy in the south came to be adopted, the Dublin-Belfast corridor as a spatial concept, was a critical and central component of both spatial strategies.

Pointers at national and international level provide strong support for the stance of the RDS and NSS in relation to the role of the corridor concept. These pointers also suggest clearly that the development of a healthy and internationally competitive all-island economy can be aided by the complementary development of nearby cities and intervening towns and rural areas as an integrated and well connected package with distinctive urban and rural elements.

The Regional Development Strategy for Northern Ireland and the National Spatial Strategy are both being implemented in a similar broad structural manner, but there are significant differences in the detail of the implementation process. Differences between planning systems in the Republic and Northern Ireland as well as differences in local political involvement in planning between North and South pose challenges that must be addressed if the Dublin-Belfast Corridor concept is to be further developed.

These challenges in particular include:

1. Defining what the Dublin Belfast Corridor means in practical on the ground considerations.
2. Working out the spatial planning implications of the corridor and establishing the public, political, and private sector buy-in to an overall approach.
3. Matching up different governmental systems, north and south of the border in addressing 1 and 2 above.

Addressing these challenges will depend on (a) harnessing current efforts in establishing regional and local planning frameworks that respond to and support the RDS and NSS and in the longer run (b) establishing a high level and tightly drawn stakeholder alliance of the key agencies, authorities and interests involved in aspects of the planning and development of the corridor. This alliance would seek to develop and strengthen links between overlapping elements of the various regional and local spatial plans and supporting programs along the corridor for collective benefit.

The National Spatial Strategy and the Dublin-Belfast Corridor

Objectives of the National Spatial Strategy

The NSS is a 20 year spatial development framework: see *Figure 3.1, National Spatial Strategy: Greater Dublin Area Diagram.* This sets out how a strengthened and expanded network of cities and towns, together with rural communities and resources, supported by appropriate social and physical infrastructure, will be mobilized to create more balanced regional development across the country. Important concepts for the corridor as outlined in the NSS relate to (a) Consolidation and (b) Economic Integrity. Developing these concepts further in the corridor will also fully support the broader objective of the NSS in relation to balanced regional development.

Consolidation

The NSS emphasizes that the performance of the economy of the Greater Dublin area and surrounding counties must be built upon so that its success, competitiveness and national role are sustained into the future.

While the NSS accepts the reality that Dublin will continue to grow in population and output terms, it emphasizes that it is not desirable for Dublin to continue to spread physically into surrounding counties. The NSS therefore envisages a physical *consolidation* of Dublin, supported by effective land use policies for the urban area itself, as an essential requirement for a competitive Dublin.

In order to achieve this physical consolidation, the NSS outlines a number of initiatives that the bodies responsible for strategic planning in the Greater Dublin Area must address, particularly in the context of reviews of the current Strategic Planning Guidelines for the Area. Such initiatives involve audits of underutilized lands, urban intensification, and generally exploring all reasonable options to accommodate the development needs of the GDA within a tight physical footprint.

Economic Integrity

In relation to the area beyond the Greater Dublin Area and between the GDA and the Border, the NSS makes further recommendations.

Recognising the potential and scale of the urban centres in Dundalk, Newry and Drogheda, the NSS emphasizes that the central portion of the Dublin-Belfast corridor needs to be strengthened in order to give that corridor greater *economic integrity*. In other words, without a strong core to the corridor, (meaning an ample critical mass in economic terms), there is a danger that Dublin and Belfast will generate commuter-driven development but not much self supporting economic activity within the corridor.

For this reason, and taking into account spatial development roles, size and infrastructure, the NSS identified Dundalk as having the capacity to develop as a gateway within the Dublin-Belfast corridor. The NSS envisages developing Dundalk so as to use its strategic location between Dublin and Belfast to underpin cross-border co-operation, particularly with neighbouring Newry. Building up the transport and business links between Dundalk and Newry will offer a scale of development and critical mass that can help drive development throughout the eastern part of the border region.

Drogheda and its environs effectively straddle the boundary between the Border region and the Dublin and Mid East regions. For this and other reasons, (such as excellent road and rail connections to Dublin), the development of Drogheda is strongly influenced by its relative proximity to the Greater Dublin Area. The NSS sees Drogheda as a major urban centre within the Dublin-Belfast corridor to be developed in concert with other key urban centres in the middle part of the corridor to build up critical mass. For these reasons, the NSS emphasizes that account will have to be taken of:

- Drogheda's relationship with its own catchment,
- its role within the Border region,
- its role as a significant port and
- its role in the spatial development of the Greater Dublin Area having regard to the town's close functional and physical links with the Dublin.

Balanced Regional Development

It can be argued that one of the reasons why a national spatial framework climbed the political agenda in the 1990s was a concern that the east coast of the Republic was developing much faster than other areas such as the Midlands, the West and the Border regions, (and becoming consequently congested).

By extension, some might argue that the development of a Dublin Belfast corridor is contrary to the concept of more balanced regional development. The NSS however, sees the concept of a Dublin-Belfast corridor as wholly consistent with achieving more balanced regional development. The NSS is not and could not be about stopping development in one part of the country and transferring it to another in the manner of a 'zero sum game'. Rather the NSS is aiming to build up a critical mass in the regions to complement what Dublin and the east coast has to offer.

The Regional Development Strategy For Northern Ireland

The Regional Development Strategy for Northern Ireland 2025 (RDS) sets out a challenging agenda which influences the future of all land uses throughout the region. See *Figure 3.2, RDS Key Diagram*. It impacts on all who have a role in taking forward its key objectives on economic, social and environmental matters. The RDS underpins the NI Executive 'Programme for Government' and the Statement by The Secretary of State on 'Progress and Priorities' on 24 June 2003.

The RDS was born to meet a political need for better strategic planning that recognizes the importance of balanced development across Northern Ireland and the interrelationships between the region and its neighbours. The Belfast Dublin Corridor, or the Eastern Seaboard Corridor as described in the RDS, as an integral part of this spatial relationship.

The RDS is the first step in an agreed change towards a plan led system. It offers coherent and strategic direction, and a shared vision, for the sustainable development of Northern Ireland. The publication of the National Spatial Strategy for Ireland 2002–2020 presents a unique context where development needs can, for the first time, be assessed against a strategic spatial background for the whole island.

The RDS is based upon an ethos of 'Plan, Monitor, and Manage' rather than the previous approach of 'Predict and Provide'. New legislation strengthens and improves the planning system in Northern Ireland. It requires planning policies, development plans and development schemes to be 'in general conformity with' the RDS. This legislation introduces a 'statementing' procedure to ensure that plans are in conformity with the Strategy.

The establishment of an Inter-Departmental Steering Group, chaired by the Minister for Regional Development, provides the focus within Government to ensure that there is co-ordinated effort to deliver the key objectives of the Regional Development Strategy and the Regional Transportation Strategy.

A paper entitled 'Implementation of the Regional Development Strategy and Monitoring and Evaluation Arrangements' was agreed with the Regional Development Committee of the Northern Ireland Assembly on 24 April 2002. That paper sets out three important principles to guide the implementation process. These are:

- A partnership and participative approach;
- The importance of monitoring and reviewing to assess progress; and
- The need to learn lessons from successful regional and inter-regional development elsewhere.

The Annual Report outlines progress under these headings and scopes the way forward. It also sets out progress on implementation of the Regional Transportation Strategy that was agreed by the Assembly on 3 July 2002.

In summary it:

- Reports on the achievements since the Regional Development Strategy was formulated in September 2001;
- Establishes a baseline against which future performance may be assessed; and sets out areas for action over the next year.

Links between the two Strategies

The high level messages of the RDS and NSS are closely related. Both strategies recognize the value of an attractive and competitive metropolitan corridor, with good physical connections and complementary development of the area within the corridor, as a key element in the development of internationally competitive economies and a healthy all island economy.

What is missing from the NSS and RDS is the detail of how planning activities at regional and local levels might support both strategies.

- How to encourage a structured approach to the development and enlargement of urban centres such as Dundalk, Newry and Drogheda to support self-sustaining economic development in the central part of the corridor.
- How to approach the development of other areas within the corridor such as smaller villages coming under pressure for considerable levels of commuter driven development in a way that supports achievement of critical mass at strategic locations.
- How to promote the diversification and renewal of rural economies so as to harness local assets in a sustainable way, such as the uplands that straddle the border.

These details are not missing in a deliberate sense. The details now need to be added through planning activities at trans-boundary, regional and local levels.

Implementation Of The National Spatial Strategy

Summary of Overall Approach

Implementation of the NSS is taking place at three main levels.

1. *At national level*, through the DoEHLG overseeing a process whereby the approach of the NSS will be embedded within the programmes and activities of Government Departments and Agencies, so that these activities support the NSS.
2. *At regional level*, through Regional Authorities putting in place regional spatial development frameworks 'Regional Planning Guidelines' that will structure and inform more local planning.
3. *At local level*, through Planning Authorities putting in place the local development frameworks and plans, particularly at the gateway and hub level, that will support the achievement of a critical mass of development at strategic locations as well as putting in place complementary policies in more rural areas.

'Embedding' the NSS

Structures and mechanisms to integrate the NSS into planning and activities at Government, Departmental and state agency level are being put in place. As these structures are developed, they will ensure that the NSS informs the spatial aspects of public sector planning in the areas of transport, enterprise development and social infrastructure investment in particular.

Already the NSS has shaped the Strategic Rail Review and the development of the Forfas regional investment strategy. The NSS will also influence the mid term review of the National Development Plan, to be completed this year.

To oversee the process of embedding the NSS at national level, an Interdepartmental Group, similar to that which oversaw the preparation of the strategy, has now been established and meets at regular intervals. As set out in the NSS, a Monitoring Group will also be put in place to oversee progress in implementing the strategy.

A particular feature of the process of embedding the NSS at national level is the preparation of 'NSS Implementation Issue Papers' by the relevant Departments and Agencies. These will focus on (a) identifying activities of the relevant Department or Agency linked to implementation of the NSS; (b) the degree to which those activities currently support the implementation of the NSS and (c) future priorities for better alignment between those activities and the implementation of the NSS.

It is intended to draw together an overall report on progress, issues and future priorities in implementing the NSS from these initial working papers towards the end of 2003.

Regional Planning Guidelines

The NSS is a high level, nationally focused strategy. Substantial elements of the implementation of the strategy depend on supporting actions at local level. To provide a framework for more detailed planning at county, city and town level, it was recognized by the DoEHLG that regional planning frameworks would be needed to link the NSS at national level with city and county development plans at local level. In Chapter 6, Yarwood gives an account of the Regional Planning Guidelines for the Greater Dublin Area.

In February 2003, *Guidance Notes for Regional Authorities on preparing Regional Planning Guidelines* were issued by the Department to all regional authorities. Regional Authorities, working in partnership with local authorities, have now commenced this work with the aim of ensuring that the guidelines are in place by 2004. For example, all the authorities have published 'Issues Papers' to act as an initial focus for public consultation. The Minister for the Environment, Heritage and Local Government made two legal instruments to support this process on 1 May 2003.

The *Planning and Development (Regional Planning Guidelines) Direction 2003*, formally directs each Regional Authority to make Regional Planning Guidelines for its region. These regulations set out a number of requirements in relation to the preparation process. In particular, it has been specified that the NSS is of relevance to the determination of strategic planning policies. This means that Regional Authorities are obliged to take account of the NSS when making Regional Planning Guidelines.

The guidelines will be focused on how to create and sustain those development opportunities in the regions that will be able to attract and retain investment and population growth and thereby support more balanced regional development. Matters that will arise in this context will include identifying key settlement patterns in the future, including where population growth needs to be maximized to deliver critical mass, including the difficult question of where investment priorities should lie in the future to support critical mass.

The 'Issues Paper', which initiated work on the Border Regional Planning Guidelines has identified inter-regional issues linked to the development of the Dublin-Belfast corridor concept. In particular these include:

- How the aims and objectives of the Regional Planning Guidelines recognize and support the Regional Development Strategy for Northern Ireland.
- The role of the Border region in the Dublin-Belfast corridor.
- Links with planning guidelines for the Greater Dublin Area.

The Issues Paper highlights the role of the Dublin-Belfast corridor as a significant inter-regional opportunity moving in the direction of the trend of co-operation between cities to enhance competitiveness.

The Regional Planning Guidelines for the Greater Dublin Area already emphasize the importance of consolidating growth in the transportation corridors radiating from Dublin to specific 'Primary Development Centres'. Completion of the regional planning guideline process will be a critical step upon which the implementation of the NSS is highly dependent. Regional Planning Guidelines play a key role under national planning legislation in structuring the type of local planning actions that will support the achievement of critical mass at strategic locations within each region, such as gateways, hubs and county towns.

Local Initiatives and Local Planning

Actions at local level, through County, City and Town Development Plans, have a pivotal role in supporting the implementation of the NSS. A key challenge in this regard is to lift the horizon for local plan making beyond local concerns alone. A criticism frequently levelled at the planning system in Ireland has been that it is excessively focused on local issues to the detriment of progressing strategic development issues and therefore finds it difficult to cope effectively with broad development trends.

The 2000 Planning and Development Act has completely overhauled the forward planning elements of our system. It is creating a much more integrated system of spatial planning at national, regional and local levels. Planning actions at each level need to support and reinforce each other to maximize the considerable potential for an effective planning system that exists in the legal structure of the Act. The Department has a vital role to play also in supporting and encouraging quality plans at local level.

The successful development of gateways and hubs, such as Dundalk, will require integrated spatial frameworks for land use planning, urban design, transport and public service delivery. In the case of Dundalk, the authorities have made much progress in this area already.

Implementation Challenges

At this stage, there appear to be three key challenges in taking forward the Dublin – Belfast corridor concept to an operational level. These challenges are:

- Developing consensus around what the concept means, particularly to those stakeholders who make planning decisions along the corridor.
- Working to bridge the differences between spatial and planning policy regimes either side of the Border.
- Moving over time to an agreed high level development vision that is supported at regional and local levels on both sides of the border and that informs local spatial planning actions.

What the Corridor means

There are two important elements in taking any spatial concept forward.

Firstly key groups located within or responsible for the development of areas to which the spatial concept relates, must see the concept as a valid one that has something to offer. In the case of the NSS, a broad consensus view emerged during the latter part of the 1990's that more balanced regional development was desirable and this gave rise to the commitment made in the National Development Plan to prepare the NSS.

Secondly, with some broad agreement as to the relevance of the spatial concept, it is vital to develop a broad consensus around what the concept means to those responsible for its promotion and or implementation.

It appears that the Dublin-Belfast corridor concept has a broad currency at governmental, departmental and agency levels. The NSS sees the value of the concept as a mechanism to deliver international competitiveness with much larger centres of population in Europe. However, it is more debatable whether the concept is fully recognized at local level.

It can be argued that more work remains to be done in outlining to the elected members in the south, how their actions have implications for, and or are linked to, the prospects for the overall corridor.

It might be argued by some that in fact there is no buy in at local level to a single corridor and that instead there are probably three or four individual sub-corridors that are recognized such as:

- The Belfast Metropolitan Area (as it relates to the corridor),
- The Greater Dublin Area (as it relates to the corridor),
- Parts of Louth along the M1,
- Portadown to Newry.

Priorities to take the Dublin- Belfast corridor forward might also include working to develop a political and institutional consensus as to what the concept of a spatial development corridor between Dublin and Belfast actually represents. It could be argued that at present there is no single image, map or framework that is supported, north and south of the border and that in the absence of a consensus, the corridor instead means different things to different people. One view might be that it represents the possibility of varied development opportunities strung out along the M1 motorway and the rail line wherever the market decides. Would this be in the interests of proper planning and sustainable development? Would it deliver critical mass within the corridor at strategic locations?

The NSS and RDS suggest instead that it will be vitally important to build up a sizeable level of critical mass centrally within the corridor to avoid the corridor becoming a reservoir of mainly long distance commuters to and from Dublin and Belfast. At the same time both strategies emphasize the importance of building up locally important levels of critical mass at locations near the main centres to both support these urban centres and capitalize on them. In other words, a planned approach means doing specific things in specific places to further higher level goals and objectives.

It might therefore be useful to seek answers to a number of straightforward questions that arise in the context of implementing the NSS and RDS and in particular the preparation of regional planning guidelines.

1. What is the spatial extent of the corridor to which specific policies should apply?
2. Is it possible to identify strategic 'segments' within the corridor that play strategic development roles for the corridor as a whole?
3. What types of broad spatial planning policies should apply to (a) the corridor as a whole and (b) any strategic segments identified within the corridor?
4. If a chapter were to appear in the two regional planning guidelines that cover that part of the corridor in the Republic, what might be the table of contents of that chapter and would it differ from current policies?

The nature of the questions above demonstrate the breadth of work that remains to be done to take the corridor concept into the chambers of planning authorities and area committee meetings of the elected members in the south and therefore ensure that it acts as an influence on local planning actions.

Implementing the RDS at Local Level

Clearly, district councils in Northern Ireland have an important role to play in implementing the RDS at sub-regional level. Indeed, many councils have already embarked on community planning exercises to develop local areas. Such an approach will advance the strategic vision for each area and encourage and develop the continued involvement of key stakeholders.

To assist this process the Department for Regional Development will, during 2003/4, facilitate a programme of four sub-regional seminars with key stakeholders, including senior government officials. These seminars will permit a shared understanding of the roles and responsibilities of each of the stakeholders and encourage better coherence and co-ordination of policies, programmes and services at region, sub region and local area. They will also assist in developing an understanding of the relationships between the Regional Development Strategy, the Regional Transportation Strategy and the Republic of Ireland's National Spatial Strategy.

The objective of each seminar will be to agree a framework for an integrated approach to the future development of each sub-region, involving key stakeholders in tracking performance of the RDS against the strategic planning guidelines and their measures and targets as envisaged by the Northern Ireland Assembly Regional Development Committee.

The RDS offers visions for the future. One of these is the potential to be released by encouraging the economic exploitation of the Eastern Seaboard Corridor and its close links to cross-border trade. The potential is huge, but on a cautionary note it must be appreciated that success is predicated on sharing the rewards throughout the west as well as the east of the island.

The RDS is a long-term spatial framework and we must not lose sight of the need to achieve its strategic objectives. The real challenge, to interpret strategic guidance in practical steps, is now being met through constructive dialogue with stakeholders and thorough monitoring and evaluation of progress. The Northern Ireland Dept for Regional Development intends that this should be an inclusive process which sees RDS objectives embedded into other strategies, inside and outside government, and empowers and enables a wide range of actors to lift their horizons to new levels.

Contrasts in Planning Systems

The Border represents not only the boundary between the Republic and Northern Ireland but also a boundary between two different ways of organising and delivering a planning service.

Developing links between the two very different operational arrangements in the two planning systems will be vital in taking forward the concept of the corridor, which is supported by the NSS and RDS, and developing political and institutional consensus around what it means.

In the Republic, planning has effectively been driven at local level, with individual planning authorities composed of locally elected councillors making local development plans and local authority officials making decisions on local planning applications with separate overseeing roles for the DoEHLG and An Bord Pleanala, (the Planning Appeals Board). Recent developments have will introduce a more strategically focused national and regional spatial framework to inform local decision making.

In Northern Ireland, the planning function is an executive one, delivered through Government Departments such as the Department of Regional Development, which is responsible for the implementation of the RDS, and the Department of the Environment, which operates the planning service.

Linking up a local politically-driven planning system on one side of the border with a planning system delivered by central Government on the other side of the border, represents a considerable challenge in taking the Dublin-Belfast corridor concept forward. Unique models and mechanisms will be needed, and theymust be tailored to the task.

Need for a shared vision

This chapter has argued for a concerted effort to take the Dublin-Belfast corridor concept beyond the level of an academic proposition and to actively seek out the potential for the concept to influence planning at local levels north and south of the border, but particularly south of the border where recent transport developments have suddenly focused minds on how close places like Dublin, Drogheda and Dundalk and Belfast are to each other.

Events such as the series of academic conferences on the Dublin-Belfast corridor play an essential role in developing a broader awareness about the concept and exploring its potential.

The process of preparing Regional Planning Guidelines in supporting the implementation of the NSS and corresponding development plan policies in Northern Ireland represent immediate and valuable opportunities to get aspects of the Dublin- Belfast corridor down on paper.

In the longer term however, attention must turn to how the existing structures responsible for spatial development might be linked in terms of co-operation and technical assistance, particularly across the border, so as to develop a sense of ownership and responsibility for the progression and implementation of the concept.

Conclusion

The NSS and RDS recognize the importance of pooling the resources and strengths of the corridor that envelops Dublin, Belfast and various urban and rural areas in between. The two strategies recognize the role that the two largest cities on the island play in its economic future. They have drawn from developing spatial planning practice in other parts of the world with which we must compete to progress and attract and sustain investment and business activity.

The nature of the corridor poses significant challenges in implementing the concept. Arguably however, the hardest element of that task is already accomplished, in that both the NSS and RDS recognize the concept.

The opening of the new M1 motorway in the south is already beginning to revolutionize how people see the stretch between Dublin, the Border and Northern Ireland generally. Putting in place the remaining motorway link will accelerate that process further.

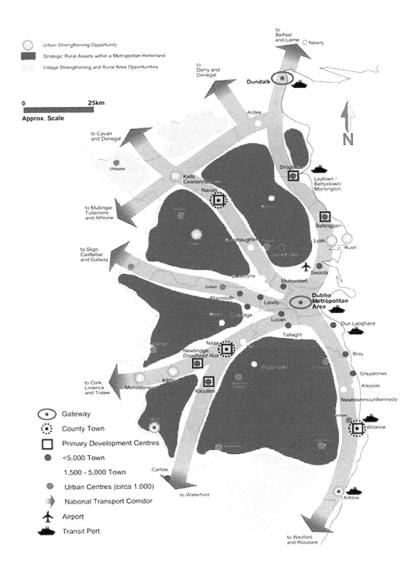

Figure 3.1   National Spatial Strategy: Greater Dublin Area Diagram

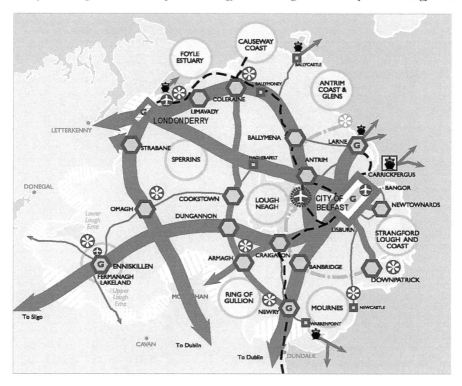

Figure 3.2   Regional Development Strategy for Northern Ireland: Key Diagram

Chapter 4

Critical Reflections on National Spatial and Regional Development Strategies for Northern Ireland

Jim Walsh
National University of Ireland, Maynooth

Michael Murray
Queen's University, Belfast

Introduction

The National Spatial Strategy (NSS) for the Republic of Ireland and the Regional Development Strategy (RDS) for Northern Ireland are policy documents of potentially immense importance for the long term development of different parts of the island of Ireland. Both documents provide spatial frameworks that are of direct relevance to the implementation of actions in many areas of public policy, and which can also significantly influence the geographical distribution of investments by the private sector. While each strategy is primarily concerned with issues related to the promotion of more balanced regional development within their own areas of jurisdiction there are of course also opportunities for achieving enhanced outcomes through greater coordination of the two territorial planning frameworks.

In this chapter we review the wider policy context within which the NSS and the RDS have been formulated and we consider some of the barriers that need to be overcome in order to achieve more coherent spatial development in the Dublin Belfast corridor. We then consider in some more detail four issues,

1. the relationship between strategic spatial planning and theories of regional development,
2. interactions between the Regional Development Strategy and statutory local plans,
3. the rural perspectives in the RDS and the NSS, and
4. implementation and capacity building in the area of strategic spatial planning.

The Context for the NSS and the RDS

The preparation of the NSS and the RDS must be viewed as part of a more general orientation towards new approaches to spatial planning in many European countries and also at EU level. A major catalyst in inserting strategic spatial planning firmly into the public policy arena was the process that culminated with the publication of the European Spatial Development Perspective in 1999. The publication of the ESDP is widely regarded as a very significant milestone in the history of spatial planning which has introduced new perspectives, policy aims and concepts that are currently being further elaborated within the context of the ESPON research programme.

The ESDP was the culmination of a lengthy preparation process that gained momentum in the 1990s as the EU sought to devise a new a geography that would be of assistance in the pursuit of the higher level goals of the Community, especially that of improving competitiveness in the global markets. Three policy guidelines inform the ESDP:

- the development of a balanced and polycentric urban system and a new urban-rural relationship,
- securing parity of access to infrastructure and knowledge, and
- sustainable development, prudent management and protection of natural and cultural heritages.

Taken together they provide a basis for reconsidering traditional patterns of territorial and spatial relations and in particular they identify opportunities where co-operation and coordination between regions could lead to enhanced outcomes. Such ideas are clearly relevant in the context of the Dublin Belfast corridor given the nature of its urban structure, the relationships between metropolitan and rural areas, and the presence of the Border.

The specific local contexts from which the NSS and the RDS emerged are also important. The National Development Plan (NDP) published in 1999 identified the promotion of balanced regional development as a core strategic objective and included a commitment by the government to prepare a national spatial strategy. This was a significant departure from the strategic goals and objectives of previous National Development Plans. The case for a spatial planning framework had been made in a number of influential reports including the Sustainable Development Strategy, the White Paper on Rural Development, and studies by the Economic and Social Research Institute and the and the National Economic and Social Council. The NDP chapter on regional development outlines the government's objective for regional policy as follows:

> To achieve more balanced regional development in order to reduce the disparities between and within the two regions and to develop the potential of both to contribute to the greatest possible extent to the continuing prosperity of the country. Policy to secure

such development must be advanced in parallel with policies to ensure that this development is sustainable with full regard to the quality of life, social cohesion and conservation of the environment and the natural and cultural heritage.

This is a rather formidable statement of objectives with a strong emphasis on development based on harnessing potential rather than on relying on redistribution between regions, and also on regional policy being advanced in parallel with other policies. This approach does not explicitly recognize the need for an overall coherent spatial framework that would be adopted by all government departments and public agencies. Later there is further evidence of caution, which is repeated in the NSS, in statements such as 'a prerequisite for implementation of the (regional) policy is the achievement of the macroeconomic objectives on which the Plan is based so that the necessary resources can be made available' (NDP, p. 46). Thus it can be seen that regional policy and the NSS are contested political, and indeed administrative, constructs which need to be nurtured over the medium to long term. The consultation processes that were employed in the preparation of the NSS helped to secure a high level of political and administrative support which needs to be maintained by ensuring that the implementation programme and structures have the support of all government departments.

Given the contextual origins of the NSS it is clear that any discussion of the potential of the Dublin – Belfast corridor must also take account of the tensions between maximising the overall level of development (usually measured by GDP per capita) and the relationship with the remainder of the island. The primary economic objective of the government is to maintain or enhance the level of international competitiveness of goods and services produced in Ireland so that there can be a continuation of economic growth. It is vitally important that the level of priority attached to balanced regional development and spatial planning in the current National Development Plan which was formulated during a phase of unprecedented levels of economic growth will be maintained in future NDPs even though the rates of economic growth may be much lower.

The RDS for Northern Ireland also had a lengthy preparation process that lasted almost four years with extensive consultation and discussion. Here the process had the added dimension of seeking to secure a consensus on future development patterns against a background of social divisions and distrust. Indeed the commitment to prepare the RDS was a component of the Good Friday Agreement in 1998. The detail of the final strategy represents a number of compromises that were achieved via the participatory processes that were employed at different stages.

The outcome from the contrasting preparation models is that while the broad structural components (gateways, hubs, regional/local urban centres, radial and linking transport corridors) are similar there are a number of significant differences. These include firstly that the NSS is more skeletal in that it provides a framework that is to be elaborated in more detail via Regional planning guidelines and later via the statutory local development plans. By contrast, the RDS is more detailed as it is a *regional* strategy, though of course it is not part of any UK level framework for spatial development as there is not any framework. This is a potentially serious constraint given the extent to which Northern Ireland is linked to the rest of the UK.

Secondly, the strategies differ in the extent to which they each refer to the remainder of the island of Ireland. Thus, in recognition of the current political realities, the RDS juxtaposes references to cross-border cooperation with discussion of linkages with Scottish regions. The point is most aptly illustrated by the truncated representation of 'key transport corridors' in the RDS maps. By contrast, the NSS provides more explicit recognition of the inter-dependencies between the North and the South. This is evident in the manner in which the transport proposals are depicted and also in the selection of Dundalk and Letterkenny as strategic frontier gateways with potential for much further development based in part on developing stronger linkages with Newry and Derry respectively. The NSS also identifies the potential offered by the ports by Belfast and Larne. The lesson to be drawn from these comparisons is that the concept of a Dublin-Belfast corridor is not particularly strongly nor coherently articulated in the two strategies. While this may be a disappointment to some it is important to recognize that any attempts to devise an integrated spatial planning framework along the east coast of Ireland, which may fit comfortably with the discourse underpinning the ESDP, will be essentially a long term project. The reflections of Professor Faludi, one of Europe's foremost thinkers on spatial planning, are pertinent here. He has noted that among the challenges of strategic planning are those of 'shaping the minds of those involved in spatial development, rather than shaping spatial development as such' (Faludi, 2001).

Against the contextual background outlined above we now consider some key issues that are pertinent to achieving the goals of the spatial strategies.

Key Issues

Spatial Planning and Regional Development Theory

The NSS and RDS both seek to promote more balanced regional development. A fundamental issue relates to the interpretation of this objective. For some, usually located outside the core regions, it is viewed as achieving a more equal sharing of opportunities and more equalisation of rewards. This perspective has been largely rejected in both strategies and replaced by a focus on harnessing regional potential through in part the realisation of critical mass in the supply of various development factors. The strategies also recognize the critical role of the metropolitan centres for international linkages and as bases for competitively producing internationally tradable economic output.

The strategies opt for a settlement framework consisting of gateways and hubs which are connected by radial and linking corridors. Special roles are also identified for small settlements and for rural areas. There is a risk that in a conceptual sense the NSS and RDS will be regarded as little more than updated versions of the plans produced in the 1960s and 1970s when 'growth centres' were in vogue. It would be a serious mistake to equate gateways with regional growth centres of the type envisaged in the 1960s. The reason for this is that the earlier growth centres were based on theories of regional development that are no longer considered satisfactory. Economically successful regions today, which include both urban and rural areas, are characterized by many diverse sets of factors including a blending of indigenous and externally driven enterprise strategies, by strong institutional capacity which is enhanced by intensive networking involving diverse sets of actors, and also by a strong commitment to innovation. There is a very extensive literature on the role, variety and potential of territorial or spatial innovation systems. Over recent years there have in fact been considerable efforts to build national or regional innovation systems. However, as argued by international theorists such as Professor Edward Malecki, a focus on territorially bounded innovation systems such as those organized by national or regional agencies may be too restrictive. Instead he proposes the concept of spatial innovation systems that consist of overlapping and interlinked national, regional and sectoral systems of innovation which are all manifested in different configurations in space. Thus the spatial innovation system approach seeks to highlight the complex and evolving integration at different levels of local, national and global forces. In order to promote development on an all Ireland basis and more specifically within the Dublin Belfast corridor it will be necessary that spatial planning coordination will be supported by coordination of other key strategic objectives as for example in relation to innovation. The concept of all Ireland spatial innovation system would benefit from further exploration.

The NSS and RDS provide the physical planning frameworks within which development may occur in the future. In order to capitalize on the opportunities presented by the two strategies it is essential that a deeper understanding of the dynamics of development in the regions of Ireland is promoted and that sectoral and regional policies take account of such dynamics and incorporate best practice models from regions in other countries. It is also important to note that the transfer of best practice from other regions is not unproblematic and will usually involve local adaptations.

In relation to the Dublin Belfast corridor there are opportunities to achieve higher levels of critical mass in a number of key areas through coordinated actions. Improvements in transport infrastructure, the possibilities offered by ICT, and the improved political context certainly offer the prospect of much increased interaction between the two cities and for enhanced development especially in a linked gateway consisting of Dundalk and Newry. However, such optimism must be restrained by a consideration of the legacy of partition.

The reality is that the histories of economic development in the North and South of Ireland are very different and therefore the preconditions that are usually required for enhanced levels of economic integration are weak. These include complementarities in production systems, strong and dynamic institutional linkages, excellent transport and communications infrastructures, and effective information dissemination. Hamilton (2004) has recently identified three sets of issues that have hindered either directly or indirectly the pace of economic integration between the North and the South.

Firstly he draws attention to the legacy of the Border. This includes physical infrastructure systems (transport, waste management, public utilities, etc.) that have been developed with little attention to coordination on an all Ireland basis. The Border has also created internal peripheries and artificially distorted the hinterlands of regional centres such as Dundalk and Newry.

Secondly, Hamilton identifies major contrasts in the industrial structures of the Republic and Northern Ireland. In summary manufacturing in Northern Ireland is much more reliant on traditional sectors which are characterized by lower productivity levels and also its service sector is much more oriented towards the non-market or public sector. Thirdly, and to a large extent related to the previous factors, the patterns of trade are very different. Not surprisingly North/ South trade is very low as a percentage of total imports/exports for both the North and the South and is mainly confined to agricultural and traditional low technology manufacturing.

These structural differences are very significant and are unlikely to change substantially in the short to medium term. A convergence in industrial structures and a greater integration of the Northern Ireland economy into the global as distinct from the UK economic systems, as has occurred in the Republic, may not necessarily lead to much closer economic integration in the form of North South trade. However, convergence might lead to more opportunities for sub supply firms to operate on an all Ireland basis, or to greater labour mobility among highly skilled workers, and more importantly to enhanced prospects for knowledge transfers, specialist business networks with a strong international orientation, and more generally social capital formation. The factors just listed have been identified in many studies as crucial ingredients in sustainable regional development. It has also been well established that Geography has a role in the transformation of regions. There is a large body of international evidence that supports the role of urban centres as locations that drive regional development. In an all Ireland context, and bearing in mind emerging trends towards polycentricity in parts of mainland Europe, the Dublin Belfast Corridor represents a geographical as well as a political, economic and cultural space that merits much more attention in relation to how it might be transformed from its current position of weakly integrated components into a region consisting of several overlapping activity spaces. The frameworks set out in the NSS and RDS can help policy makers and others to make this transition if the analytical framework is extended beyond considerations of purely physical planning.

Development Strategy – Statutory Plan Interactions

The Regional Development Strategy for Northern Ireland provides a set of housing growth indicators designed to guide the distribution of housing within the region over the period to 2015. However, within the Republic of Ireland this task is being carried forward by Regional Authorities which have been charged with the preparation of Regional Planning Guidelines to give effect to the National Spatial Strategy at regional level. While each strategy, therefore, successfully maps future spatial relationships within the context of the European Spatial Development Perspective, the prospects for area based development at a local authority scale are located in and are being devolved to the regional tier. In this regard it could be argued that, at present, the strategic planning framework for Northern Ireland is considerably more advanced in its guidance than the reciprocal strategic planning framework for the Republic. Nonetheless, there are issues surfacing in the rolling out of the Northern Ireland Regional Development Strategy across the sub-regional statutory planning process that require immediate debate and which have implications for development activity within the Belfast-Dublin Economic Corridor as whole, especially should the Northern Ireland methodology be more widely embraced.

The Northern Ireland Regional Development Strategy provides housing growth indicators for each District Council area out to the time horizon of 2015. Thus, for example, the Belfast Metropolitan Area Districts are allocated 51,000 residential units, Down District – 7,750 units, Banbridge District – 4,000 units and Newry and Mourne District – 8,500 units. As noted by the Strategy, the allocation rationale reflects:

> the inherited pattern of population in these districts, population growth trends, and a broad assessment of the economic role and range of cultural, leisure, social and commercial activities available in each district. It acknowledges that some districts exert an influence and pull beyond their own immediate locality, due in part to the magnetic power of the district town. Over the longer term, some *districts are more likely to generate a larger demand for housing consistent with their higher levels of population growth (p118).*

At present a number of emerging Area Plans are seeking to disaggregate these indicators into settlement housing targets in order to inform land use zoning and the phased release of housing land. The precision applied to the distribution of housing across each District Council settlement hierarchy in line with its regional strategy indicator contrasts with the opaqueness of how the various factors cited above have been balanced against each other. Moreover, the apportionment of housing downwards from each hub or gateway implies the determination of development quotas which, because of limited numbers, not only are giving rise to disquiet among elected representatives, but also are running against alternative technical calculations which point to a stronger growth dynamic than that provided for by the Regional Development Strategy. So, for example, an analysis of building rates over the period since 1998 (the base year for the Regional Development Strategy) would suggest that the required 2015 housing growth indicator for Newry and Mourne is of the order of 12,500 units, with that for Banbridge District being almost 6,000 units. The great danger is that a land supply which is unreasonably constrained will exacerbate imperfections within the housing market related to availability and price. This could well serve to undermine the competitive position of these Districts and their respective hubs of Newry and Banbridge which because of their location are acknowledged as having pivotal status on the Belfast-Dublin Corridor.

Dealing with this tension between a mechanistic approach to strategic demand and local concerns over inadequacy will require no small amount of political mobilisation which can transcend emotional advocacy. At the same time the Northern Ireland planning system, unsatisfactorily divided in terms of authority between the Department for Regional Development and the Department of the Environment, must demonstrate greater responsiveness to the collective goal of driving forward the revitalisation of cities and towns and to do this with greater transparency and accountability. In this vein it would seem only appropriate that local authorities should be able to challenge and re-negotiate regional allocations, either upwards or downwards, thus moderating a coercive and regulatory approach to development strategy – statutory plan interaction through a deeper process of dialogue and collaboration.

The Rural Perspective in Development Strategies

Both the Regional Development Strategy for Northern Ireland and the National Spatial Strategy for the Republic of Ireland give considerable attention to rural matters. The former devotes a complete chapter to rural Northern Ireland and where appropriate includes mention of the rural under other development themes. The latter presents a deeper analysis of rural diversity and links this with regional planning responses. Both highlight the issue of single dwellings in the countryside as *the* spatial policy issue to be addressed, though again political sensitivities would seem to have warranted caution on being overly prescriptive. The preferred *modus operandi*, certainly within the Northern Ireland policy arena, is that of stealth and patience whereby the housing indicator approach discussed above, when combined with extensive Green Belt and Countryside Policy Area designations within statutory plans, and supported by a forthcoming and overarching Planning Policy Statement on the Countryside to guide development control decision-making, will provide a rigorous policy rationale for a strong presumption against housing in the countryside. Within this context a plausible scenario for the Belfast-Dublin Corridor is the demise of dispersed rural communities. In working through the application of this spatial concept it is appropriate that the profile of hubs, gateways and transport networks should dominate. The countryside as a living and working territory should not, however, be marginalized to a so called 'rural residual'.

It is unfortunate that any assessment of the merits and drawbacks of single houses in the countryside is never more than one-sided when it comes to planners assessing costs and benefits. The content of a draft policy discussion paper on this topic, published recently by the Irish Planning Institute, is evidence of that neglect. But the parameters of this debate go well beyond the issue of approving or refusing planning permission for a countryside dwelling and rest fundamentally on how rural society is valued. The Regional Development Strategy for Northern Ireland and the National Spatial Strategy for the Republic of Ireland have exposed a gaping fault line between rural planning and rural development: the former looks for problems and the latter for solutions. In this context the enduring frustration with rural planning, certainly in Northern Ireland derives from its preference to de-socialize the territories it claims an affinity with. The pre-eminence of landscape protection policies on planning policy maps fosters a sense of rural space that, in short, is envisioned as being socially empty. Rural areas and not least those within the Belfast-Dublin corridor deserve a better fate.

Essentially, what is called for in this chapter is a strong rural development perspective in the delivery of initiatives to help realize the potential of the corridor project. That perspective should be informed by the following ten considerations:

- Realising the potential of multi-sectoral development
- Community development as an approach to change
- Stakeholder participation, responsibility and empowerment
- Equity, equality and social justice
- Spatial differentiation which accommodates rural diversity and cultural distinctiveness
- Collective problem solving through collaborative governance
- Stewardship of land and environment
- Rural – urban interdependence, rather than urban dominance
- Quality, competitiveness, added value and innovation
- A willingness to learn from comparative rural development experiences.

The task ahead, therefore, must be to ask fundamental questions about what policies are required for the rural territories of the Belfast-Dublin Corridor, and how such policies can be delivered within each jurisdiction and on a cross-border basis. This in turn may well raise additional questions about institutional design and the most appropriate division of labour between central government departments and agencies, local authorities, other public bodies, the private sector and civil society. These matters go well beyond the content of the Regional Development Strategy for Northern Ireland and the National Spatial Strategy for the Republic of Ireland. Moreover, they are matters which transcend the rural. The important point is that those charged with policy formulation and implementation must ensure that the rural dimension is strongly represented in the operationalization of the Belfast – Dublin corridor concept.

Implementation and Capacity Building in the Area of Strategic Spatial Planning

There is an urgent need to strengthen the capacity for strategic spatial planning as an on-going activity in the context of the implementation of the NSS and the RDS. While administrative structures have been put in place to oversee implementation it is imperative that systems are developed to ensure that the practice of strategic spatial planning becomes an on-going rigorous and robust process that will be able to effectively support the ambitious goals of the strategies as spatial frameworks to be adhered to by all government departments and development agencies. Critical issues that need to be addressed in this respect are (1) coordinated development of digital spatial databases, (2) development of expertise in spatial modelling so that alternative scenarios can be developed and evaluated and so that crucial evidence can be produced in support of claims for resources to achieve the strategic goals, and (3) mechanisms to ensure on-going dialogue between policy makers in both the political and administrative arenas, the diverse range of actors involved in activities related to regional and local development, and researchers on an all Ireland basis so every opportunity is used for cooperation and coordination of actions in support of the long term goals and objectives of the strategies.

Here we focus only on the issue of data assembly and dissemination in a coordinated manner. Both NSS and the RDS provide the basis for requiring a very strong territorial focus in the design and delivery of a wide range of public policies. More significantly, each strategy recognizes the need to co-ordinate strategic territorial planning between the North and the South, and especially in the Border zones. Meeting the diverse needs of policy makers, local and regional development organisations, private sector actors, political leaders, educators and others at this time can be most efficiently and effectively addressed through the development of an integrated and dynamic approach to collation, analysis and dissemination of digital spatial data.

There is now an urgent need for a broadly based initiative in this area. There are a number of key stakeholders who already have some statutory responsibilities in this area. The Ordnance Surveys (North and South) have responsibilities in relation to the collection, management, storage and dissemination of data recorded at a variety of geographical scales. They also guarantee the quality of the data and ensure that the practices in Ireland are in conformity with international standards. The Department of the Environment, Heritage and Local Government in Dublin has recently been assigned responsibility for developing a National Spatial Data Infrastructure. This initiative is very timely even though it is primarily concerned with data provision in the Republic of Ireland.

On a practical level over the short to medium term a cross border structure needs to be established, maybe under the auspices of the North South Ministerial Council that will be responsible for developing an integrated and dynamic approach to the collation, analysis and dissemination of digital spatial data. The structure might include representatives of the ministries with responsibility for spatial planning in Belfast and Dublin, the two Ordnance Surveys, the Central Statistics Office Dublin and the Northern Ireland Statistical and Research Agency, the Regional and Local Authorities, other agencies with responsibility for collection and management of spatial datasets, the GIS user groups, and researchers in spatial analysis.

The structure could provide assistance at two levels. At the high level of strategic policy development it could assist the governments in Dublin and Belfast in the preparation of policies to guide the long term development of digital spatial data infrastructure for the island of Ireland. At an operational level it could oversee a range of actions to be undertaken by the main stakeholders with responsibility to:

- Establish a data management and integration system for spatial datasets
- Develop an integrated virtual Spatial Data Archive consisting of generalized spatial datasets.
- Co-ordinate the development of metadata across partner institutions on an all-Ireland basis.
- Develop and implement data transfer protocols to communicate with the data archive.
- Investigate ways of identifying, measuring and communicating geographic data quality indicators.
- Provide an advisory service to researchers in order to encourage and facilitate greater usage of spatial datasets and spatially referenced databases.
- Promote greater usage of spatial data for analyses undertaken by researchers and among policy makers through the development of a web interface for users, production of promotional literature and organising workshops/seminars and conferences.
- Maintain promotional material on an on-going basis.
- Co-ordinate as a medium term project the production of a multi-thematic digital *Atlas of Ireland* which will be a major resource for researchers and for informing wider audiences on spatial aspects of the economy, society, environment, culture, etc. It will also be a major promotional tool for all of the agencies engaged in the collection and processing of spatial data.

On a practical level a first module in the production of a multi-thematic Atlas of Ireland could be a comprehensive spatial analysis of the data from the Censuses of Population taken in Northern Ireland in 2001 and in the Republic in 2002 with comparisons back to the 1991 data. This is a major project that will have to overcome substantial technical issues related to differences in definitions, the geographical scales at which data are provided, and for mapping purposes unharmonized digital boundary systems. Nevertheless, it is imperative to develop as quickly as possible a thorough understanding of the spatial trends that emerged over the last decade and for these trends to be examined on an all Ireland basis using micro level data so that the extent of spatial imprints can be more clearly identified.

The tasks outlined above are fundamental building blocks for a new and more rigorous approach to spatial planning. While accepting the limitations of quantitative data analysis and quantitative models there is an urgent need for more sophisticated tools to assist the promotion of spatial planning. There is a need to develop a comprehensive spatial model that will be able to explore the interactions between economic, social and environmental indicators and provide alternative scenarios to guide policy formation. This is a very large task that will require a number of years to accomplish, partly due to the paucity of data to calibrate any model. However, there are possibilities to learn from experience in other parts of Europe as for example the Netherlands where comprehensive models have been constructed to assist in the preparation of strategies for the next 25–30 years. The current reality is that much of macroeconomic and sectoral planning is guided by models that permit investigation of different scenarios and which are also used in the bargaining process with the Finance ministries to secure public resources. Without a similarly rigorous approach to spatial planning there is a risk that the aspirations in the NSS and the RDS will be assigned lower priority than sectoral or other objectives. The pursuit of an integrated and coherent approach to territorial cohesion as envisaged in the NSS and RDS frameworks could be frustrated from the outset.

Conclusions

The National Spatial Strategy and the Regional Development Strategy are important starting points for a new era of comprehensive spatial planning at a time when the broader political and economic contexts are more supportive of an approach towards a coherent development strategy for the island while recognising that policies must in the first instance be formulated within each of the jurisdictions. They represent the beginnings of a process that will need to be supported on an on-going basis over the long term. A crucial part of the process is that explicitly spatial goals are maintained as core objectives of all development strategies in the future and that the frameworks established by the Strategies are adhered to, subject to adjustments following rigorous periodic reviews. Responsibility for spatial planning and the pursuit of goals related to territorial cohesion must be shared by all government departments and public agencies, while accepting that one Department must take on the lead role in each jurisdiction.

We have highlighted a number of areas where further work is needed in order to advance the spatial planning agenda. These relate to the need to incorporate into spatial planning a deeper understanding of the dynamics of spatial development and especially of the interactions that occur at, and between, different geographical scales so that the regional perspective can deal with locations and spatial units in a relational as well as in an absolute sense. There is also a need for a planning perspective that facilitates development that is sustainable in every sense with particular attention to different types of settlement and to the distinctive characteristics of local landscapes in both rural and urban contexts. Finally, we argue that there is an urgent need to develop more sophisticated methodologies to support strategic spatial planning on an all Ireland basis.

The Dublin Belfast corridor, whatever its extent, undoubtedly has the potential to become a significant axis of development within the framework of northwest Europe. However, this will be a long term process as there are significant legacies to be overcome. The NSS and RDS provide a basis for a more coherent development strategy along the east coast of Ireland. While a vigorous approach to supporting development in the corridor may pose a threat to other parts of the island this need not be the case. Rather, more inter-regional competition may provide a springboard to support more radical long-term proposals involving the other major urban centres as is also envisaged especially in the National Spatial Strategy.

References

Dept. for Regional Development (2001), *The Regional Development Strategy for Northern Ireland* (Belfast, Dept. for Regional Development).

Department of Environment, Heritage and Local Government (2002), *National Spatial Strategy: People, Places and Potential* (Dublin, Stationery Office).

European Commission (1999), European Spatial Development Perspective: *Towards Balanced and Sustainable Development of the Territory of the European Union* (Luxembourg, Office for Official Publications of the European Communities).

Faludi, A. (ed.) (2001), *European Spatial Planning* (Cambridge Mass. Lincoln Institute of Land Policy).

Hamilton, D. (2001), *Economic Integration on the Island of Ireland* Administration 49 (2), pp73–89.

Ireland: *National Development Plan 2000-2006* (1999), (Dublin, Stationery Office).

Malecki, E.J. (1997), *Technology and Economic Development: the Dynamics of Local, Regional and National Competitiveness* (London, Addison Longman).

Murray, M. and Greer, J (2002), *Participatory Planning as Dialogue: the Northern Ireland Regional Strategic Framework and its Public Examination Process* Policy Studies 23(4), pp 283–294.

Oinas, P. and Malecki, E.J. (2002), *The Evolution of Technology and Space: from National and Regional to Spatial Innovation Systems.* International Regional Science Review 25(1), pp102–131

Walsh, J.A., The National Spatial Strategy as a Framework for Achieving Balanced Regional Development. In McDonagh J., (ed.) (2002), *Economy,*

Society and Peripherality – Experiences from the West of Ireland 55–79 (Arlen House, Galway).

————, Planning for regional development in a peripheral open economy: the case of Ireland. In Byron, R., Hansen, J.C. and Jenkins, T., (eds.) (2004), *Regional Development on the North Atlantic Margin* 125–149 (Ashgate Publishing, Aldershot).

————, Spatial Planning for Territorial Cohesion: Linking the urban and Rural Domains. In O'Cinneide, M. (ed.) (2004), *Territorial Cohesion: Meeting new challenges for an enlarged EU* 83–98 (Department of Community, Rural and Gaeltacht Affairs, Dublin).

Chapter 5

The Structure of the Greater Dublin Area

John Yarwood

Former Director, Urban Institute, Ireland

Introduction

This chapter presents an analysis of certain structural characteristics of Dublin and the Greater Dublin Area It is based upon work done as part of the Irish contribution to the POLYNET consortium, which is undertaking an EC-funded research project (INTERREG IIIB) entitled 'The Sustainable Management of Polycentric Mega-City Regions in North-West Europe'.

After a brief physical overview, identifying the most important towns outside Dublin, we record their populations and project them forwards by twenty years. Secondly, we consider the labour market, and project employment forward by twenty years, identifying the current ratio of jobs to resident workforce by county. Thirdly, we present the commuting flows between urban centres, and comment on their characteristics. The final part of the chapter uses this data to calculate measures of the polycentricity of the area in three ways. Finally, we make some largely qualitative observations on structural change, such as the gentrification of the urban core, the emergence of an 'edge city', and 'counter-urbanisation'.

I suggest that the Greater Dublin Area is not a polycentric structure, by comparison with some other regions in North-West Europe. The concluding remarks comment on what the significance of this might be. The chapter after this one describes the regional planning guidelines, which are to some extent based on the analysis here.

Regional Physical Overview

We begin by a brief examination of the region. Refer to Figure 5.1, Regional Overview. This map is based upon the 2002 'Corine' image, in a simplified version. Land use categories have been combined for simplicity and legibility. Urbanized areas are shown, as well as major rural uses, motorways and principal roads, railways and important rivers, ports and airports. We have also noted sensitive landscape zones, such as the Dublin and Wicklow mountains, the Boyne Valley, the coastal strip, and the Mountains of Mourne. Such constraints have exercised a powerful role for many decades in shaping the regional-urban form.

The first general observation is that the structure seems to be intensely radial, with roads and railways fanning out from a dominant mono-pole towards the other major cities of Ireland, which lie around the coast and are relatively distant. There has been little investment in orbital or tangential movement in this city-region, however. The hinterland contains no other major settlements. The transport links from the minor towns lead mainly to Dublin, with links between one minor town and the others being generally poor.

We focused upon the Greater Dublin Area, comprising the four metropolitan counties, (Dublin City, Fingal, South Dublin and Dun Laoghaire-Rathdown), and the three counties of the Mid-East Region, (Meath, Kildare and Wicklow). This is essentially the hinterland of the city. We excluded the southernmost part of Wicklow and we added County Louth, (which is within the Border Region), because it contains two substantial towns, Drogheda and Dundalk. County Louth also forms a part of the potential Dublin-Belfast Corridor. Dundalk is the only town near Dublin which was identified in the National Spatial Strategy as a 'Gateway', designated for major growth of population and investment.

The POLYNET project assumed the standard criteria for defining a Functional Urban Area 'core' (i.e. the urban area of a town) to be a minimum of 20,000 jobs and a density of 7 jobs per hectare, within a cluster of contiguous census districts; (i.e. NUTS 5 area). This was agreed after discussions with the various European regions involved in POLYNET, as being most appropriate.

The Irish censuses for 1981 and 1991 give workers' residence, but not the workplace location. The 2002 census gives the workplace location, but this data has not yet become available. At the time of writing, therefore, we have used the Employment Survey prepared in 2002 by the Dublin Transportation Office (DTO). However, this survey excludes County Louth, (i.e. Drogheda and Dundalk), and for this we used the census data on resident workers and factored it down by a comparable 'Jobs Ratio', (Table 5.6) or the proportionate net out-commuting, (Table 5.7).

In the case of Greater Dublin, only Dublin itself meets the stated criteria. Therefore, in order best to capture the detail of the Irish situation, we undertook a supplementary study, which has selected several other minor urban centres for study, on the basis of more relaxed criteria. These selected towns, as well as Dublin itself, are shown on Figure 5.2, Base Map of Cores and Rings.

The relaxed criteria are that (a) there should be a minimum of 4,000 jobs in each cluster of contiguous survey zones and (b) the density in constituent zones should exceed 0.8 jobs per hectare. This might be taken as showing how ruralized Ireland is, compared to North-West Europe as a whole. The stricter criteria worked well for France, England, Belgium, Holland, Germany and Switzerland. But in our case, there were no towns other than Dublin big enough to choose for study. For this reason, it was agreed to relax the norms for the Irish case only.[1]

The 'ring' around the core was defined as the contiguous survey zones from which 10 per cent of workers or more commute to the core. Using the Dublin Traffic Model (DTM) and 2003 survey data, this contour has been shown: see Figure 5.2. Almost the entire GDA lies within the ring, which goes over the GDA boundary into adjacent counties.[2] The enclosing counties, (i.e. NUTS 4 areas), are also shown.

However, we have also shown a second inner contour, namely the ring from which 20 per cent of residents commute to Dublin. This is based upon the DTM, and may be regarded as reliable

Applying these criteria in a strict, comprehensive way, we have identified the following urban centres. The survey zone names, (if any), within each cluster, are placed in brackets:

- Maynooth (Leixlip, Celbridge, Maynooth)
- Bray (Bray 1, 2 and 3, Rathmichael)
- Naas
- Newbridge
- Navan
- Wicklow
- Drogheda, (Drogheda Municipal Borough, St Mary DED, St Peter DED)
- Dundalk, (Dundalk urban, Dundalk rural, Haggardstown DED).

The job numbers, zonal areas and densities are shown in Table 5.1, Identification of Urban Centres.

However, note that in the case of Drogheda and Dundalk, we showed the census districts which enclosed the urban areas, (drawn from the Corine image of 2002).

---

[1] The justification for such apparently undemanding criteria is as follows. First, by adopting a low size threshold, we can avoid excluding Wicklow, which has just over 4,000 jobs, as well as a port and a railway. Secondly, the low density is necessary because the survey zones adopted by the DTO are of variable size. Some important employment centres have large survey zones, which creates a misleading impression. For example, Navan has nearly 8,000 jobs, with a density of only 1.3. Maynooth has nearly three thousand jobs (including the National University), with a density of 0.83, (although it is part of a group of contiguous zones totalling 13,450 jobs with a net density of 2.10).

[2] In order to determine the full extent of the ring, we were unable to use the DTM, since it covers only the GDA. Instead, we took from the 2002 census those districts from which more than 20 per cent commuted more than 20 km. We assumed that at least 50 per cent of such journeys went to Dublin, (believing that this approximation, whatever its difficulties, was the most reasonable possible), and used this line to extend the ring beyond the GDA boundary.

Table 5.1   Identification of Urban Centres

Urban Centre Name	Survey Zone Names	Jobs	Area (Ha)	Jobs/Ha
Maynooth	Leixlip	8611	1147	7.51
	Celbridge	2026	1753	1.16
	Maynooth	2813	3393	0.83
	(Total)	13,450	6293	2.10
Bray	Bray 1	1316	58	22.69
	Bray 2	4319	230	18.87
	Bray 3	4070	141	28.86
	Rathmichael	1470	875	1.68
	(Total)	11,175	1304	8.57
Naas	Naas	13,579	3189	4.26
Newbridge	Newbridge	7331	1988	3.69
Navan	Navan	7959	6100	1.30
Wicklow	Wicklow	4146	3723	1.11
Balbriggan	Balbriggan Urban	2017	215	9.90
Drogheda	MB	8394	1346	6.24
	St. Peter DED	2556	3180	0.80
	St. Mary DED	1908	3554	0.54
	(Total)	12858	8080	1.59
	Factor (0.45)	5786	----	---
Dundalk	UD	11,880	592	20.01
	RD	9840	2476	4.00
	Hagardstown	2262	2036	1.11
	(Total)	23,982	5140	4.70
	Factor (1.08)	25,901	----	----

Note:
For Drogheda and Dundalk 2000 Census figures were factored by author as described in text. All other centres based on D.T.O, Employment Survey 2002.

For case study purposes, and for heuristic reasons, we decided to include Balbriggan. This is regarded with great interest as a key growth centre in terms of 'official' planning, being the largest settlement closest to Dublin on the Dublin-Belfast Corridor.

Population

Population Census Figures

The population statistics have been obtained from the censuses for 1981, 1991 and 2002. See Table 5.2, Population Data.

Table 5.2   Population Data

a)   Total Population

Town	1981	1991	2002
Dundalk	29737	30340	31120
Drogheda	27528	28873	30974
Navan	13125	13964	21426
Balbriggan	4786	8378	11132
Maynooth	17797	28909	40324
DMA	1003164	1040904	1141051
Newbridge	11387	12790	17377
Naas	8837	11661	19422
Bray	22853	26836	29826
Wicklow	7455	8629	11621

Source: *CSO Censuses*

b)   Intercensal Population Change (per cent)

Town	1981-1991	1991-2002
Dundalk	2.02	2.57
Drogheda	4.88	7.28
Navan	6.39	53.44
Balbriggan	75.05	32.87
Maynooth	62.43	39.50
DMA	3.76	9.62
Newbridge	12.32	35.86
Naas	31.96	66.56
Bray	17.43	11.14
Wicklow	15.75	34.67

c) Population Density: Persons per Km^2

Town	1981	1991	2002
Dundalk	589.90	601.90	617.30
Drogheda	366.60	384.50	412.40
Navan	217.70	231.60	355.30
Balbriggan	167.00	292.30	388.40
Maynooth	259.20	421.10	587.40
DMA	1086.00	1127.00	1235.00
Newbridge	464.60	521.80	709.00
Naas	275.80	364.00	606.20
Bray	1152.00	1353.00	1504.00
Wicklow	160.00	185.30	249.50

These data illustrate rather dramatically that (a) the towns outside Dublin are still very small in relative terms; (b) all the minor towns, (except Dundalk), have nonetheless grown very fast compared to Dublin, which has grown in percentage terms rather slowly; and (c) gross densities have increased, particularly in Dublin, (and particularly in the inner city).

Regional Trends, Projections and Future Policies

It may be helpful to sketch out the likely future of the regional population, according to the Greater Dublin Area Regional Planning Guidelines, (as described in the next chapter). These reflect official development policy objectives. It is envisaged that the GDA will grow from 508,096 households in 2002 to 773,929 households in 2022. Within this household projection was added a 'headroom' of 38 per cent to allow for second homes, relocation of families, vacancies etc. (Another matter requiring close attention in Dublin is the drastic reduction in household size. The number of households in typical villages or small towns will increase, even if the population were to remain static or decline).

Ireland has an exceptionally high amount of house-building activity – five times the UK or German level, and three times the EU level in 2002. (See: McCarthy C., Hughes A., and Woelger E., "Where have all the houses gone?" Davy Stockbrokers. November 2002 Dublin). The housing completion returns seem to indicate a number of households almost 40 per cent higher than the 2002 census. This is due to a huge number of second or third homes, and it is thought that this is driven by cheap mortgage finance plus a desire to tie up spare cash in investment in 'bricks and mortar'. It is widely suspected that Ireland is overproducing dwellings, although prices have risen to scarcely affordable levels.

The GDA planned totals are based on CSO national growth scenarios, constrained by a policy goal of retaining a constant ratio of GDA population to national population, which is 39 per cent. On the other hand, various chosen urban centres outside Dublin should be expected to more than double in size, even on a low scenario. For example, (according to studies for the Regional Planning Guidelines), the population will grow from 2002–2017 as follows: Navan from 21,428 to 48,211; Balbriggan from 11,709 to 30,096; Maynooth from 44,679 to 70,676; Naas/Newbridge from 40,535 to 84,182, and Wicklow from 14,074 to 52,774. From a local point of view this would have a transforming effect. It also illustrates the effect of a policy of concentrating growth into growth centres, (as opposed to rural dispersal.) See Atkins Ireland, Urban Institute Ireland, Goodbody Economic Consultants, and Tom Phillips and Associates, Background papers for the GDA Regional Planning Guidelines, 2003.

In the case of Dublin, however, the metropolitan area (DMA) would increase by densification and infill (2002–2017) from 371,111 to 468,034 households. As part of the total GDA population, this is a reduction from 82 per cent to 74 per cent, and obviously the population of the remainder, including minor towns and rural areas, will correspondingly increase, from 18 per cent to 26 per cent. Even so, the small towns outside Dublin, chosen as growth nodes, would individually by 2017 have populations around a mere 5 per cent to 8 per cent of the GDA total.

Employment

Regional Output

The work of the RPG consultants on employment, and particularly Bernard Feeney of Goodbody Economic Consultants, is acknowledged as the basis of this discussion.

In the year 2000, regional output in the Greater Dublin Area (GDA) amounted to €43bn and accounted for almost half (47 per cent) of the output of the national economy as a whole. Between 1995 and 2000, regional output grew by 95.3 per cent in nominal terms. This was similar to economic growth nationally. As a result, the share of regional output has remained broadly static over the period.

There are now almost 750,000 people employed in the GDA. Over the period since 1995, employment in the region increased by an additional 237,000 persons. See Table 5.3, Output and Employment in the GDA 1995–2003.

Table 5.3 Output and Employment in the GDA, 1995–2003

	1995	2000	2003
Output (€ millions)	22,061	43,089	N/A
Employment (000s)	512.2	721.8	749.6

Source: *CSO*

Of the total regional output of €43 bn in 2000, output of the service sector was almost €27bn. The industrial sector accounted for €16 bn, with the agricultural sector making up the balance at less than €0.5 bn. Thus, the service sector accounts for 62 per cent of regional output, (or about 75 per cent of employment). This compares with a 54 per cent service sector share of national output. The predominance of services in the region largely reflects the role of Dublin City as a centre for Government (to date, although this may be reduced somewhat through the decentralisation of Government departments) and public sector activity and a focus for the provision of business services.

The industrial sector in the GDA has performed strongly over the period since 1995, increasing its share of regional output from 34.6 per cent to 37.4 per cent in 2000. This reflects the strong performance of both the construction sector and the manufacturing sector, and particularly the foreign owned manufacturing sector in this period. See Table 5.4, Output and Employment in the GDA, by sector, 2000. The projected growth in the national economy presents a considerable challenge for the regional economy. Given that the GDA accounts for nearly half of national output, the achievement of expectations with regard to national economic growth will require a very strong economic contribution from the region.

Table 5.4   Output and Employment in the GDA by Sector, 2000

	Output		Employment	
	€ millions	%	000s	%
Agriculture	407	0.9	15.7	2.2
Industry	16,115	37.4	174.9	24.2
Services	26,712	62.0	531.2	73.6
Total	43,089	100.0	721.8	100.0

Source: *CSO*

The manufacturing sector in the region will not have as profound an impact on economic growth in the future as in the recent past. Ireland is no longer a low cost environment and there is strong competition from countries such as China and India for inward investment in manufacturing. The labour market in the GDA region is more constrained and infrastructural resources are more pressurized. As countries develop into high wage economies, employment tends to rise in high value-added activities in manufacturing, such as research and development. The importance of the market service sector as a source of employment also grows. These trends are likely to impact strongly on the region over the next twenty years.

The importance of the service sector to the region is demonstrated not only by the high level of service sector employment, but also by the fact that over one-third of that employment is in business services, including financial services. Internationally traded services are very important to the region, with, for example, two thirds of IDA supported firms in the GDA region being in internationally-traded financial and other services.

The Labour and Jobs Markets

The labour force in the Greater Dublin Area stood at 749,676 people in 2002, compared to 630,401 in 1996. This represents a total increase of 18.9 per cent, or an average annual growth rate of 2.9 per cent. In 2002, 72.7 per cent of the labour force fell into the 25–54 year old age bracket. The most active age bracket in the labour force was the 25–34 year old bracket, making up over 31 per cent of the total labour force.

Labour force participation varies according to age and gender. The rate of participation in the labour force by people in the 15–24 year age bracket has fallen somewhat for both men and women. This is a clear indication of increased participation in third level education. Whereas male participation rates for other age groups on the whole have remained reasonably steady over the period, there have been some significant changes in the proportion of women entering the labour force.

The most significant changes have occurred in the age brackets for 35–44 year olds and 45–54 year olds. In the 35–44 years age bracket, the labour force participation of females increased from 41.5 per cent in 1991 to 63.6 per cent in 2002, while the 45–54 years age bracket saw an increase of 23.8 percentage points from 35.1 per cent to 58.9 per cent in the same period. The indications are that more women are now returning to work after starting their families. These trends reflect both the higher educational qualifications now being attained by women, the increased availability of jobs, and for some, the need to supplement family income to meet housing expenses.

The trend over the last decade for male participation rates in the labour force has been for very little change. For this reason, when predicting future participation rates, the focus will inevitably be on female involvement.

Employment in the Urban Centres

As stated above, according to the standard POLYNET criteria, Dublin is the unique eligible centre in the region. However, we identified other urban centres using reduced criteria: see above. There are two sources of data. Firstly, the censuses have identified the labour force in each census district in terms of the workers' residence, but not the location of the workplace. (The 2002 census reveals more, but the data has not yet been analysed and made available). Secondly, the Employment Survey 2002 of the Dublin Transportation Office gives the job numbers located in each Traffic Zone. There is no such survey earlier than 2002, unfortunately. The DTO survey zones equate to census districts or aggregations (or subdivisions) of them. The difficulty is that some zones are relatively big, and so give a misleading impression of density.

Refer to Table 5.5 Employment Data for Dublin and Minor Towns 1981, 1991 and 2002, Intercensal Change and Densities.

Table 5.5   Employment Data for Dublin and Minor Towns

a)   Total Employment

Town	1981	1991	2002 (CSO)	2002 (DTO)
Dundalk	9528	8547	10942	0
Drogheda	9071	8997	12858	0
Navan	4317	4308	10039	7959
Balbriggan	2518	2489	4978	2209
Maynooth	6506	10285	19092	13450
DMA	359648	358346	508030	617599
Newbridge	3563	4116	8025	7331
Naas	3050	4403	9489	13579
Bray	7241	5296	6939	11175
Wicklow	2333	2529	4638	4146

b)   Intercensal Employment Change (per cent)

Town	1981-1991	1991-02 (CSO)	1991-02 (DTO)
Dundalk	-10.30	28.02	0.00
Drogheda	-0.82	42.44	0.00
Navan	-0.21	133.03	84.75
Balbriggan	-1.15	100.00	-11.25
Maynooth	58.08	85.63	30.77
DMA	-0.36	41.77	72.35
Newbridge	15.52	94.97	78.11
Naas	44.36	115.51	208.40
Bray	-26.86	31.02	111.01
Wicklow	8.40	83.39	63.94

c)   Employment Density (jobs/ha)

Town	1981	1991	2002 (CSO)	2002 (DTO)
Dundalk	1.89	1.70	2.17	0.00
Drogheda	1.21	1.20	1.71	0.00
Navan	0.72	0.71	1.66	1.32
Balbriggan	0.88	0.87	1.74	0.77
Maynooth	0.95	1.50	2.78	1.96
DMA	3.89	3.88	5.50	6.69
Newbridge	1.45	1.68	3.27	2.99
Naas	0.95	1.37	2.96	4.24
Bray	3.65	2.77	3.50	5.64
Wicklow	0.50	0.54	1.00	0.89

Neither data source is ideal, and for this reason we have presented both. The DTO figures are mostly greater than the CSO figures for 2002. This can be explained by the obvious fact that the resident workers are for many places greater than the local job numbers, as the 'Jobs Ratio', (Table 5.6) and the out commuting data, (Table 5.7 and Figure 5.7) make clear.

The 1981 census probably gives a reasonable figure because most people lived and worked in the same town. This was particularly true for Dublin. By 2002, however, it was no longer true, and the DTO figures are more useful than the census. For this reason the growth figures 1991-2002 in are calculated on the basis of the DTO 2002 survey and not the census 2002. This creates a difficulty, because the 1991 figures (CSO) show the resident workforce, whilst the 2002 figures (DTO) show the number of jobs. There is no jobs data for 1991, however. The last intercensal growth is probably underestimated as a result. The DTO employment 2002 survey excludes County Louth, (i.e. Drogheda and Dundalk.) Here, for the want of better sources at the moment of writing, we have been obliged to take the 2002 census data and estimate an adjustment to them. We have factored the census data by a percentage equivalent to the 'Jobs Ratio' for the adjacent county, (Table 5.6) checked against the net out-commuting figure, (from Table 5.7) This suggests a factor of 0.45 for Drogheda and 1.08 for Dundalk. This method is hardly perfect, but it the best we could do at the time of writing.

Spatial Mismatch of Jobs and Labour Force

The growth in the labour force indicates that some 14,500 net additional jobs will have to be created each year up to 2010, if unemployment in the region is not to rise. The total number of jobs will rise by over 116,000 by that date. From the point of view of land use planning, the distribution of the jobs throughout the region is important. Table 5.6, Spatial Distribution of Jobs and Labour Force by County, 2002, below, presents an overview of the distribution of jobs throughout the region in 2002, and the corresponding distribution of the labour force.

Table 5.6   Distribution of Jobs and Labour Force by Local Authority in DA 2002

Local Authority Area	Jobs	Labour Force	Jobs Ratio
Dublin City	393,221	250,330	1.62
DLRCC	77,471	86,896	0.87
Fingal	68,477	98,448	0.69
South Dublin	85,683	119,632	0.72
Kildare	54,271	79,220	0.67
Meath	31,272	63,134	0.49
Wicklow	30,615	52,016	0.59
All	741,000	749,676	0.99

Source: *Labour Force from CSO, Jobs from DTO*

As would be expected, Dublin City accounts for over half (53.1 per cent) of all jobs in the region. South Dublin is the next most important with 11.6 per cent of jobs.

Only Dublin City has more jobs than the resident labour force, (168 jobs for every 100 resident workers,) with all the other local authority areas having a labour force that exceeds the jobs available in their area. This imbalance between jobs and labour force outside Dublin City is not unexpected, as the pattern of in-commuting to the city centre is well established. However, the scale of the imbalance is a matter of concern, especially in relation to Meath and Wicklow.

The Jobs Ratio is the total number of jobs divided by the labour force. This is as low as 0.49 for Meath and 0.59 for Wicklow. This Jobs Ratio has been used to measure the sustainability of settlements, and although very little research has been undertaken on this issue, it has been suggested that on sustainability grounds, the ratio should not fall below 0.75

Commuting

Flow Diagrams for Personal Movements at Morning Peak

Based upon 2003 traffic survey data, the Dublin Transportation Model (DTM) has been used to create Origin-Destination data for the urban centres identified above. I acknowledge here the invaluable help of the DTO, particularly John Henry, the Director, and Mick MacAree and Eoin Farrell. See Table 5.7 Origin-Destination Matrix. See also Figure 5.4 Commuting Networks.

Comments on Commuting Patterns

The total number of personal journeys at morning peak with origin and destination within the entire area is 222,553. Of these, 113,572 trips, (or roughly half), have both origin and destination inside the metropolitan area. Only 38,455 trips start in the hinterland towns and rural areas and end in Dublin. Of these trips,

Table 5.7 Origin-Desintation Matrix

| | destin | | | | | | | | | | | |
origin	**1** DMA	**2** maynooth	**3** bray	**4** naas	**5** newbridge	**6** navan	**7** wicklow	**8** balbriggan	**9** drogheda	**10** dundalk	**99** other	
DMA **1**	113572	452	940	240	95	72	51	43	39	18	4265	**119787**
maynooth **2**	3888	708	10	112	16	10	1	1	2	0	1010	**5758**
bray **3**	2081	8	1433	5	0	2	32	0	1	0	287	**3849**
naas **4**	1521	48	3	1022	114	1	0	1	0	0	568	**3280**
newbridge **5**	710	20	1	359	614	2	0	3	1	0	501	**2209**
navan **6**	1087	31	3	24	3	971	0	0	35	11	596	**2764**
wicklow **7**	388	1	119	1	0	0	554	0	0	0	256	**1319**
balbriggan **8**	521	2	1	0	0	2	0	135	6	1	142	**810**
drogheda **9**	1154	15	2	1	3	30	0	28	2035	119	590	**3977**
dundalk **10**	78	2	0	0	0	1	0	1	17	863	89	**1051**
other **99**	27027	811	934	1747	649	1244	451	136	1289	3549	39912	**77749**
	152027	**2098**	**3446**	**3511**	**1494**	**2335**	**1092**	**348**	**3425**	**4561**	**48216**	**222553**

| | destin | | | | | | | | | | | |
origin	**1** DMA	**2** maynooth	**3** bray	**4** naas	**5** newbridge	**6** navan	**7** wicklow	**8** balbriggan	**9** drogheda	**10** dundalk	**99** other	
DMA **1**	95	0	1	0	0	0	0	0	0	0	4	**100**
maynooth **2**	68	12	0	2	0	0	0	0	0	0	18	**100**
bray **3**	54	0	37	0	0	0	1	0	0	0	7	**100**
naas **4**	46	1	0	31	3	0	0	0	0	0	17	**100**
newbridge **5**	32	1	0	16	28	0	0	0	0	0	23	**100**
navan **6**	39	1	0	1	0	35	0	0	1	0	22	**100**
wicklow **7**	29	0	9	0	0	0	42	0	0	0	19	**100**
balbriggan **8**	64	0	0	0	0	0	0	17	0	0	18	**100**
drogheda **9**	29	0	0	0	0	1	0	1	51	3	15	**100**
dundalk **10**	7	0	0	0	0	0	0	0	2	82	8	**100**
other **99**	35	1	1	2	1	2	1	0	2	5	51	**100**

Source: *Dublin Transportation Office.*

only 11,428 start in the nine selected centres, and the remaining 27,027 start in smaller towns, villages and rural areas.

Only 6,215 trips originate in Dublin and end outside it, illustrating the intensity of the tidal flow inwards at peak. There are 16,367 trips with both origins and destinations within the hinterland, of which only 5,557 are between one POLYNET urban centre and another. This is 2.49 per cent of all trips.

This illustrates the extreme monocentricity of the region in terms of movement flows, and is consistent with the data we presented earlier on the concentration of jobs in the metropolis as well as the low populations of centres outside Dublin.

The dispersal of development is shown by the high figures for the 'other' category; (i.e. smaller towns, villages and rural areas). There are 77,749 trips originating there, (35 per cent of all trips), of which 39,912 have also destinations there.

From more detailed analysis done with DTO data but not reported here, one can see that the great majority of traffic is flowing from the hinterland to destinations in Dublin City, which occupies the core of the Dublin metropolitan region. Here the greatest flows come from County Kildare, from the west, (Maynooth, Celbridge, Leixlip, etc.) and from the south-west, (Naas and Newbridge, and so on) Smaller flows come from the north and the south, (Wicklow and Drogheda), although centres closest to Dublin, (Bray and Balbriggan), have moderate flows, as would be expected. This certainly raises questions about the current reality of the corridor, a topic on which Chris Paris makes comment in his chapter.

One can clearly see from study of the detailed data that commuting to the other three counties of Dublin region come mainly from the radially adjacent hinterland counties. Thus commuters to South Dublin come mainly from County Kildare; to Dun Laoghaire-Rathdown mainly from Wicklow; and to Fingal from Meath. However, one can see also that commuting between Lucan, (in the north-east corner of Co.Kildare) and Swords/Balbriggan, is substantial. This implies orbital movements, which are doubtless associated with the M50 Ring Road.

The use of public transport is very low, with a modal split worse than 90:10 in most connections. Public transport, particularly by rail, is strongly radial, with limited capability to make through connections from one radial rail to another. This might be ameliorated by the proposed tunnel between Heuston and Connolly stations. As regards direct intra-hinterland public transport links between the minor urban centres, there are no new practical possibilities for rail linkages. Rail services have been improved in recent years by the purchase of new commuter rolling stock, and the upgrading of the permanent way and signalling. However, the main underlying problem is the dispersal of development, and the low densities that make it difficult for most travellers to interchange with rail.

Measuring Polycentricity

Rank-Size Analysis

This analysis is shown in Figure 5.5, Rank-Size Graph. This is based upon a logarithmic scale of population, but even so the gradient between centre 1 (Dublin) and centre 2 is very steep, whilst from centre 2 to centre 10 the gradient is consistently far flatter. The concave 'blips' in the graph arise because the rank is shown for 2001, even using the data for earlier censuses, although the rank order changed between censuses. Here again, the non-polycentricity of the area and the dominance of Dublin are clearly illustrated.

Self-Containment

We have shown the morning peak trips into each centre and out of each centre based on the above-mentioned Origin-Destination data; (see Table 5.7) "Self-Containment", (i.e. trips with both origin and destination within each centre,) is shown on the main diagonal of the matrix. The in-commuting for each centre is shown by the column totals for each centre, and out-commuting by the row totals. See Table 5.7 for the O-D data and also the pie-charts in Figure 5.6, Self-Containment.

Dublin is highly self-contained, with 95 per cent of trips originating in Dublin also ending there. Only Dundalk is similarly self-contained, with 82 per cent of journeys starting there also ending there. The middle category, with 35–50 per cent, includes Wicklow, Navan and Drogheda – in other words, the middle ring of towns. The lowest category, with 10–35 per cent includes the towns closest to Dublin. On the whole, the closer the town is to Dublin, the lower is its self-containment.

Calculation of Polycentricity

The appendix to this chapter contains a technical note explaining the statistical method for calculating polycentricity, which has been used for the Dublin case and similarly by the POLYNET team for seven other "mega-city regions" in North-West Europe.

We focus on the functional polycentricity arising from in-commuting and out-commuting. In each case, the method will yield a value between 0 for no polycentricity and 1 for perfect polycentricity. A value of 1 would mean that there was an even distribution of linkage and flow, or to put it another way, the commuting to each centre was the same as for all other centres. A value of 0 would mean that there were no such linkages between centres.

The calculations presented in the appendix indicate functional polycentricity for in-commuting is 0.057 and for out-commuting is 0.062. This is certainly an indication of monocentricity, as one can see from the measurements for other city-regions in North-West Europe, given in Table 5.8, Comparative Measures of Polycentricity for Regions in North-West Europe.

Table 5.8   Comparative Measures of Polycentricity for Regions in North-West Europe

	Special Functional Polycentricity Index (In-Commuting)	Special Functional Polycentricity Index (Out-Commuting)	General Functional Polycentricity Index
South East England	0.14	0.16	0.15+
Delta Metropolis	0.16	0.15	0.16
Central Belgium	0.04	0.04	0.04
Rhine-Ruhr	0.20*	0.17*	0.19*
Rhine-Main	0.97	0.09	0.08
Northern Switzerland	0.03	0.03	0.03
Ile-de-France	0.02	0.02	0.02
Greater Dublin	0.06	0.06	0.06

*   Calculation based on 151 NUTS 5 units, not on FURs.
+   Calculation based on 2001 data with rings at NUTS 4.

Source: *Hall, P. (2005) POLYNET Action 1.1: Commuting and the definition of functional urban regions: Summary Report. London: Institute of Community Studies/The Young Foundation & Polynet Partners, p. 64.*

General Observations on Changes to City Structure

Counter-Urbanisation

The tendency to permit isolated 'one-off' housing of a suburban style in the countryside has become a major public issue. It has been driven by the desire of farmers to sell plots, which is to a significant degree legally possible, allied to an apparent desire on the part of many people to live in rural isolation. We note the recent publication by the Government of *Draft Guidelines for Sustainable Rural Housing* (2004), the government planners acknowledge that one third of new houses in the last five years have been built in open countryside or small villages. An Taisce has been active in appealing decisions to An Bord Pleanola, (the

Planning Appeals Board), against one-off housing, but this has by no means stopped the problem.

Traditional towns, such as Trim, Navan and Portlaoise, have had constant or declining populations, whilst nearby country districts have expanded considerably: for example by 21.4 per cent in Kildare and 22.1 per cent in Meath. This is visually obvious both from observation on the ground and from the inspection of large scale maps. Many country lanes are lined by detached houses at intervals of one or two hundred metres. If this phenomenon were to continue, it would presumably undermine the planned concentration of growth in urban centres.

See Figure 5 7, Map of Percentage Change in Population for Census Districts in Intercensal Period 1991–2002. It identifies the large rural areas of > 15 per cent increase. The form shows a pattern paralleling certain main radial roads from Dublin to the north, north-west, south-west and south. This phenomenon is discussed also in Chapter 10 in a different context.

Central Area Regeneration

Turning now to the central area of Dublin, there has been generous financial encouragement by the government to encourage investment in regeneration of the central areas, including a 10-year remission of local taxation, the offset of half of construction costs against tax for investors, the write-off of twice annual rent against tax for tenants, and the ability to claim half the value of new property against tax for owner occupiers. This succeeded in stopping the extensive dereliction of the centre, and succeeded in creating much office space. When supply too much exceeded demand, with 42 per cent vacant space in 1992, developers shifted their attention to apartments. The result was to drive out poor communities. Between 1995 and 2002, average industrial earnings grew by 43 per cent and house prices by 181 per cent. Social classes 1 and 2 rose from 21 per cent of the central population in 1991, (in the 'inner forty wards') to 39 per cent. Land value rises threatened the economic viability of social housing, and the tenure balance changed, with a marked decline in social housing at a time of increasing homelessness. The social geography of the centre has greatly changed.

Emergence of an 'Edge City'

We next turn to consider the emergence of an 'Edge City'. In the 1960s there were 41 office buildings constructed, of which 39 were in Dublin 1, 2 and 4. In the 1970s 140 were built, with 70 per cent in Dublin 2 and less than 10 per cent in the suburbs. In the 1980s, 382,000 square meter of office floor space were built, bringing the total to 975,000 square meter, of which 75 per cent were in the office core, 16 per cent in a secondary fringe, and only 9 per cent in the suburbs. In the 1990s and particularly between 1996 and 2002 was an unprecedented boom, adding 2,362,079 square meter. to the stock, of which 67 per cent was in suburbia, particularly west and south near the M50 ring road. Similar messages could be given as regards industrial stock and retailing. The emergence of nodes spread around a fringe belt served by major roads, but usually not well by public transport, has led to observations about the emergence of an 'edge city' since 1990. This has been driven by the marked reduction of central government funding to local authorities, which have sought active partnership with private investors in order to create development with maximum financial benefits for the local tax base. Proposals to connect satellite towns together so as to further the policy of polycentric development, (by an outer orbital route), have been criticized for risking consolidating and accelerating the growth of an edge city.

I must acknowledge that I drew here extensively upon unpublished research by Menelaos Gkartzios, (UII researcher), and Dr Mark Scott (UCD Dept of Planning) regarding counter-urbanisation, and by Sinead Kelly (UII researcher) and Dr Andrew MacLaran (Trinity College Dept of Geography) on regeneration of the core and the 'edge city' phenomenon.

Conclusion

This chapter might have been sub-titled: 'Is the Greater Dublin Area emerging as a Polycentric Region?' The answer would be that on the basis of the evidence here, it is not. Also, we might reasonably assert that the Dublin-Belfast corridor is not emerging as a similarly-functioning corridor. However, we could ask another question. If Dublin (or Dublin-Belfast) were managed so that it started to emerge as a polycentric region, would this help resolve its structural difficulties and would it improve its ability to seize its opportunities or mobilize its potential in future? The answer to this might be 'yes'.

If Dublin-Belfast were to emerge as a polycentric region, what might this boil down to in concrete terms? The key point is that more growth would be located in some or all of the constituent towns, and not only in Dublin. Also the balance of jobs and residences would be more equal within each individual urban node, and they would be better connected in terms of transport, communications and institutional liaisons. The next chapter concerns the Greater Dublin Area Regional Planning Guidelines, which are based to some extent on these ideas of polycentricity, and we have explained how this would ameliorate its structural difficulties and improve its ability to mobilize its potential in future.

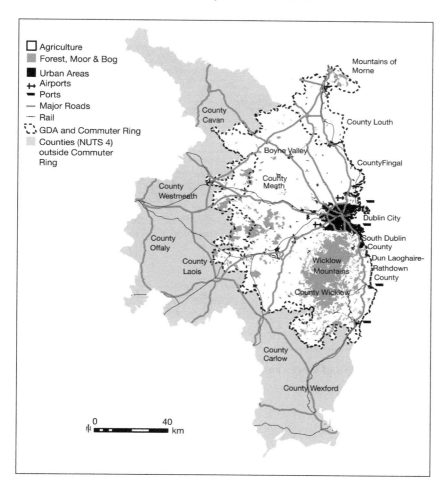

Figure 5.1   Regional Overview Map

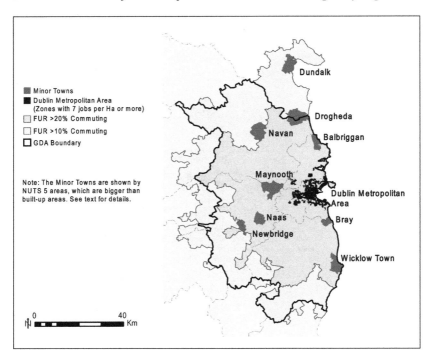

Figure 5.2   Base Map of Cores and Rings

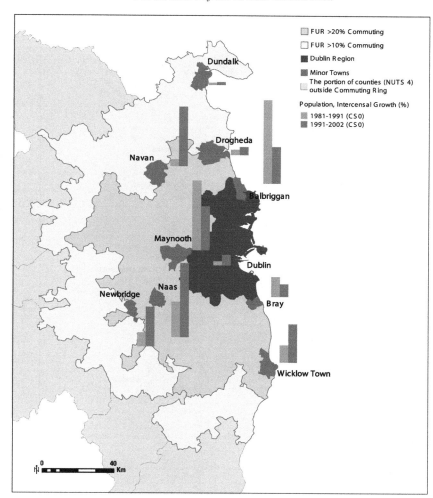

Figure 5.3   Histograms of Intercensal Population Growth

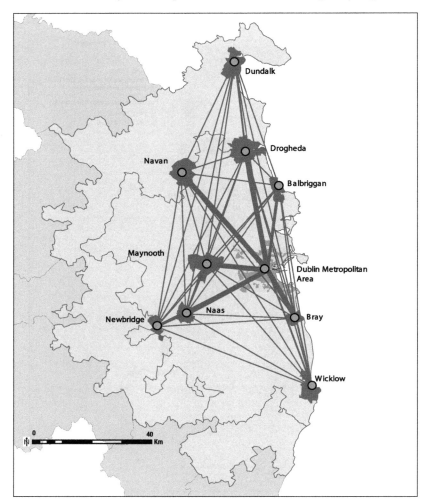

Figure 5.4   Commuting Network

TOWN	Rank '01	Population 1981	Population 1991	Population 2001	
DMA	1	1003164.0000	1040904.0000	1141051.0000	
Maynooth	2	17797.0000	28909.0000	40324.0000	
Dundalk	3	29737.0000	30340.0000	31120.0000	
Drogheda	4	27528.0000	28873.0000	30974.0000	
Bray	5	22853.0000	26836.0000	29826.0000	
Navan	6	13125.0000	13964.0000	21426.0000	
Naas	7	8837.0000	11661.0000	19422.0000	
Newbridge	8	11387.0000	12790.0000	17377.0000	
Wicklow	9	7455.0000	8629.0000	11621.0000	
Balbriggan	10	4786.0000	8378.0000	11132.0000	

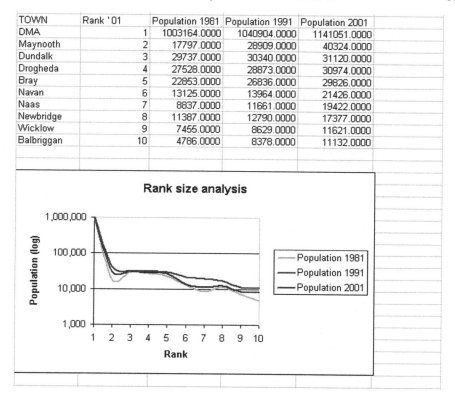

Figure 5.5   Settlement Rank-Size Graph

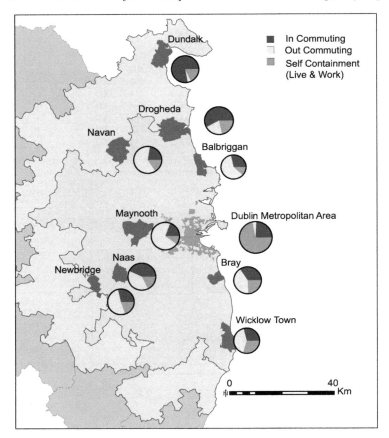

Figure 5.6   Pie-Charts of Self-Containment

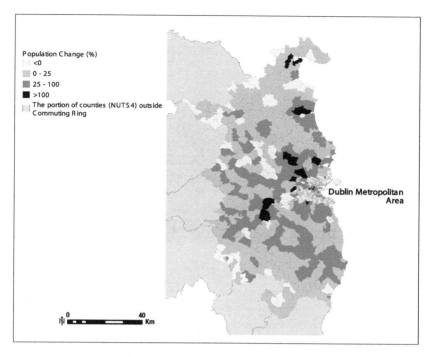

Figure 5.7   Map of Population Change by Census District

View of Riverfront

New Architecture in Dublin Docklands

Figure 5.8   Images of Central Area Regeneration

Ballymun

City West Project

Figure 5.9   Images of the Edge City

Appendix to Chapter 5

Technical Note on Polyconcentricity

Gearoid O'Riain
Consultant, Dublin

Nick Green
Institute of Community Studies, London

Introduction

Polycentricity can be seen as a combination of spatial topography and interconnectedness. A polycentric region might be conceived as a network of settlements such as the urban centres in the Dublin area. While the word 'polycentricity' addresses spatial topology, it does not itself address function, and a qualifying term, 'functional' is added to create the more specific term, *'functional polycentricity'*. In this note, the function under consideration is commuting, both into and out of urban centres. If there are no functional connections between nodes, then functional polycentricity cannot be said to exist.

In a network, the more evenly distributed the functional linkages, the less likely that any single node will stand out from the others. Thus in a network that has a perfectly even distribution of linkages, there will be no node that is better connected than any of the others. In the case of commuting in the Dublin region this would mean that the amount of commuting into centres (such as Navan, Naas-Newbridge, or Wicklow,) would be the same as Dublin itself. While clearly this is not the case, one might expect it to be more true for a region such as the Randstad, which has a number of urban centres of similar size.

Using formulaic notation, we let PF stand for polycentricity for a function F (e.g. commuting,) and assign to polycentricity a minimum value 0 (no functional polycentricity) and maximum value 1 (perfect functional polycentricity).

In seeking to appreciate the concept of Functional Polycentricity, it is useful to note a number of facets. First, polycentricity is defined as a network theoretic function. It is thus fundamentally aspatial, and therefore scalable – and so could be used equally for analysis at county or continental scales. Second, the definition includes density of the network which means that the level of interaction between places is taken into consideration. It thus has a bearing on the extent to which a network of places may be considered as a single system.

Lastly, it defines polycentricity in functional terms, and can thus be used to describe polycentricity across a variety of functions within the same geographical area. For example, rather than measuring in-commuting or out-commuting, one could look at telephone conversations, movement of goods, or leisure related travel using the same network analytic techniques. In this way, the many different levels and types of polycentricity within a region of any size can be analysed and compared, and a more layered model of polycentricity developed. To carry out this calculation of polycentricity across a number of functions, we can simply calculate the mean polycentricity for a variety of different specified functions to derive a figure for *General Functional Polycentricity*.

Application of the Functional Polycentricity Concept

For the Polynet project, data on inbound and outbound commuting for a number of urban centres in the greater Dublin region was made available to us by the Dublin Transportation Office. This data was organized into a matrix format so that the in and out bound commuting from any centre to any other centre could be readily identified. Thus we had data for a functional network of ten urban centres (a functional network of ten nodes), that can be expressed in notation as $NF = \{n1, n2,...n10\}$.

We begin by removing all data that relate to self-containment, (i.e. workers from a centre working in that same centre and thus not commuting.) We do this by deleting all values along the diagonal of the matrix).

Then the first step was to sum all in and out bound commuting for each centre. This was done by summing across the rows to calculate the out bound commuting total for each centre, and summing down the columns to calculate the in bound commuting totals. (See Table A). Each of these boxes in the matrix indicates a flow between a pair of centres and can be termed a *linkage*. As a formula, $L = \{l1, l2,...lg\}$ is thus the set of lines between the centres denoting linkages for function F. We can calculate Li (total number of linkages for in commuting) and Lo (total number of linkages for out commuting) by summing the in commuting figures and out commuting figures for all the urban centres, (a value of 14,593 in Table A).

In order that functional polycentricity falls to zero where the number of linkages is zero, we must also measure the density of the network or graph Δ such that $0 \leq \Delta \leq 1$. We do this using the calculation $\Delta = L / L_{max}$. We have calculated Li and Lo already and now calculate Lmax by calculating the maximum number of linkages possible in the network of urban centres. In this case we imagine that commuters from all other centres commute into the smallest centre. In the study area case we calculate the number of linkages were all commuters to commute to the centre with the smallest commuting population, (i.e. Balbriggan).

Taking the commuter figures as set out in Table A, the following values are arrived at:

Li = 14,593
Lo = 14,593
Lmax = 143,964

... therefore Δ = 14,593 / 143,964 = 0.101.

It is possible to measure the distribution of linkages by analysing nodal degree within the network, and generating a ratio of actual variance of nodal degree within the network to a notional maximum variance. This gives a value of 0 for a completely regular graph. However, with very large values of nodal degree, using the variance, becomes problematic, since it scales exponentially. An alternative is to use standard deviation, which scales linearly, and thus avoids this problem.

Formally $P(F,N) = \sigma F / \sigma F max$ *where* $P(F,N)$ is Ordinary Polycentricity with regard to a particular network relation F in a network N, such that 1 indicates monocentricity and 0 indicates perfect ordinary polycentricity, and σF is the standard deviation of nodal degree being measured. Thus, for the study area, it is the standard deviation of the standard deviations for all the urban centres, (those values in the light grey filled cells in Table A). Here $\sigma F max$ is the variance of a 2-node network Nz where degree $n1 = 0$ and degree $n2 =$ the degree of the node with the highest degree value in network N. Thus, for the study area, it is the standard deviation of the centre with the highest standard deviation for commuting (Dublin Metropolitan Area in the case of in-commuting, and Maynooth in the case of out-commuting), and zero.

Thus in the case of in commuting, $\sigma F = 3519.27$, and $\sigma F max = 8080.816$; and in case of out-commuting $\sigma F = 1116.93$, and $\sigma F max = 2856.711$.

Dividing standard deviation by a notional maximum possible standard deviation for the network is a means of normalising the index of standard deviation.

We are now in a position where we can derive a value for functional polycentricity for a single function. This we call *Special Functional Polycentricity*. Formally:

$$P_{SF}(N) = \left(1 - \frac{\sigma_{\partial}}{\sigma_{\partial max}}\right) \bullet \Delta$$

where:
PSF is *Special Functional Polycentricity* for a function F within network N;
$\sigma \partial$ is the standard deviation of nodal degree;
$\sigma \partial max$ is the standard deviation of the nodal degree of a 2-node network *(n1,n2)* derived from N where $dn1 = 0$ and $dn2 =$ value of the node with highest value in N.
Δ is the density of the network.

In this case we are calculating functional polycentricity for two separate functions – in and out commuting.

PSF (in-commuting) is calculated at 0.057.
PSF (out-commuting) is calculated at 0.062.

To carry out the calculation of polycentricity across a number of functions, and thus to derive a figure for *General Functional Polycentricity*, we simply calculate the mean polycentricity for the individual special functions.

Formally:

$$P_{GF}(\mathcal{N}_1, \mathcal{N}_2, \ldots \mathcal{N}_n) = \frac{\sum_{n=1} \left(1 - \frac{\sigma_\partial}{\sigma_{\partial max}}\right) \bullet \Delta}{n}$$

where PGF {N1,N2...Nn} is general functional polycentricity for functional networks; the sum is taken over all *PSF* , and *n* is the number of networks.

Thus for the study area *PGF* is calculated to be $((0.057 + 0.062) / 2) = 0.0595$.

Table 5.9 Matrix of Commuting Value based on Dublin Transportation Office Data, 2004

Origin/ Destination	Dublin MetroArea	Maynooth	Bray	Naas	Newbridge	Navan	Wicklow	Balbriggan	Drogheda	Dundalk	Out-Commuting Totals	Standard Deviation Out-Commute
Dublin Metro Area	0	452	940	240	95	72	51	43	39	18	1,950.00	304.86
Maynooth	3888	0	10	112	16	10	1	1	2	0	4,040.00	1,290.16
Bray	2081	8	0	5	0	2	32	0	1	1	2,129.00	733.40
Naas	1521	48	3	0	114	1	3	0	0	0	1,690.00	501.42
Newbridge	710	20	1	359	0	2	0	1	1	0	1,094.00	250.10
Navan	1087	31	3	24	3	0	0	3	35	11	1,197.00	357.99
Wicklow	388	1	119	1	0	0	0	0	0	0	509.00	130.35
Balbriggan	521	2	1	0	0	2	0	0	6	1	533.00	173.18
Drogheda	1154	15	2	1	3	30	0	28	0	119	1,352.00	378.27
Dundalk	78	2	0	0	0	1	0	1	17	0	99.00	25.71
In-Commuting Totals	11,428.00	579.00	1,079.00	742.00	231.00	120.00	87.00	77.00	101.00	149.00	14,593.00	
Standard Deviation In-Commute	1,156.23	146.21	309.94	131.56	45.23	23.97	18.69	15.76	15.59	41.11		

Chapter 6

Remarks on the Regional Planning Guidelines for the Greater Dublin Area

John Yarwood
Former Director, Urban Institute, Ireland

Introduction

In the Irish system, the purpose of Regional Planning Guidelines (RPGs) is to interpret the National Spatial Strategy (NSS) vision for 2020 in detail at the level of a region so as to guide the local planning authorities in the preparation of their own County Development Plans. The aim is to ensure that the county plans, (taken together), add up to a coherent regional strategy, and beyond that, the regional strategies add up to the national strategy, (as portrayed in the NSS). In the case of Dublin, however, the RPGs apply to the Greater Dublin Area (GDA), which comprises two regions, namely (a) the Dublin Region, (comprising the local planning authorities for Dublin City, South Dublin, Dun Laoghaire-Rathdown and Fingal; and (b) the MidEast Region, (comprising Meath, Kildare and Wicklow). This guidance should accord with the scope specified in the Planning and Development Act 2000 section 23(2), and also with the directive from Government *Preparing Regional Planning Guidelines Guidance Notes*, issued in February 2003, and revised by further guidance dated October 2003 and November 2003. Section 23(2) of the directive specifies eleven topics, comprising projected population trends and settlement and housing strategies; economic and employment trends; location of industrial and commercial developments; transportation and public transportation; water supply; waste disposal; energy supply and communications; education, health, retail and community facilities; environmental protection, cultural and natural heritage; environmental impact and 'other'.

The two Regional Authorities (which constitute the GDA) formed a joint committee for the purpose of preparing these Regional Planning Guidelines. Consultants were appointed. The Urban Institute Ireland was asked by the consultancy team to join it. The team was led by Atkins Ireland, and included Goodbody Economic Consultants and Tom Philips and Associates, as well as Urban Institute Ireland. When making the initial presentation to the client, I spoke about the potential of polycentricity as a planning policy, and offered an interpretation of its meaning. Also we made reference to the corridor as a contextual factor. These topics, which are, of course, themes in this book, were on the agenda at the start of our work on the RPGs. This chapter describes the RPGs, but includes comments from the perspective of polycentricity and corridor planning.

This chapter does not cover all the content of the RPGs. In the interests of brevity, I have focused on settlement strategy and movement, as well as certain spatial planning principles. This discussion has also fed into later chapters, particularly Chapter 15, in which these RPGs have been incorporated in a hypothetical plan for the Dublin-Belfast Corridor as a whole.

There does appear to have been a long-standing concern in theory in Ireland about regional planning. This was evident in the work of Abercrombie, Myles-Wright, ERDO and Buchanan, at least. However, in *practice* regional planning seems to have been something of a dead letter until the preparation of the Strategic Planning Guidelines, published in 1999.[1] Before this time, county planning authorities prepared plans for their own areas within little or no wider formal spatial framework. In the most dynamic regions, these plans consequently suffered from a failure of coordination between adjacent counties. The SPGs were an attempt to redress this difficulty for the Greater Dublin case. The Planning and Development Act 2000 took up this theme at a national level, and provided for the National Spatial Strategy (NSS).[2] The Act envisaged that each Regional Authority would prepare RPGs to act as 'bridge' between the NSS and the County plans. Although very little time had gone by, the RPGs replaced the SPGs, and their legal status, arising from a new Act, was stronger.

Strategic Urban-Regional Form

We had a preconception of the city-region as a polycentric group of towns, comprising the Dublin Metropolitan Area (DMA) and towns clustered around it, with three characteristics: (a) the towns would be spatially distinct and separated by strategic greenbelts, giving easy access to open country; (b) they would have differentiated but complementary economic and cultural life, with an internal balance of residential and economic functions; and (c) they would be held together by multi-modal movement spines, with activity well connected into these spines so as to form *integrated activity/movement corridors,* a topic discussed by Prosser in Chapter 8.

We also spoke about the 'compact-dispersed model' of settlements, whereby growth would be dispersed at the regional level, but the settlements themselves,

---

[1]   See *Strategic Planning Guidelines for the Greater Dublin Area* (1999), prepared by Brady, Shipman and Martin.

[2]   *National Spatial Strategy* (2000), published by the Dept. of Environment and Local Government, Dublin.

considered separately, would be compact. This compactness would help urban services to be viable, and in particular, would allow public transport services to be attractive to customers. The settlement hierarchy, in terms of size and function, was spelled out, on the basis that smaller settlements were clustered around higher-order settlements. This would maximize accessibility to the full range of services and 'life-chances' from any one location, whilst also attaining the urban scale and concentration or critical mass necessary to make services sustainable. This concept aims to balance service access from remoter areas with critical mass at each point. See Table 6.1, Settlement Hierarchy. (However, this hierarchy could not be agreed by all of the seven local planning authorities, and it was eventually agreed to omit it altogether from the published version).

The strategy selected a small number of satellite towns for major growth, with the key criterion that they must have the potential to be optimally integrated into a system of public transport (road/rail) movement corridors connecting the towns to Dublin, to other major cities of Ireland, and also to each other. Towns with little potential for strong linkage into an efficient regional movement system should not be allowed to expand very much, because this would encourage car dependency, and exacerbate congestion and pollution, lengthening journey times beyond the already preposterous levels. Such congestion would work against polycentricity by accentuating the dominance of the Dublin monopole.

The strategy sought to achieve an internal balance within each town between the resident working population and the number of jobs so as to minimize the amount of obligatory commuting. (As the previous chapter indicates, there are 168 jobs for every 100 residents in Dublin, whilst in Meath there are only 49. It is no surprise that massive commuting is required, and that poor public transport infrastructure leads to congestion).

The patronage levels for public transport are determined in part by the convenience of moving between the dwelling or workplace (or whatever) and the station/stop. Distance is one factor, but danger, inconvenience and unpleasantness are also involved. This entails great attention to detail, particularly detail of layout, local planning and urban design, which is an enormously influential factor affecting the propensity to choose public transport.

Common sense would therefore favour concentration of population growth in a small number of large and internally compact satellite towns, with good communications between them. But it was immediately clear that the political will was in favour of a larger number of smaller developments, and there was a particular wish to facilitate, (or certainly not to obstruct) 'local need' demand for rural and village housing. I am inclined to see this as part of a 'ruralist' vision embedded in Irish cultural values. Certainly local politicians in rural constituencies are impatient with technical/logical arguments to the contrary.

The housing growth in the MidEast region, (the rural hinterland), has been faster than the Strategic Planning Guidelines proposed, and the growth of the Dublin Region, the metropolis, relatively slower. This may be due to the relative ease with which greenfield land was delivered in country areas, and the relative difficulties in delivering land at a reasonable price in the city. In any event, politicians from urban constituencies felt there was a need to rebalance the growth in favour of the city by a policy of infilling, consolidation or densification; or, in other words, to get back 'on track'. The RPGs thus combine elements of metropolitan consolidation and small town/rural growth. The effort to achieve enough development intensity outside the metropolis to allow a really strong public transport system to be created has not so far been embraced.

The RPGs warned of the implications of current trends.

> The result of imbalance between jobs location and residential location has been an increase in long-distance commuting. The enormous spatial sprawl of housing development has made the provision of attractive public transport difficult. The consequent travel mode decisions lead to a car-based commuting pattern, and increasing congestion.

> If current trends persist, jobs will continue to be predominantly located in the Metropolitan Area, whilst the population will grow greatly in the Hinterland Area. This will increase the amount of commuting and congestion. By 2016, much of the Greater Dublin Area may have the following characteristics:

> - Some of the countryside will resemble an ultra-low density suburb (or 'ex-urb') and consequently the designated urban areas will not be as fully developed or as consolidated as currently planned.
> - There will be difficulties in the management of water resources, and aquifers will be increasingly polluted, with emerging public health risks.
> - Jobs will remain relatively concentrated in the Metropolitan Area, and the absolute number of homes in the Hinterland Area will grow. If, in practice, less Metropolitan land can be delivered than in the past, hinterland growth could soar.
> - Since dispersed development will continue at a substantial scale, public transport services will often be unviable and car use will continue to be high for journeys to work, shops and schools. There will be worsening congestion at peak times, even in some villages and rural lanes. The suburbs and inner city will be more congested than otherwise will be the case due to commuting to Metropolitan job locations.
> - Major destinations will disperse to the edge of towns, as congestion in the whole regional territory grows, and an edge-city or 'doughnut' economy will emerge by degrees. As a result, Dublin City may decline economically and socially.[3]

---

[3]   See RPG Draft Dec 2003 page 31

Table 6.1 Settlement Hierarchy: Early Draft

Settlement Type	Population Range	Accessibility	Typical Distance from higher level settlement	Economic Function	Service Function		
					Retail	Public	
Metropolitan Consolidation Towns	40,000 to 100,000	Quality Bus Corridors / Rail / Major radial routes	Close to City Centre	Main attractor for major investment. Strong international marketing	Regional / Major Town Centre	Hospital. Secondary education Possible Third Level facility
Large Town I ("Satellite town")	25,000 to 40,000	At junction of major radial and orbital multi-modal transport corridors. Commuter rail	Within 40 km. from Dublin	Main attractor for major investment. Strong international marketing	Substantial comparison retail (mall) Retail park Leisure centre Etc.	Hospital. Secondary education Possible Third Level facility
Large Town II	15,000 to 25,000	On major radial multi-modal transport corridor. Commuter rail	15 km from satellite or Dublin	Subsidiary attractor for investment	Comparison retail. Etc.	Clinic or small hospital. Secondary education

Moderate Town	5,000 to 15,000	On or near multi modal transport corridor. Rail if possible	10 km from Large Town	Attractor for substantial investment	Limited comparison retail. Good convenience. Medium supermarket(s)	Secondary education. Clinic
Small Town	1,000 to 5,000	On national primary or secondary road. Good bus links to railway and major settlements	10 km from Large Town	Attractor for investment	Small and medium convenience. Some local retail centres Specialty retail	Primary schools (and secondary in more peripheral areas). Post Office. Clinic
Village	Up to 1,000	Improved Rural Road. Bus links to Railway and larger settlements	10 km from Small Town (or other town)	Small rural-based enterprises	Small convenience units and a neighbourhood centre	Primary School. Surgery Sub-Post Office

The RPG study proposed to choose key satellite towns for major growth, which were dispersed across the area, (but were also the largest towns). They were Drogheda,[4] Navan, Maynooth-Celbridge-Leixlip, Naas-Newbridge and Wicklow. The strategy was seen as polycentric in nature, and therefore we wanted to create a network linking the main 'satellite' centres to each other. We therefore envisaged integrated activity-movement corridors connecting Dublin to each of these towns. These radial corridors would be based on existing rail lines and major roads, with modal interchanges linked closely in to important investment nodes. The land for these would be pro-actively delivered, and the development would be briefed and controlled so as to promote attractive public transport access and high patronage levels.

These multi-modal spines would be radial in nature of course, but the orbital movement, which can be met at the moment only by the use of minor, unsatisfactory country roads, would be catered for by a modified version of the recently-designed Dublin Outer Orbital Route (DOOR) project.[5] This orbital route could not have a parallel railway, but a high speed coach route would parallel the DOOR, intersecting with the radial railways at stations. Each town would lie at the intersection of a radial and the orbital. The overall form resembles a half-wheel, with Dublin at its hub, radial corridors like spokes, and a rim of orbital connected satellite towns.

There is also a second orbit further out from Dublin, connecting Dundalk, Ardee, Kells, Mullingar, Tullamore, Portlaoise, Carlow and Enniscorthy. These towns lie outside the Greater Dublin Area, and were therefore not incorporated into our detailed proposals. Evidence exists that there is some out-commuting from these towns, and much of it goes to Dublin. This orbital follows a route of existing roads which is in the upgrading programme of the National Roads Authority. These two orbitals are concentric. See Figure 6.1 and 6.3. The plans show major roads, rail lines, stations and settlements, (including 'Multi-Purpose Investment Nodes'). This highlights the key strategic goal of integrating major origins and destinations with multi-modal movement facilities, (within activity/movement corridors).

The Strategic Planning Guidelines of 1999 and indeed the NSS itself were based on a purely radial structure for Dublin. See Figure 6.2, Key Diagram of the Strategic Planning Guidelines. The implication was that traffic would travel inwards to Dublin, around the M50, and then out again, thus maintaining the primacy of the mono-pole. A polycentric policy, however, would suggest that the smaller towns should be connected to each other more directly. We advanced this

---

[4]   Drogheda lies on the Meath/Louth border, but is just within Louth. It is thus part of the Borders Region, not the Greater Dublin Area. In reality it is a commuter town for Dublin, although the Regional Planning Guidelines for the Border Region deal with it. In this chapter, we have incorporated in to the GDA vision for simplicity and clarity.

[5]   Refer to Dublin Outer Orbital Route Study Report prepared for the National Roads Agency by Oscar Faber and Partners. July 2001.

idea, but it met with initial resistance. The objection was that such linkage would make the small towns too attractive as business locations, and would undermine Dublin's economy. But, of course, the aim was precisely to attract business to the smaller towns in order to rebalance the jobs/workforce ratio, whilst Dublin had already far more jobs than it could support without huge in-commuting.

Demographic Studies

Principles[6]

The initial discussion tended to see Dublin as dominant and the region as monocentric, and we speculated about the region of the future comprising also a variety of medium-sized towns well integrated into a polycentric network. We suggested that several towns be planned with relatively high growth targets, but argued against excessively large numbers of settlements, which would tend to 'spread the jam thinly', (because the allocation of growth was to be a zero sum game). Large towns could be provided with a larger mass of services. They would be better connected and more accessible and would be easier to market to inward investors than a proliferation of small places. We were particularly keen to create more jobs in the hinterland, and to persuade location decision-makers that they should open their businesses in such towns, in order to reduce commuting distance and dependence on the motor car. In the past, location decision-makers tended to regard the small towns as remote and disconnected, preferring Dublin, which was perceived as the only place with major market access.

Projections

The 2002 Census of Population has raised two fundamental issues for the demography of the GDA and indeed for the Republic as a whole. Between the censuses of 1996 and 2002, household formation was much lower than had previously been assumed. The increase in household numbers was well below the number of dwellings that had been constructed in that period. Household headship rates in 2002 were little higher than in 1996. The consultants questioned whether the gap between household formation and housing construction could be explained by increases in vacancies or second homes, or by a reduction in sharing. It is most probably due to replacement of dwellings that have been demolished or abandoned. Looking at census data on the age and condition of the current housing stock, it appears unlikely that this rate of demolition will be sustained in the future. A much larger proportion of future housing completions may therefore be absorbed by increasing headship rates.

---

[6]   Most of the demography discussion here is taken from an unpublished background paper prepared by David Jordan in 2003.

Between the two censuses the population growth rate of the GDA was not much higher than in the rest of the Republic. Although the GDA captured a large share of international migration, it also had a net migration loss to other parts of Ireland. Contrary to current diagnoses, these losses cannot be explained as 'overspill' from the GDA. The main destinations of out-migration include the competing centres of Cork and Galway while the GDA had net losses to most counties. It is likely that these trends have considerable inertia.

Because of the structure of the NSS model, the projections run forward from 2002 in 5-year jumps – to 2007, 2012, 2017 and 2022. Totals were produced for the RPG years 2010, 2016 and 2020 by linear interpolation. See Table 6.2.

Table 6.2   Projections of Population and Households for the GDA, 2002 to 2020

LO projection

	2002	2010	2016	2020
Total Population	1,535,446	1,695,877	1,787,450	1,831,992
Households	508,096	641,694	720,000	757,111

HI projection

	2002	2010	2016	2020
Total Population	1,535,446	1,774,891	1,947,659	2,048,980
Households	508,096	670,559	783,587	844,011

The LO projection gave a 2020 population of 1.83 million, with 0.76 million households, implying an average household size close to the prevailing West-European-level of 2.4 persons, substantially down from the GDA level of 3.0 persons in 2002. This appears to be consistent with the current Dept. of the Environment view of the most likely position with regard to total population and average household size. The HI projection gave a 2020 population of 2.05 million with 0.84 million households, which is consistent with the Dept. of Environment 'high' view of a national population of around 5.0 million with 40 per cent living in the GDA. This population was generated by feeding into the NSS model a net migration of 14,000 per year in the early years, reducing to 10,000 at the end of the projection period. This would entail an acceleration of recent international migration gains and a reversal of the GDA's internal migration losses and should therefore be regarded as an unlikely maximum.

It will be seen that under both projections the number of additional households appears high compared with the number of additional persons. This is because the reduction in average household size applies to the whole population, generating a substantial number of additional households from the existing population size. Thus, even if there were no population increase through migration or through natural increase, there would still be a substantial increase in the number of households. Similarly, the existing housing stock will accommodate far fewer people in 2020 than it does now. This has implications for the methodology of forecasting growth at the zone and county level, as shown below.

Growth at Zone and County Level

We divided the study area into 56 zones, each of which was built up from a number of Electoral Districts (EDs).[7] The four inner zones were the four counties of the Dublin region, less the northern part of Fingal County, which was divided into separate zones. The remaining zones consisted of urban areas (such as Navan, Trim, Naas and so on) together with their surrounding rural hinterlands. All these zones nested within counties, so that a total for the seven counties of the region could be assembled. We also distinguished a *metropolitan area* which consisted of the Dublin Region, plus parts of the other counties. The remainder of the GDA, outside this *metropolitan area,* is termed *the hinterland.*

For each zone, the numbers of households and persons were calculated using ED-level information from the 1996 and 2002 censuses. As in the demographic work for the NSS, we did not distinguish between the private household population and those living in institutions. Estimates of household size derived from the data are therefore slightly exaggerated.

The projected reductions in average household size mean that the number of persons living in the existing housing stock will fall sharply over the plan period. New dwellings must be produced for this 'overspill population' over and above the dwellings that are needed to accommodate population increases. An analysis based on households rather than persons makes these processes explicit, and gives a more direct indication of the amounts of additional housing needed in each zone. The zonal forecasts were therefore carried out by allocating the additional households forecast in the HI and LO projections to individual zones. This was done on the basis of two alternative scenarios:

- The 'Do Nothing' scenario, in which present spatial trends continued, and
- The 'Planned Growth' scenario, in which growth allocations are implemented by planning controls and land delivery.

Zone household forecasts were first made for each zone for both HI and LO projections assuming a *do nothing* situation with regard to development strategy, planning controls etc. We took this to mean that each zone would continue to absorb the same share of the total GDA household increase that it absorbed in the period 1996 to 2002. Thus, between 1996 and 2002 the number of households in zone 7, for instance, increased by 2,543, which was 4.1 per cent of the total GDA

---

[7]   EDs were formally known as DEDs. The CSO said that there were no changes in boundaries between the 1996 and 2002 censuses so that a direct comparison is possible.

increase, 61,665. For the HI projection *do nothing* scenario, it is assumed that zone 7 will absorb 4.1 per cent of the projected increase 2002 to 2007 (99,432 households,) then 4.1 per cent of the projected increase 2007 to 2012 (105,000 households) and so on. The same procedure was followed for the LO projection *do nothing* scenario. As pointed out above, the HI and LO projections run forward from 2002 in 5-year jumps – to 2007, 2012, 2017 and 2022. County totals have been produced for the RPG years 2010, 2016 and 2022 by linear interpolation.

We next made a set of 'planned allocations' based upon the settlement hierarchy: see Table 6.1 above. The planned allocations were controlled, as above, to the household increases projected in the GDA HI and LO projections. The basic allocations were made for the entire period 2002 to 2017, and were then interpolated to 2007, 2012 and 2022, using a 'same share' procedure. The 2002 to 2017 control was 293,200 additional households under the HI projection and 223,800 under the LO projection.

For the *hinterland* we made allocations according to the following indicative rules:

- Large growth centres type 1 (for example Wicklow) received around 20,000-40,000 extra households.
- Large growth centres type 2 (for example Balbriggan) received around 10,000 extra households.
- Small growth centres (or example Kildare) received either 1,000 or 2,000 extra households depending on whether they had railway stations.
- Key villages (for example Ennis Kerry) received an extra 800 households

This left a number of rural zones that did not contain any centre of the types set out above. For these zones we made a notional allowance of around 20 per cent of the 2002 households, which is the scale of increase needed to counterbalance population losses with reducing household size.

These allocations for the *hinterland*, were applied to both the HI and LO projections. For the *metropolitan area* we made allocations under the following headings:

- Major metropolitan consolidation areas (for example Swords, Tallaght and Bray) received 10,000 to 20,000 extra households
- Each county received an allowance for minor sites, densification and dwelling subdivision.
- Moderate growth centres (for example Ashbourne, Greystones,) received 5,000 extra households
- Small towns (for example Rush, Lusk) received 2,500 extra households each

The draft settlement map is shown in Figure 6.1, Settlement Strategy Plan. Drogheda is shown on this plan, but it is just on the county boundary. (However, it was subsequently decided to show it as part of the Borders Region guidelines, and at the insistence of Meath County Council, nearby Navan was upgraded to a satellite town status, a higher settlement category).

Economic Development Strategy

The RPGs contain a substantial regional economic analysis, the main points of which are covered in Chapter 5.[8] Certain general policy prescriptions were also discussed, and they are recounted here. The priority for economic policy in the region is thought to be the relief of supply constraints in relation to infrastructure and some categories of labour, as well as improvements to the jobs/labour ratio, so as to reduce the extent of the "dormitory role" of settlements outside Dublin. A high level of investment in economic infrastructure and human capital is required, as an essential prerequisite for:

- Attracting new high-tech manufacturing and internationally-traded services sector inward investment;
- Enhancing the scale and competitiveness of indigenous firms; and
- Expanding the research and technological development capacity of the regional economy as a whole.

To be successful in attracting inward investment and growing indigenous industry, the Greater Dublin Area must offer:

- A high quality economic infrastructure, and land availability;
- A large and varied labour market;
- Availability of appropriate education infrastructure; and
- A high quality built environment.

Inward investors require good transport to allow access to ports and external markets and to widen labour catchments. Competitive and effective telecommunication services, including broadband services, not only help to attract the inward investment of international services, but also facilitate manufacturers in accessing business services and in marketing their products. Obviously an important theme of the RPGs and indeed this entire book, concerns multi-modal movement spines, and their coordination with key activity nodes within a frame of 'Activity/Movement Corridors', as we explain above and Prosser argues in Chapter 8. Compact urban forms and reasonably high densities will be a big help here. Airports and ports should be 'plugged into' corridors, so that they serve the whole urban-regional system, and not only their locality, as Chapter 15 aims to illustrate.

---

[8]   The lion's share of the credit for this work must go to Bernard Feeney of Goodbody Economic Consultants.

Efficient and cost-effective waste disposal infrastructure and services are now a requirement of modern industry. Servicing of sufficient land for both industrial and housing requirements and putting in place a coherent solid waste management strategy will be central to the economic development of the region. In Chapter 10 Scott, Redmond, Moore and Gkartzios stress the importance of pro-active delivery of land and its coordinated servicing, according to plans, at the right place, time and cost.

Access to a skilled and flexible labour market is a key requirement of firms that are on higher levels of the value chain. The larger the available market, the more likely it is that it will meet these requirements. Within the region, hinterland towns have a drawback in this regard in that the labour market in their immediate catchment may be relatively small. Good transport links can overcome this disadvantage by allowing access to labour markets outside the urban area, and indeed this is one of the most important benefits of a corridor plan.

In the changed environment for industrial development, the educational sector has a vital role to play in the delivery of a highly trained workforce, the relevant technological expertise, and a strong research and innovation capacity. The tertiary education sector is crucial to this process.

Inward investors wish to locate in places that provide a high quality environment that not only is attractive to their staff, but also reflects an image of quality that they wish to associate with their firm. Thus, planning authorities have a role to play in promoting a high quality built environment in relation to housing, streetscapes, green spaces, amenities and leisure facilities.

Conclusion

The Dublin City area has consistently performed more strongly as an economic generator and attractor of employment sources and opportunities than the remainder of the Dublin and Mid-East Regional areas. Outside Dublin City centre, a number of major employers have been established in recent years, which can be attracted to existing centres that are well served by major transport corridors and offer ease of access to Dublin Airport and Dublin Port.

The major pulling attraction of Dublin City centre (given its extensive employment base coupled with the significant population dispersal to locations outside the Metropolitan Area) has resulted in the increasing trend for a number of centres (especially those located close to railway lines or national roads) to take on a dormitory function. These centres serve as commuter towns with their inhabitants often travelling significant distances to go to their places of employment.

Planning Authorities should:

- Encourage mixed-use settlement forms, in which jobs and residences are relatively close, thus encouraging short trips and greater use of walk and cycle modes, while discouraging longer trip lengths and dispersed settlement patterns that result in extensive car use.
- Ensure the provision of adequately zoned and serviced industrial and commercial sites, at high quality locations preferred by industry, within the centres selected for future growth as presented in the settlement strategy.
- Facilitate high quality transportation and other economic infrastructure serving such locations.
- Promote the delivery of a high quality built environment in the urban centres to ensure the attractiveness of these centres to employers.
- Provide good educational and research facilities in appropriate centres.
- Encourage and foster local enthusiasm, enterprise and initiative.
- Where appropriate, play a proactive role in the development of business parks and business centres in consultation with the appropriate bodies and in the decentralisation of Government offices.

My final observation is that the real test of guidelines and of the Regional Authorities themselves will be whether the Authorities are able to implement them. That will be seen. My experience of sitting in many meetings on this matter has taught me how proud the Counties are of their independence, and how this might well limit the grasp of a regional strategic overview. But, to be fair, two regions and seven counties did indeed come together around a single document. That is testament to a desire for unity of purpose, and so we can go forward in hope.

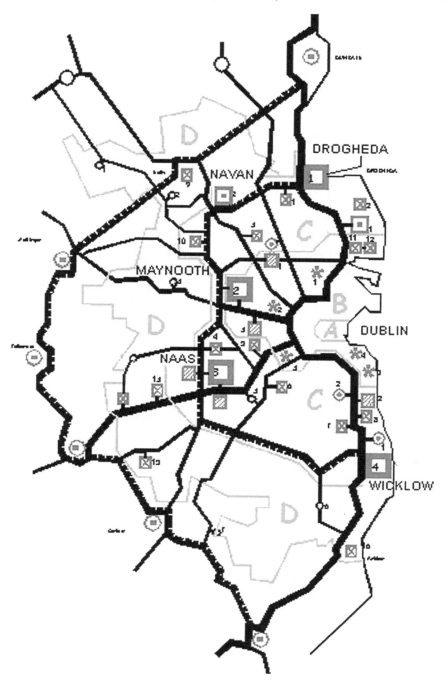

Figure 6.1 Settlement Strategy: Draft Plan

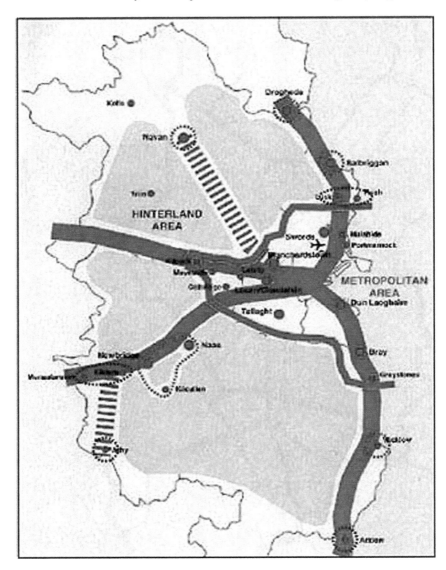

Figure 6.2   Strategic Planning Guidelines: Key Plan

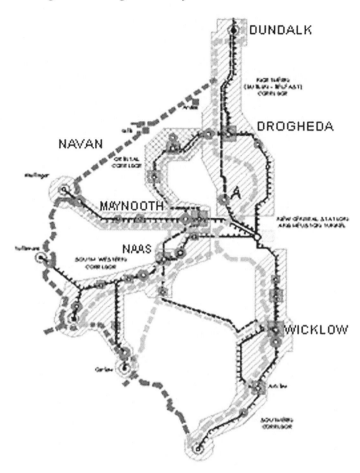

Figure 6.3   Movement and Activity Corridors: Draft Plan

Chapter 7

A Review of Local Planning within the Dublin-Belfast Corridor

Malachy McEldowney
Queens University, Belfast

Derry O'Connell
University College, Dublin

Introduction

Prior to the recent evolution of strategic spatial planning north and south of the border at the turn of the present century – the Regional Development Strategy for the Northern Ireland (RDS) and the National Spatial Strategy for the Republic (NSS) – local planning in both jurisdictions lacked an established strategic planning context. Although the format of local plans differed – Area Plans produced by Divisional Planning Offices of the DoE in the north, County and Town Development Plans by local authorities in the south – they shared the characteristic of being (a) relatively autonomous and locally focused and (b) pre-occupied with functional regulation.

They also tended to adopt a promotional role, particularly south of the border. The emergence of the Dublin-Belfast Corridor concept, within a climate of wider spatial planning awareness, has provided the opportunity to take advantage of a very positive initiative – particularly in relation to advertising the accessibility of strategic nodal sites for economic development and employment generation. Plans exist at national, regional and local level on both sides of the border, although no statutory plan crosses the border in the scope of its area of operation. Since the rank and tier structure of plans also varies on both sides of the border, the easiest way to gain an initial understanding of their relationship is to consider them in sequence from one end of the corridor to the other – in this case from north to south.

There are some disparities in the approaches adopted within the two jurisdictions, and these are reflected in the discussion below. Recent Area Plans in Northern Ireland have been based on the amalgamation of several previous Plan areas within a new composite Plan area, so although there are fewer Plans north of the border, they tend to be more comprehensive in their coverage. In addition, interviews with planning officers have been carried out in the three Divisional Planning Offices in Northern Ireland, as well as in the DoE Headquarters, and this provides some reflective comment from practitioners on the Corridor concept and on its relevance to their particular Area Plan.

Local Plans in Northern Ireland

The catalyst for current and future thinking on the subject as far as local plans are concerned is the RDS, which, after a slow start, has become thoroughly outward-looking and internationalist in its perspective. The European planning context has been influential here (ESDP, Europe 2000 etc.) as have the economic arguments (Quigley, 1997) and the consultation process (McEldowney and Sterrett, 2001)). More specifically, the Corridor concept, particularly the Eastern Seaboard Corridor, has been repeatedly emphasized in both planning and transportation strategies, and has been impressively enforced in the discussion of issues for the more recent Area Plans (Larne/Ballymena, Belfast Metropolitan Area Plan or BMAP, Newry/Banbridge). How the improved rhetoric translates into practical planning remains to be seen, but the RDS's positive image in European planning (Albrechts et al., 2003) is a reflection of its serious intent.

The analysis of each case study area starts with a brief consideration of the Issues Papers for its Local Plan within the RDS context. Then we focus on the attitudes and reactions of local planners involved in its preparation. The first part is therefore retrospective while the second part probes the significance of the Corridor concept in current thinking and looks forward to its future implications. It is complementary to the analysis of local plans south of the border in the second part of the chapter.

The three local plans discussed in the first part of the chapter are significantly different from previous local plans in Northern Ireland. They have been prepared under a process known as the 'Issues Approach' and they are all subject to a new protocol which ensures that local plans are in general conformity with regional strategy as outlined in the RDS (DRD 2003). 'Issues Papers' are produced instead of Preliminary Proposals for the purpose of widening public debate on the underlying key issues rather than concentrating too immediately on detailed locational proposals. This should facilitate a speeding-up of the often-protracted development plan process. In relation to a concept such as the Dublin-Belfast Corridor they should theoretically provide more scope for strategic discussion by a wider population, and indeed all the Plans considered show positive evidence of this more considered approach.

Antrim and Ballymena Local Plan

See Figure 7.1. This Plan was the subject of an Issues Paper in May 2002 – covering an area previously the subject of three Area Plans and their statutory alterations during the nineties. The benefits of this amalgamation are presumably the same as indicated above, but the disadvantages of the composite approach become clear in relation to the Corridor concept. A key section of the Corridor between Belfast and Lame is outside the scope of this particular Plan and is included within the Belfast Metropolitan Area Plan (below). Thus Larne, a key inter-regional gateway in the RDS, is left isolated from its links to other gateways such as the International Airport and the port/airport of Belfast, and from the rest of the Eastern Seaboard Corridor.

The Issues Paper is very positive in relation to the opportunities presented by the hubs/corridors/gateways proposals in the RDS and the development potential they offer. Under 'transportation' the location of both Ballymena and Larne on strategic corridors is highlighted:

> ... Ballymena is located on the Northern Corridor... the RDS identifies the Northern Corridor as also providing access to the Antrim Glens and Coast and facilitating Londonderry to Dublin links by direct connection to the Eastern Seaboard Corridor ...

> ... Larne Borough is located on the Eastern Seaboard Corridor which the RDS identifies as being an important north-south route between Belfast and Dublin and onwards to Larne ... in the long term the RDS indicates that this will involve the continuing development of high quality road and rail links between the two cities, such as the completion of the Larne-Rosslare TENS route to facilitate long distance freight movement.

See Figure 7.2 Northern Corridor and Figure 7.3 Eastern Seaboard Corridor (both from the RDS 2025).

In relation to tourism the Issues Paper makes the interesting point that the RDS concept of favourable 'first impression points' for visitors arriving in Northern Ireland applies to both Larne as a ferry port and to Aldergrove as an International Airport. Specifically in relation to the airport it stresses that:

> ... the RDS recognizes Belfast International Airport as one of Northern Ireland's regional gateways ... it identifies its potential for promotion as a key regional economic development opportunity offering the potential of clustering economic development to create a strong magnet for regional growth.

Of particular interest in relation to the Corridor concept is the Issue Paper's endorsement of a key component of the Corridor diagram:

> ... a circular passenger rail service on the Belfast-Bleach Green-Antrim-Lisburn-Belfast section of the rail network that would have connection to Belfast International Airport ... such an option was identified by the RDS.

Planners in the Ballymena Divisional Planning Office were very positive about the

Corridor concept. This is slightly surprising in view of the area's relatively peripheral location. The potential benefits for Larne are recognized - an opportunity for a port town in some danger of decline to 'plug in' to an exciting transnational project which would accentuate the town's strategic position in relation to future links between Ireland, north and south, northern Britain and ultimately mainland Europe. Freight services would be particularly important, and the Port Authority was looking for additional land to accommodate larger ferries. Potential industrial land was already available in the vicinity of the port, although there were some possible environmental conflicts. The upgrading of the A8 road would be welcome and the improvement of the inadequate existing rail service would be a high priority. The town's tourism potential as a 'destination resort' and gateway to the "Causeway Coast" could be more fully exploited.

The other strategic Gateway in the plan area is the International Airport which was also a major development site. Lands adjacent to the airport had existing planning approvals for industrial/commercial proposals with an emphasis on large-scale distribution services, and any potential conflict with Antrim town centre would be a key Area Plan issue. Potential major distribution development on the adjacent 'Nutt's Corner' airport site is also an issue and should be considered along with the International Airport within the Corridor concept. RDS suggestions in relation to rail links to the Airport should also be taken up. However, other ideas advanced at the 2003 Conference, particularly the bridge/tunnel from Larne to Scotland and the motorway around the north of Belfast were the subject of some scepticism.

The Belfast Metropolitan Area Plan 2015

This is the most significant of the new generation of RDS-influenced area plans. Its Issues Paper was launched in December 2001 and its public consultation carried out during 2002. The Draft Plan is expected in the winter of 2004. As compared with the above plans, the BMAP Issues paper makes few specific references to the Dublin-Belfast Corridor concept or to corridors in general for that matter. Being the most important Gateway may mean that Belfast feels it is less reliant on proclaiming attachment to a strategic corridor than lesser urban areas. Nevertheless, the indirect implications of many of its key issues are significant for the corridor concept. The Issues Paper underlines the city's European credentials at the outset:

> ...The Belfast Metropolitan Area Plan will aim to secure the long-term status of the Belfast Metropolitan Area as one of Europe's successful metropolitan regions – one where the political developments of recent years provide a much more favourable context for development than in the past.

It also affirms its consistency with European and wider UK policy – the European Spatial Development Perspective (Faludi and Waterhout, 2002) and UK Urban

Renaissance (Urban Task Force 1999) in particular. It stresses the city's role as an international city as well as a regional capital and locates Belfast at the centre of the RDS's ambition to:

> ... create an outward-looking, dynamic, and livable region with a strong sense of its place in the wider world ... where diversity is a source of strength rather than division.

Having identified a problem of employment growth (in comparison with Northern Ireland and UK growth rates over the past decade,) the Issues Paper highlights the RDS's point about:

> ... the need to identify and safeguard Strategic Employment Locations... which will attract and accommodate major inward investment projects as well as expanding local enterprises ... accessibility to the Regional Strategic Transport Network will be an important factor in their identification.

The significance of Belfast harbour as a freight and passenger port is emphasized:

> ... Belfast Harbour caters for nearly 10,000 shipping arrivals per year and is the largest ferry port in Northern Ireland handling over 35,000 freight vehicles, 2 million passengers, and over 450,000 passenger cars each year ....

and the existence of a series of economic focal points is underlined:

> ... Belfast has a number of vital economic, employment and commercial locations outside the city centre including the Port and Harbour Estate, City Airport, Queen's University, the Odyssey Centre and the major hospitals.

Beyond this there is little explicit reference to Corridor concepts. An obvious reason for this is the fact that transportation issues are dealt with by its sister plan, the Belfast Metropolitan Transport Plan (DRD 2003), which developed in detail the metropolitan implications of the Regional Transportation Strategy (DRD 2002). This emphasizes key and link transportation corridors. Another reason is the one indicated above, namely that as a focal point of the Corridor concept, the Metropolitan Area's priority is reinforcing the strength of the focal point, and the city's claims to European and international significance in its own right. This priority is stressed by local planners in the BMAP team, whose views are outlined below.

The Belfast Metropolitan Area Plan team is responsible for the Belfast Metropolitan Area Plan which, like both the above examples, has been the subject of Issues Paper consultation and is now at Draft Plan preparation stage. Planners in this team were also positive about the Corridor concept and supported RDS references to Belfast as a significant city on the European stage and a member of the international network of cities. The TENs Corridor was important in this context. Within the BMAP area, the corridor concept has been seen as the key metropolitan transport element which provided the framework for planning. Belfast's port and airport were also key focal points in the transportation network, but were still in competition with the port of Larne, the international airport and, increasingly, (as the Dublin-Belfast road links improve), with Dublin Port and Airport. Improvements to the corridor heightened the potential for such competition, so it was necessary to take a large-scale strategic view for planning purposes.

This competition/complimentarily debate applies also to the tourism market - Northern Ireland and the Republic were now co-operating on tourism promotion at the macro scale but such co-operation was limited at city scale, although Belfast is now included in many all-Ireland tourist bus routes. Belfast badly needs a 'must see' major tourism facility to reinforce its attraction to the Irish tourist market - the Odyssey project is one example of this, but more are needed. The Dublin/Belfast Corridor south of Belfast was a possible location, but current rumours of a major international theme park around Dublin Airport could obviate such an opportunity.

Strategic Employment Locations were the subject of serious planning consideration and there was much competition between District Councils in relation to them. Possible locations within the BMAP area – West Lisburn, Newtownabbey, Castlereagh and the Harbour Estate – were all well related to the metropolitan corridors, (West Lisburn, near motorway and rail interchanges, and Newtownabbey, on the Belfast-Larne corridor, being particularly well positioned.) The provision of adequate housing sites in proximity to employment locations was another key planning consideration. Views on the Corridor diagram were similar to previous ones – general acceptance of the public transport concept, but some scepticism about our new motorway proposal that had Larne rather than Belfast as its prime destination.

The Banbridge/Newry and Mourne Area Plan 2015

See Figure 7.4: The Banbridge/Newry and Mourne Area Plan 2015: (Banbridge District.) This Plan covers the area once occupied by no less than five Area Plans in the 'nineties - separate urban and rural plans for Banbridge and Newry and a plan for the Mournes which focused on an Area of Outstanding Natural Beauty. The concentration of these into a single Plan will obviously make for efficiencies of scale, but may run the risk of including disparate elements - certainly it has benefits for the Corridor concept in that a substantial section of it will now be within a single Plan and subject to a single public local inquiry. The RDS is given prominence in the policy context as well as in its housing growth indicators. In the transportation section, its location on the Eastern Seaboard Corridor and the Belfast-Dublin road and rail link are highlighted. The RDS proposal to strengthen this will provide benefits of a better public transport system and a stronger regional economy.

With particular reference to Banbridge it is argued that:

... it has an excellent strategic location on the Belfast-Dublin transport corridor and is within easy travelling time of the region's ports and airports and the major urban centres of Belfast, Lisburn and Craigavon ... Given its strategic location the town is well placed to accommodate further growth including the potential for industrial/commercial development accessed off the AI.

This endorsement of the benefits of the corridor concept is echoed in specific reference to Newry:

....the town occupies a gateway position on the Belfast-Dublin road and rail transport corridor and benefits from its close proximity to the border in terms of trade with the Republic of Ireland.

See Figure 7.5, Banbridge, Newry and Mourne Area Plan 2015: (Newry and Mourne District).

Craigavon Divisional Planning Office is responsible for the Banbridge, Newry and Mourne Area Plan for which the Issues Paper consultation has been completed and the Draft Plan is under preparation. Again, planners here positively acknowledged the relevance of the Corridor concept to their work, but stressed that the translation of an economic Corridor concept into a development plan process was a difficult objective to achieve. They have had extensive consultations with the Department of Regional Development (DRD), they have kept their local Council informed, particularly in relation to potentially-controversial housing growth indicators, and they have liaised extensively with colleagues across the border in Louth and Monaghan County Councils, in Dundalk Urban District Council and in the East Border Region group of Councils. Obviously this is not a cross-border plan but they share common infrastructural concerns and, indeed, some strategic designations – both Newry and Dundalk are 'gateway' cities, although the definitions may vary – so it is important to agree on common understandings and approaches.

In relation to roads infrastructure, the completion of a dual-carriageway link on the Al between Banbridge and the border is essential, and firm programmes are now in place to implement this south of Loughbrickland – the ultimate completion of such a link to Lisburn, Belfast and the MI is desirable but may have to await a roll-forward of the Regional Transportation Strategy. As far as rail is concerned, the improvement and possible re-location of Newry Station is under consideration and the RDS suggestion of a high-speed rail link (with motorway) from Lisburn via Banbridge and Poyntzpass to Newry is acknowledged as a long-term objective.

Strategic employment locations linked to the corridor concept are the subject of much debate and both District Council areas have candidate sites in mind- Carnbane in Newry and Cascum Road in Banbridge. However, the planners felt that employment location would in future be more fine-grained than in the past and that a series of smaller employment centres (some related to brownfield sites), would be necessary. The idea of a high-speed rail link, (shown here in Chapter 15,) was welcomed but it was felt that dualling the A1 was a higher priority than building a new motorway. Some scepticism was expressed about the danger of the corridor concept exaggerating and exacerbating present commuter patterns. Already Banbridge is a commuter settlement for Belfast and Newry is beginning to be the same for Dublin. There may be a problem of retaining a 'living and working' heart to the plan area if these trends really were exacerbated.

While most of the comments from planning officers (above) were positive in relation to the Corridor concept, there was also much uncertainty as what it really meant in economic terms. Such scepticism was underlined and amplified by comments from the Department of the Environment Headquarters planners in Belfast, who agreed that the corridor principle was hard to challenge but that too many corridors, with too many growth points on them, dilute the value of selectivity. If we have to promote Belfast as the prime focal point, can we also promote Larne, and Banbridge, and Newry, not to mention Dromore or Warrenpoint? In addition, how do we continue to have a 'living and working countryside'? By the same token, how many Selective Employment Locations are justifiable, if every District Council wants one, and there are ample corridors on which to locate them? Selective Employment Locations depend on investment, prompted by Invest Northern Ireland and complementary functions such as third-level educational facilities, but not on political bargaining nor on planning designations based on land availability or accessibility.

In relation to the Dublin/Belfast Corridor it is interesting to compare Newry with Dundalk. Newry has only a modestly increased housing target, while Dundalk has substantial economic and educational investment underpinning extensive housing growth. What are the mechanisms within the Corridor concept which will make the towns complementary, since Newry may find it difficult to compete? On a more negative note, what are the mechanisms in the concept which will protect a town like Dromore, which is ideal as a commuting base, but increasingly unattractive as a commercial focus? What are the benefits to a particular locality of major investments (IKEA, for example) which is looking for an accessible all-Ireland base? How can public transport be promoted if car-based accessibility is the criterion for locational decision-making?

Local Plans in the Republic of Ireland

South of the border, the corridor is covered by three County Development Plans, with a number of specific plans within them, such as those for Dundalk and Drogheda. The dominance of the corridor varies in its relationship to each of these plans: Fingal and Louth, for example, sit almost entirely within the influence of the corridor, while for Meath the coastal corridor is very much an annex, the characteristics of which are not those of the body of the county. Although the focus of this discussion is on local planning, it is important to comment briefly on the national planning context.

The National Spatial Strategy (NSS) (DoELG 2002) is very much a plan about settlement interaction at a national scale, proposing a settlement plan for Ireland, outlining both the role of settlements within this plan and their relationship to each other. As in the Regional Development Strategy for Northern Ireland (RDS) (DRD 2001) it identifies linkages between settlements and develops the concept of corridors of activity around these linkages. Although it does explore cross-border relationships between Derry and Letterkenny in the north-west, for example, there is little concentration elsewhere on cross-border corridors at this scale. It does, in its diagrammatic representations, indicate desire lines of association northwards from Dundalk, along the Dublin-Belfast Corridor.

Louth County Development Plan 1997/2003

As the county immediately south of, but contiguous to, the border, and midway between Dublin and Belfast, Louth has the potential to play a significant role in the development of the Dublin-Belfast Corridor. The strategic location of the county is reflected in the current Development Plan in terms of policy on transportation, employment opportunities, and tourism and it is clear from the Plan strategy that the County Council is committed to fostering cross border co-operation in generic terms.

The Louth County Development Plan 1997 identifies the county's strategic position as a key strength. The development of the Euro-route E01 (Larne/Belfast-Dublin-Rosslare, focused on the N1 road, together with the Belfast-Dublin rail line,) increases access to both of these major cities from County Louth. The accessibility of the county is further enhanced via the Corridor by its relative proximity to the international airports of Dublin and Belfast and also to the major ports in these two cities and in Larne. The protection and improvement of this strategic transportation infrastructure is the aim of the County Council as reflected in Development Plan policy.

In relation to employment policy, the County Development Plan identifies the possibility of exploiting the county's strategic location, by attracting new industries to the area. It is stated Development Plan policy:

… to promote the county's strategic location between Dublin and Belfast, together with its transport and communications links, to industrialists and other potential employers.

The fact that County Louth generally has lower land prices as compared with the major cities on the east coast is also identified as a key strength.

In terms of tourism, the potential links between Northern and Southern Ireland are stressed in the plan. Louth is viewed as a gateway to Ireland for tourists from Northern Ireland, Scotland and the North of England. At a more detailed level it is Development Plan policy to explore the potential to create walking trails which cross the border in the Cooley Peninsula, linking trails in the Carlingford Mountains to trails in the Mourne Mountains.

As is the case in the current Plan, the new Draft Plan, on display until April 2003, identifies and stresses in its Vision Statement the County's strategic position midway between Dublin and Belfast, the two main urban centres on the island:

> ... by reason of its strategic location on the Dublin/Belfast Economic Corridor, accessibility to East Coast ports and international airports and the rapidly improving road and rail infrastructure, the county is well placed to continue to grow in population and economic terms into the foreseeable future.

In relation to economic development and employment, the Plan refers to the potential to capitalize on the county's location and to utilize the key transportation infrastructure:

> ... Much of County Louth's strength as a source and provider of employment lies in its strategic location, the continued development of the M1 / EO1 Euro-route motorway, together with the up grading of the rail network. When completed, it will strategically link the key ports and airports of Larne, Belfast, Dublin and Rosslare. Dundalk, Drogheda and Ardee provide the main locations for employment uses in the county. The influence of the M1 /EO1 Euro-route has the potential to transform the county of Louth as a whole and impact on the development of its towns, including settlements located some distance from the motorway.

The County Council has further explored the potential of the M1/EO1 route as a generator of economic activity. In this regard the Council commissioned the production of an Interchange Strategy from Murray O'Laoire Architects and Planners. This interchange strategy examines the potential of motorway interchanges and makes detailed recommendations with regard to their appropriate development.

Dundalk Development Plan 1996

As the major settlement closest to the midway point between Dublin and Belfast, Dundalk is in a position to capitalize on the development of the Dublin-Belfast Economic Corridor, and most of its planning documents underline this point.

The Dundalk Development Plan 1996 recognizes the strategic locational position of Dundalk, fifty miles from both Dublin and Belfast. It is stated that Dundalk's hinterland stretches across the border and that the town serves as a major commercial service centre for parts of the adjoining counties of Monaghan, Armagh and Down in Northern Ireland. The town's location on the Euro-Route EO1, on the main Dublin-Belfast rail line and its accessibility to both Dublin and Belfast International Airports, are seen in the plan as major locational advantages, particularly in terms of developing the town's industrial and service base. It is

Council policy to emphasize the strategic position of the Town on the east coast 'Golden Corridor' linking Dublin and Belfast in its promotion of Dundalk as an ideal locale for industrialists and other potential employers. The town's strategic position also affects the retail policy in the plan, as it is the Urban District Council's policy to strengthen the role of the town centre as the primary retailing centre for both the town of Dundalk and County Louth.

Drogheda Development Plan 1999

Of the three major development plans in Louth, the Drogheda Development Plan makes least reference to the strategic potential of the links between Dublin and Belfast. Given the town's position in the south of the county, the emphasis in development policy is towards links with the neighbouring county of Meath so as to counter the growing influence of Dublin.

While Louth's strategic position between Dublin and Belfast is clearly recognized in the county's Development Plans, it is not translated into detailed development policies or objectives to the extent that might be the case if there was a more concerted effort to develop the economic corridor. For example, what specific roles might Dundalk and Drogheda play in such an economic corridor? Does such a concept have implications for land use policy, particularly in Dundalk? Furthermore, does an economic corridor pose threats for Dundalk and Drogheda, as the pull from both Belfast and Dublin increases, and the accessibility to the two major cities improves? None of these questions are seriously addressed.

Meath County Development Plan 2001

The Meath Development Plan refers specifically to the Dublin-Belfast Corridor in its intentions for the town of Drogheda, which occupies a strategic position on the Corridor, and is the focus of a growing economic axis, supported by rapid mainline rail and developing motorway (M1) networks. Its economic significance is aided by its attractive setting in the Boyne Valley and adjacent to the Irish Sea coastline, close to the archaeological attractions of the Boyne Valley.

The Development Plan states that it is an objective of Meath County Council to facilitate and promote the development of Drogheda on the Dublin-Belfast economic axis, as a major development centre and in co-operation with the adjacent planning authorities of Louth County Council and Drogheda Corporation. As a major growth point on the Corridor it will be supported by sustainable water services, transportation and social infrastructure and will retain its primacy as a location for central-place functions.

Another reference to the Corridor concept is to be found in the Meath County Council East Meath Sub-Region Development Plan 2000 which describes its sub-region as … *lying within the Dublin-Belfast (Economic) Corridor*…although, conversely, the Meath County Development Board Strategy for the Development of County Meath to 2012 makes no direct reference to the Corridor.

Fingal Development Plan 1999

The Fingal Development Plan makes many explicit references to the Dublin-Belfast Corridor. While most of its policy statements and objectives are general in intent, the focus is firmly on the opportunity to generate economic development and employment. It suggests that the Corridor has

> ... the potential to provide one of the most significant economic development entities in the country ... due to improvements in transport and other infrastructure, the economic boom, the 'peace dividend' and the single market ...

and that Fingal, in particular, is in an advantageous position to avail of the developments in trade and widening of markets because of an increase in demand created by the growth of population, income, and market integration.

The Plan's Policy Statement locates the Corridor within the European Commission's broad aim of:

> ... improving transportation networks between and feeding major cities, in order to stimulate inter-regional and international economic co-operation ...

and its general Economic Objective is to

> ... enable Fingal to make a distinctive contribution to the Dublin-Belfast Economic Corridor objectives of maximising economic growth and sustainable employment opportunities, for the benefit of the population of the county.

Specifically this means focusing future development along the corridor to enhance the county's existing computer-based, IT, pharmaceutical and electronics industrial clusters as well as developing indigenous support, service and tourism industries on the strength of enhanced investment. It also means a particular focus on the equitable distribution of investments to less developed parts of the county.

There is a specific objective to develop a variety of facilities at the motorway interchange at Courtlough which is uniquely positioned in that it is not required to directly serve an urban area. This provides an excellent opportunity for the location, directly adjoining the motorway, of facilities associated with the Dublin-Belfast Economic Corridor, motorway services and a major service facility for the rural area. Such facilities could include a major wholesale fruit and vegetable market, motorway services, warehousing facilities for the Corridor and a science and technology park.

Summary and Conclusion

Local planning in Northern Ireland has evolved considerably over the past ten years – in the early and mid-nineties it suffered from the lack of an influential strategic context and was localised, perhaps parochial, in its focus and strictly functional in its approach. There was some relevant identification of international and cross-border features and issues, but no serious recognition of their potential. The advent of the Belfast City Region and subsequent Regional Strategies has provided an essential strategic framework, while causing short-term delays in the local plan system. Allied to the 'issues approach' for public consultation, this has served to broaden and deepen the discussion on concepts such as the Corridor. It has also encouraged much improved cross-border co-operation at local and strategic level.

Post-RDS local plans have enthusiastically adopted the rhetoric of the Corridor concept, largely through RDS influence on the Eastern Seaboard Corridor. While most references are to transportation issues, selective employment location and tourism policy are also frequently related to the concept. The Belfast Metropolitan Area Plan as the key focal point of the strategy, stresses its role as an international city but relies less on direct identification with the corridor than do smaller neighbouring plans, which perhaps see the concept as an investment promotion opportunity.

Local planners are generally enthusiastic about the concept also, although most expressed vagueness about its exact economic implications and the problem of translating rhetoric into reality. Most support was based on the facilitation of much-needed infrastructure, particularly roads and public transport, and the improved accessibility of long-standing industrial sites which could be promoted as selective employment locations. They were also generally enthusiastic about new planning processes which widened consultation and professional liaison within and beyond traditional boundaries.

Common throughout all of the plans in the Republic of Ireland is an absence of preoccupation with the Corridor beyond the opportunities which it might offer for ease of linkages northwards or southwards from a particular subject area. The Fingal Plan is possibly that which goes farthest in its recognition of the potential for long distance connections of function which might be achieved only because of specific proximity to the Corridor. There is a synergy between the plans of both jurisdictions across the border but in a latent manner which follows from the natural relationship of activities. Although none of the plans have particularly strong policies to develop the corridor, they do not have policies which hinder it either. They recognize its existence as a positive opportunity.

Serious questions were also raised about the concept. There is now a proliferation of 'corridors' in Northern Ireland and there is a proliferation of 'gateways' in the Republic, so the value of selectivity is undermined, particularly when major and minor 'hubs' and a 'living and working countryside' are added to the mix. More particularly, how can smaller settlements within the corridor protect themselves from becoming commuter dormitories or redundant commercial centres? How can the conflict/complementarily balance be achieved, not just between Belfast and Dublin, but also between the likes of Newry and Dundalk?

And on a more general note, how can local planning, traditionally a facilitator rather than a generator of investment decisions, move from the rhetoric of support to the practice of implementation in relation to this and related concepts?

There is little doubt that the Belfast Dublin Corridor is generally perceived 'as a good thing'. It provides planners with a basis for selectivity, which has been a traditional planning modus operandi. It chimes with the concept of sustainability, which is a current planning article of faith; it presents a coherent and positive image, which is increasingly what planners aspire to. However, local planning is, and should be, dominated by local requirements and perhaps parochial perceptions. People ask what the locality is 'getting out of' a strategic proposal. There are many questions in relation to this that proponents of the concept must answer.

Copies of maps are provided by David Houston, School of Environment Planning, Queens University Belfast.

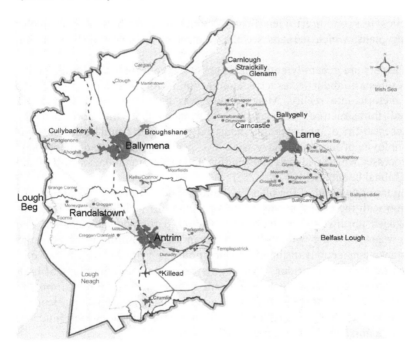

Figure 7.1   Antrim and Ballymena Local Plan

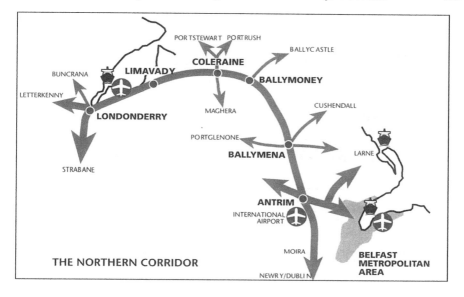

Figure 7.2   Northern Corridor

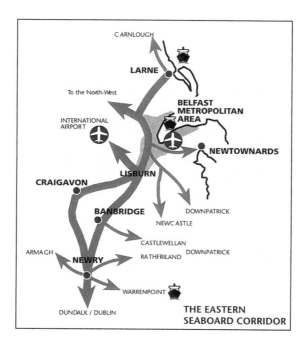

Figure 7.3   The Eastern Seaboard Corridor

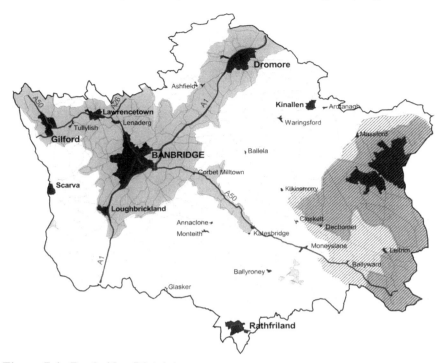

Figure 7.4   Banbridge District

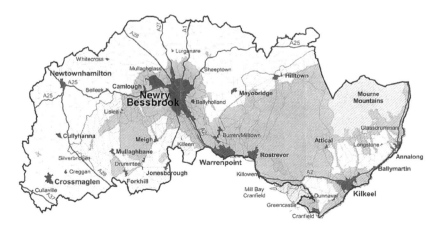

Figure 7.5   Newry and Mourne District

References

Albrechts, L., Healey, P. and Kunzmann, K. (2003), Strategic Spatial Planning and Regional Governance in Europe, *Journal of the American Planning Association,* **69,** 2, 113–129.

DoE (Department of the Environment Northern Ireland) (2001), *Banbridge, Newry and Mourne Area Plan 2015 Issues Paper* (Belfast: DoE).

————, *Antrim, Ballymena and Larne Area Plan 2016 Issues Paper* (Belfast: DoE).

DoE (2001), *Belfast Metropolitan Area Plan 2015 Issues Paper* (Belfast: DoE).

DoELG (Department of Environment and Local Government) (2002), *The National Spatial Strategy 2002-2020: People, Places, Potential* (Dublin: Stationery Office).

DRD (Department of Regional Development Northern Ireland) (2001), *Shaping our Future: Regional Development Strategy for Northern Ireland 2025* (Belfast: DRD).

————, (2002), *Regional Transportation Strategy* (Belfast: DRD).

————, (2003), *Shaping our Future...together,* First Annual Report (Belfast: DRD).

Faludi, A. and Waterhout, B. (2002), *The Making of the European Spatial Development Perspective* (London: Routledge).

Fingal County Council (1999), *Fingal County Development Plan 1999* (Swords: Fingal C.C.).

Healey, P. (1983), *Local Plans in British Land Use Planning* (Oxford: Pergamon Press).

Louth County Council (1997, 2003), *Louth County Development Plan 1997, 2003* (Dundalk: Dundalk C.C.).

————, (1999), *Drogheda Development Plan 1999* (Dundalk, Louth C.C.).

————, (1996), *Dundalk Development Plan 1996* (Dundalk, Louth C.C.).

McEldowney,M., Sterrett, K. (2001), *Shaping a Regional Vision: the Case of Northern Ireland Local Economy* 16,1, 38–49.

Meath County Council (2001), *Meath County Development Plan 2001* (Navan: Meath C.C.).

Quigley, G. (1997), Regional Economic Challenges, paper to *Shaping our Future* Conference 22 November 1997 (Belfast).

Urban Task Force (1999), *Towards an Urban Renaissance* (London, Spon).

Chapter 8

Mass Transportation within Development Corridors

John Prosser
University of Colorado, USA.
Visiting Fellow, Urban Institute, Ireland

John Yarwood
Former Director, Urban Institute, Ireland

Introduction

Urbanization comprises two realms: ways and places. Essentially, the city is a place for the production and exchange of goods and services. In the 10,000–year evolution of the city, without essential transportation (communication, infrastructure, etc.) there could not have been trade, economic development, jobs, education, cultures and civilizations. Extending, expanding, diversifying and maintaining the critical networks for commerce are paramount. That is the crux of the Dublin- Belfast 100-mile corridor vision.

Doubtless though, the funding must be based on beneficiary charges or surcharges to pay for the needed multi-modal systems and utility corridors, ('utilidors'). It is intriguing to note that ancient texts dating back to the 4th century BC in India mention the use of tolls. Tollgates, too, are referenced in the English Doomsday book of 1095 and the tolls on London Bridge date as far back as 1286.

The early economically powerful cities are strategically placed on the water transportation resource funnels of the major world rivers: Tigris/Euphrates, Nile, Rhine, Danube, Volga, Thames, Mississippi/Ohio/Missouri, Paraguay, Changjiang and Ganges, to name but a few. In Ireland, the Liffey and Shannon became such nourishing branches and, nearly without exception, the many river networks are supplemented by ubiquitous canal ways. Remarkably, New York City became the commercial capital of North America once the Erie Toll Canal from the Hudson River was completed to the Great Lakes. In turn, the Gulliver profits generated by this waterway established Wall Street.

In lieu of these internal waterways, the Greeks, Arabs and Vikings took to the seas while the Romans also webbed their Empire with some 25,000 miles of highways (comparable to the 40,000 mile US Interstate system in relative scale) and claimed as well the entire Mediterranean as *Mare Nostrum*. So too did the

Venetians and Genoans keep the sea as theirs, once Islamic fleets were defeated in the sea battle of Lepanto in 1571.

Interestingly, in that same era, China – with the largest ocean going fleet up to that time – turned completely inwards, following the Manchu Conquest, until recommencing a naval build up in the twenty-first century.

With the coming of the 'Age of Discovery' in the sixteenth century following Columbus' voyages, the Atlantic-facing nations exploited the wealth of the world for almost 500 years. The spoils from their global violence eventually fuelled the industrial revolution and underwrote the earlier resurgence of Christianity, through the Reformation.

With the birth of the Industrial Revolution, the entrepreneurial rail systems slashed through the country sides, using the same ancient Roman chariot wheel axle widths for what became standard-gauged vehicles. Besides the sheer commercial bonanza, the railroads precipitated what today is the behemoth hospitality industry with hotels, conference centres, spas, resorts and retreats, which (with travel and tourism) is now the world's largest economic generator at $3 trillion (US).

The Dublin-Belfast Corridor development scenario depends upon the entire multi- modal spectrum of trains, trams, bikes, taxis, buses, autos, electric carts, ferries, trucks, aeroplanes, jets, supersonics and so on, not forgetting facilities for pedestrians. In parallel, fire, smoke, oil lamps, torches, cold and hot water, drainage and waste systems, bells, mirrors, clocks, steam and electricity were the keystones for the 500,000-year communication and infrastructure transformations up to and beyond the electronic cathode ray tube (first conceived in 1873).

US Comparisons

It could be useful to look at US data compiled by the Federal Highway Administration (FHA). Although Ireland is the most car dependent country in the world at 24,400 km per year, America is next at 19,000 km.

- Households with two vehicles grew from 17 to 40 million between 1969 and 1995; three vehicle households went from 3 to 19 million, and only 8 per cent of all households had no vehicle.
- Travel by private vehicle accounts for 86 per cent of all person-trips and 91 per cent of all person-miles. (In the EU today private vehicles account for 80 per cent of person miles). Walking is next at 5.4 per cent of all trips with mass transit at 1.8 per cent. (Work-only trips by private vehicles are 91 per cent and transit 3.5 per cent).
- Carpooling peaked at 22 per cent of all work trips during the early 1970s fuel crisis and is now less than 9 per cent. Occupancy has fallen to 1.14 persons per vehicle.

- Notably, less than 25 per cent of all trips are to/from work and account for merely 18 per cent of person trips, whereas shopping accounts for 44.4 per cent and recreation for 37.9 per cent.
- During rush hours, 6:00–9:00 am and 4:00–7:00 pm, less than one of three person trips are to or from work.
- Surprisingly, the average travel time to work is still only 20 minutes but the distance has increased by over 36 per cent from 8.5 to 11.6 miles due to faster commute speeds rising from 28 to 34 miles per hour.

Urbanization patterns precipitated by these trends are then significantly affected with the construction and/or enlargement of freeways/motorways/toll roads and beltways/ring roads. While population growth and declining densities forge ever-larger cities, they contribute immensely to the overall 50 per cent population decline in central cities everywhere over the past 30 years. It is a push/pull development scenario – better ways, worse places.

Studies by the US Department of Transportation (DOT) and other agencies also dramatically indicate the impact these mega road systems have on settlement patterns. In the 50-year implementation of the national networks, countless enormous 'Edge Cities' and edgeless cities have risen beside superhighway corridors and interchanges. The paradigm is much the same as the beginning of the city where commercial, business, retail, office, government, health, religious and multifamily uses were arranged within half a mile from the typical Main Street and Broadway (High Streets and Cross Roads) intersections. In general, both cluster and corridor developments are more likely to occur in metropolitan areas with highly organized freeway networks, including radials and beltways. DOT specific findings nationally are the following:

- Suburbanisation occurs regardless of the transportation systems. (The obsession with escaping to the country was recorded at Ur in 2000 BC).
- The radials and rings are a great attractor of multi-family housing.
- Higher accessibility and lower land costs are incentives for manufacturing, warehousing, service employment and for industry itself. Some cities show 30 per cent–80 per cent construction increases on their edges.
- Retail follows population regardless, especially with greater traffic access.
- Office parks and employment follow that population growth as well, reflecting the extent of market exposure. In fact, this attraction appears to be greater as the distance from the city centre increases.

As the FHA observes, the movement trends reflect changes in travel patterns, the number of women in the labour force, the decline of nine-to-five work schedules and an ongoing lack of transportation alternatives. Furthermore, there are no indications that such changes will affect the fundamental forces making US society ever more dependent on personal transportation in the near future. Additionally, the FHA concludes; 'The myth of Americans' love affair with their cars may actually be a marriage of convenience. Contemporary land use patterns require the use of private vehicles whether or not we do love those vehicles.'

Unfortunately the inability of many communities to provide adequate facilities has made traffic congestion and sprawl into leading national issues. The pullback of Federal and State budgets (due to extreme economic, social, political and military constraints) has made the two problems almost insurmountable. The deterioration of the entire infrastructure (and the resultant costs in time and efficiency) defeats the very core of trade and economic development. According to the Rebuild America Coalition supported by the American Public Works Association, the present cost to bring public infrastructure up to acceptable condition is more than $1.4 trillion US dollars.

The 'New Urbanism' and Compact Cities

Contemporary urban design ideas at the level of city-regions are to a great extent based on the proposition that public transport should generate urban form ('Transit-Oriented Development') so as to optimize the propensity to patronize it. Integrated movement strategy and layout design are two sides of the same coin, in other words.

'New Urbanism' is a movement originated in the US, and its best known practitioners are probably Andres Duany and Elisabeth Plater-Zyberk. Peter Calthorpe is also a notable proponent. The key book is 'Charter of the New Urbanism'. In Ireland and Britain, the terminology is not the same, (the term 'Compact City' would be better recognized), but there are few doctrinal differences. The exponent with the greatest design charisma is Leon Krier. A useful academic text would be Jenks, Burton and Williams, *The Compact City*.

The gist might be summed up as follows. Densities should be higher than was normal in suburban projects in recent times. Cities should be subdivided into "quarters", which are small enough for the inhabitants to traverse on foot, and within this compass, all land uses, activities and facilities (associated with day-to-day existence) should be mixed. 'Urban village' is another term which has been used to convey a similar idea. The urban street-system would not be car-dominated, and most journeys would include (or even be dominated by) the pedestrian mode. Each urban unit, whether a village, a small town or the quarter of a large city, should have a clear edge, (which might signal, for instance, the point at which the urban entity terminates and the rural landscape begins. This is what the words 'compact' and 'city' imply).

The doctrine indicates that a city based on these principles would be able to offer a much better lifestyle than the usual metropolis based on strict zoning, large catchments, long journeys and car-dominated movement, surrounded by a sprawling penumbra of pseudo-urbanized countryside. So far as lifestyle and urban culture are concerned, the major authors to be consulted are probably Jane Jacobs and Richard Sennett. If this is to be more than utopian, it will obviously be necessary to retrofit existing city fabric, and this fact has been recognized and tackled by researchers.

The important point for this chapter concerns public transport, of course. At the centre of each village or urban village would be a station/stop, which may be on a railway, tram, guided bus or quality bus route. The access would be pedestrian, within say 10 minutes walk. To attain viable patronage levels it would be necessary to have (a) a frequent service, (say every 10 minutes) (b) quick journey times, with no delay in traffic jams; and (c) routes to destinations with minimum necessity to change mode, route or vehicle.

The concept of a Dublin-Belfast Corridor could be catastrophic, if it developed as a 100-mile suburb serving both Dublin and Belfast by means of a car-dominated movement system, (a danger which several other authors in this book have pointed out.) This is why the (a) self-containment principle and (b) the linkage of urban form to public transport, both of which are associated with the new urbanism, are peculiarly important for this corridor.

Transit-Oriented Development: Some Irish Case Studies

The Cork Area Strategic Plan 2020 (CASP)

One example of an Irish regional plan characterized by Transit-Oriented Development is the Cork Area Strategic Plan. The Greater Dublin Area Regional Planning Guidelines, (discussed in Chapter 6), was based on similar thinking.

Cork city is surrounded by an inner ring of small settlements, which are near the city, (although separated from it by open country), including Blarney, Glanmire, Glounthaune, Carrigtwohill, Cobh, Carrigaline, Ballancollig, and others. Beyond that is an outer ring of relatively autonomous towns, namely Mallow, Fermoy, Midleton, Youghal. Kinsale, Bandon and Macroom. There was considerable popular resistance to the idea of large scale expansion on the urban fringe of the city, and importance was placed on the proximity of open countryside. (On the other hand, the popular desire was to have an isolated house in the countryside, and this syndrome was tending to spoil the rural hinterland here as everywhere in Ireland). In addition, there was a lot of pressure to expand the outer ring of towns. Surprisingly, there is no rural protectionism yet in the case of Ireland. On the contrary, each town wants to get (at least) 'their share' of growth.

This phenomenon gave rise to some contradictions and difficulties, which the Cork plan tried to resolve by a polycentric policy. The plan tried to facilitate regional competitiveness and economic growth. Conventional wisdom would seek to enhance the urban mass of the city, whereas spreading growth more thinly over a large number of small places would be thought less likely to deliver the conditions for a continuing boom. The plan sought to reconcile the demand for growth with the resistance to expanding the city by spreading the growth among a number of settlements, and linking them together to form a polycentric city-system.

The road-based alternative plan was tested by traffic modelling, and the result was very expensive and environmentally unacceptable, but more than that, the projected congestion and delay was tremendous. Additionally, a car-based strategy would make it impractical to regenerate the city core. Inner Cork has very narrow roads, and it was agreed that the necessary widening and demolition was not going to be politically acceptable.

There was therefore a general acceptance that the plan should be public transport-led. The parts of the rail system which had been closed would be reopened, with new track and signalling, and the existing portions would be upgraded. As many new stations as technically possible would be built, (nominally at two kilometre intervals), and land would be delivered for development (or densification) packed closely around the stations.

See Figure 8.1, Structure Diagram for Metropolitan Cork. This shows a rail line from Midleton in the east to Blarney in the west, through the central city, (Kent station.) A branch line accesses Cobh. There are settlements around the line like pearls on a string. See also Figure 8.2, Sketch of typical Transit-Oriented Project, (which was prepared for discussion purposes, but not published). This shows a kilometre square development with a railway station in the middle, apartments to one side, a business park and retail mall to the other side, plus multi-storey car park and bus station connected to the rail station. This should be regarded purely as a model. The main message is that detailed design of layout near stations is a necessary part of the whole development process. The topic of greatest importance is how to achieve the highest density and simultaneously to promote highest quality of life, since high densities will maximize the proximity of travellers to stations and thus increase patronage and viability. It is good news that the government has approved the rail finances and the County Council is commissioning consultants to undertake the local planning and urban design work.

The plan also proposed the regeneration of the city centre, by rebuilding the "Cork Docklands" at high density. The Kent Station site would be rebuilt so as to link the station by foot-bridge/travelator across the river to the Docklands. This would deliver large numbers of workers and visitors to Docklands without the need for major urban motorways and car parks.

Of course, in Cork it is usually not possible to build entirely new railway lines, and here the plan proposed Guided Bus Ways, based mostly on existing roads. They would also terminate at Kent Station to facilitate cross-town journeys. Where the public transport provision is limited, for whatever reason, the new development will be correspondingly limited. To conclude, the Cork case is a small-scale corridor and possibly the best Irish case upon which to model the Dublin-Belfast Corridor. It is gratifying that the Irish government, and particularly the Department of Transport, is taking it very seriously.

The Approach of the Dublin Transportation Office (DTO)

The Dublin Transportation Initiative (DTI) Strategy 2000-2016, 'A Platform for Change' report prepared by the Dublin Transportation Office (DTO) is a regional long range comprehensive vision for Greater Dublin which has essential applicability to the entire cross border 100 mile interconnection potential. While obviously primarily addressing the ingress to and egress from central Dublin itself, the study fully encompasses the problems of hinterlands and 'journey to work' areas beyond County Dublin into Fingal, Meath, Kildare and Wicklow counties. The map indicates the five key transportation corridors of the M1/NI, N3, M4, M7 and M11/N11 and designates the highly impacted primary and secondary development centres including those to the north (Lusk/Rush, Balbriggan, Drogheda and Navan), along the corridor.

It is essential that a balance be achieved between environment and economics, ways and places. Here the DTO has been diligent in pursuing the broad strategic green belt designations and in paralleling the Dutch methodology of concentrated decentralization into the outlying communities while promoting critical public transportation extensions and/or reinforcement. While the Departments of Environment and Transportation are not always fully integrated in the overall planning process, DTO pursues a holistic transit and land use approach.

It is notable that in the 10 years prior to the completion of this DTO report, traffic growth in Greater Dublin has far outstripped the projections in the 1995 DTI Strategy. While population in the area grew by 110,000 or just over 8 per cent, the GDP increased 79 per cent and auto ownership per 1000 population rose over 70 per cent. Equally telling is the dramatic climb in the number of houses built annually in Ireland, totalling 21,391 in 1993 up to 68,819 in 2003 with 2004, for the first six months, running 21 per cent more than the previous year. In a 10-year period to 2002, one third of those units were rural one-off homes. The above data is quite remarkable considering that Ireland was relatively moribund in 1988, that special year celebrating the Dublin millennium.

Significant too, but not surprising, is that urban generated households in rural America face an annual cost of living $9,000 to $14,000 higher than their civic counterparts. For example, a study by the international transport think tank UITP found that homes and workplaces which are in close mutual proximity in diverse cities such as Copenhagen and Singapore resulted in annual transport expenditures of $3000 less *per inhabitant* than in a sprawling Houston or Atlanta.

Further indication of the effects of an aggregation of these multiple impacts is vividly defined by the fact that travel speed on primary routes within the Dublin Metro Area dropped from 22 kph in 1991 to 14 kph in 1997 with current averages far less. In 2002, moving a five-kilo package five kilometres in Dublin took 57 minutes, (relative to London at 13 and New York at 17).

In the four years since the adoption of the 2000 Strategy report, the DTO response for the multi-county region has been extremely diligent, inclusionary and comprehensive. Actual planning results to date provide a cross section of diverse prototypes ranging from general city sites to edge city, satellite and stand-alone remote locations. From the entire existing background generated from what is categorized historically as a 'boom town' or 'instant city', the DTO is in final draft of a *modelling the transport city* report. In total, the methodologies formulated and applied by DTO coupled with the outstanding conceptual urban design, form a basis for implementing sensible and sensitive planning. This could achieve the Dublin Belfast Corridor urbanization potential within an environmentally sound land use pattern.

Between the island's two international transportation, social, educational, technological, commercial and political capitals the 160 kilometre corridor must not become a twentieth century ribbon city. Best would be to echo the formulations of the 19th C. Spanish planners, I. Cerdá and A. Soria y Mata, for their 'network based' and/or 'linear city' urban planning approaches. Already along the Dublin-Belfast Corridor, the key existing towns and small cities are spaced approximately every 15 to 20 kilometres, comparable to the pre-industrial day trip time; (i.e. the distance from/to a farm and its main marketplace).

Fortunately, in the past four years, following the 'Platform for Change' guidelines, DTO has commissioned several outstanding examples of comprehensive reports for village, sub area, town and city planning solutions with local, national and international consultants. Among those studies, which would be very applicable to future 'transport city' problems in the entire corridor, are the ones for Balbriggan Integrated Area Framework (Draft Report, August 2000); 2020 Vision for Naas (Final, May 2003), Arklow Town and Environs Integrated Framework Plan for Land Use and Transportation (Final Report, October 2003) and 'Moving Dublin: Modelling the Transport City' (Draft Report March.2003).

It appears that all these and others, including the approved Adamstown Development zone, could not be more timely (with the State population exceeding 4.0 M for the first time in over a century.) Importantly, housing completion for the Greater Dublin catchment region reached 12,898 units in the first six months of 2004, representing over one-third of the entire country totals. Adding Co. Louth, at 1,239 houses, brings the figure to 14,137, showing further the immense growth pressures impacting the environment and all systems along this sector of the Irish Sea coastline and elsewhere.

What is impressive about the various DTO multi scale development planning efforts are the extremely complete correlation, cohesion and integration of every transit mode within the full scope of land uses. The population numbers and needs are always paramount in their problem solving processes. Notwithstanding nor ignoring the ubiquitous car, the essential focus is consistently on alternative levels of movement networks and not just individual projects. In this respect a critical overriding parameter is the necessity to typically density at 60-70 dwelling units per hectare to yield adequate populations for transit rider-ship service with 15-minute headways.

Without exception, the existing infrastructure is accounted and everyone is within a 10-minute walk or one kilometre of transit stops and entirely mixed-use 'development centres'. Such 'Transit Oriented Developments' (TODs) in the U.S., have a spacing of about one mile between light rail or bus rapid transit stations. Development permits include large bonuses, (square footage, activity and parking bonuses), if they are within 1500 feet or a five-minute walk of the stop. A further aspect of the American approach is to concentrate (i.e. either to avoid or regenerate strip business activities between transit points and reintroduce high density (25 to 75 dwelling units/hectare) housing interrelated with recreation and open space. Wherever possible crossing streets and curb cuts are also restricted or deleted as redundant.

In the urban development plans cited here, (that DTO has produced), it is extraordinary what a distinctive quantity and quality of comprehensive planning has been achieved. The studies listed are means to accomplish the type of desirable long-term planning required for the individual communities within the corridor itself. What must be avoided is politically charged, chaotic zoning.

1. Arklow, a secondary centre on the coast, with the population doubling.
2. Naas, a primary, vigorous centre with a superb main street design limiting daytime traffic. Population to double.
3. Balbriggan, a primary centre on the coast, adjacent to the M1, that could become self-supporting as the population triples from 10,000 to 30,000.
4. Adamstown, a 550-acre area with phased 10,000 new homes. 10 miles from Dublin city centre via rail, bus and car. Until a new station and substantial rail link capacity increase, the project is capped at 4,000 new dwellings. There are to be complete biker, jogger, hiker and walker networks related to transit, businesses, schools and open space. It could readily be transposed to the US as a classic 'New Urbanism' general layout.
5. 'Modelling the new Transport City' prototype is the ultimate scheme, which could be applied to infill, attachment or stand-alone development centres. It is quite simply a distinguished synthesis for new town planning in the 21st C. In many respects it summarizes for the next millennium the work of the past 100 years time established within the two masterful books, Unwin's *Town Planning in Practice* and Peter Hall's *Cities of Tomorrow*.

Conclusion

Finally, so far as this corridor is concerned, we should stress the need to base the entire edifice of planning and management on the regional plan. It is typical to regard the 'new urbanism' as a very local matter, the essence of which can be tackled at the scale of the village, the small town or the quarter, and this is reassuring for parish pump politicians. It is a misunderstanding, as Peter Calthorpe explains in 'Charter of the New Urbanism':

The aspect of New Urbanism that addresses the issues of where growth is most appropriate, is its call for regional design. New Urbanism proposes to create a definitive physical map of the metropolis, its boundaries, open spaces, connections and centers. This idea of 'designing' the region, much like one could design a neighbourhood, has been passé since the time of Daniel Burnham .... But it is central to addressing the issue of where development should happen and how it fits into the whole. Without regional form-givers, such as habitat and agricultural preserves or urban growth boundaries, transit systems and designated urban centers, even well-designed neighbourhoods can contribute to urban sprawl. (p 180.)

Without a whole-hearted acceptance of regional planning and attendant governance, the Dublin-Belfast Corridor will not merely fail, it could become a catastrophe. This point is nowhere more important than with respect to mass transportation.

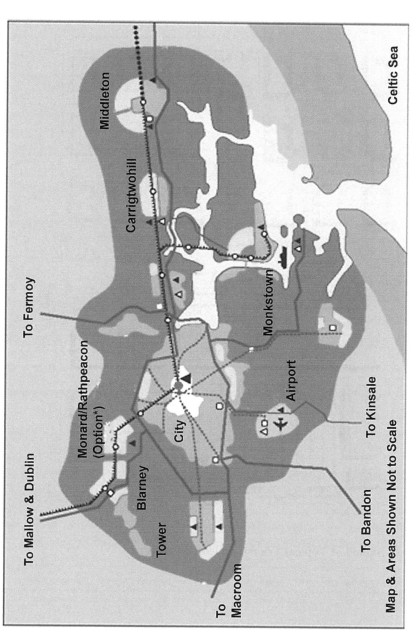

Figure 8.1 Structure Diagram: Metropolitan Cork

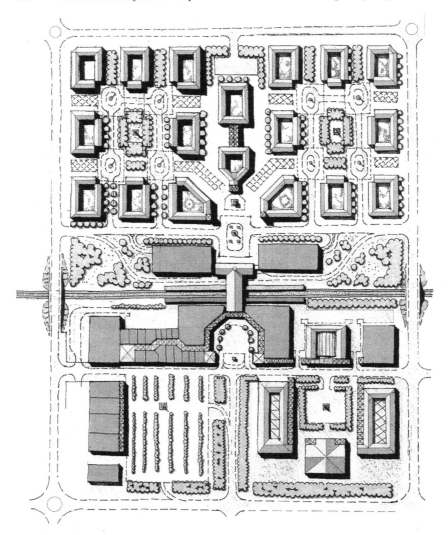

Figure 8.2   Sketch of Typical Transit-Oriented Project

References

Atkins, I. and Roger, T. and Partners (2001), *Cork Area Strategic Plan 2001–2020* (Cork County Council and Cork City Council).

Calthorpe, P. (1993), *The Next American Metropolis: Ecology, Community and the American Dream* (Princeton A.P., New York).

Congress for the New Urbanism (2000), *Charter for the New Urbanism* (McGraw-Hill, New York).

Coyle, M. (2002), *Transport Corridors: A Place for Urban Design Frameworks* "Tracings" Vol.2 pp 66–76.

Dublin Transportation Office (2001), *DTO Strategy 2000–2016: A Platform for Change.*

————, (2004), *Moving Dublin; Modelling the Transport City.(Draft Final Report).*

Jenks, M., Burton, E. and Williams, K. (2000), *The Compact City: A Sustainable Urban Form?* (Spon, London).

Krier, L. (1992), *Architecture and Urban Design 1967–1992* (St. Martin's Press, London).

Parsons Brinckerhoff Limited. (2003), *Naas Integrated Framework Plan for Land Use and Transportation* (Kildare County Council, Dublin Transportation Office et al.).

SIAS/Grontmij (2000), *Balbriggan Integrated Area Framework (Draft.)* (Fingal County Council, Dublin Transportation Office et al.).

WSP Ireland and Tiros Resources Ltd. (2003), *Arklow Town and Environs; Integrated Framework Plan for Land Use and Transportation* (Wicklow County Council, Dublin Transportation Office et al.).

Chapter 9

Service Firm Connections in the Dublin-Belfast Corridor

Chris van Egeraat
*Research Fellow, Department of Geography/National Institute for Regional and
Spatial Analysis, NUI Maynooth*

Martin Sokol
Research Fellow, Urban Institute Ireland

Introduction

The notion of an economic corridor suggests the existence of linkages of some sort between the constituent urban nodes. Research tends to analyse commuting flow data to investigate the existence of economic corridors. Other linkages, notably those involving the flow of resources, goods, services and information are believed to be important, but are seldom analysed in detail, due to the lack of readily available statistics. This chapter aims to address this gap with an investigation into the intra-firm *information* flows in the context of the Dublin-Belfast Corridor.

The chapter presents material collected as part of the POLYNET research project – an EU-funded research project that aimed to compare polycentric tendencies in eight mega-city regions in north-west Europe. Part of the study involved the collection of quantitative data on the office networks of advanced producer service firms. These were used to compute connectivity measures that can serve as a proxy for the information flows between urban centres. The analysis in this chapter adopts the conceptual framework guiding the POLYNET research project.

One of the case-study regions was the Dublin mega-city-region[1], pragmatically defined at the start of the project as the area stretching from Wicklow to Dundalk, along the Dublin-Belfast Corridor. As such most of the data presented in this paper pertain to the southern part of the conceptual corridor but additional computations were carried out to provide some insight into the links with Belfast and Newry.

---

[1] The other regions in the comparative international study were: South East England; Delta Metropolis; Central Belgium; Rhine-Ruhr; Rhine-Main; Northern Switzerland; Bassin Parisien

Below we start with a brief discussion of the theoretical background, notably that regarding the concepts of economic corridors and polycentric urban development. In section three we outline the methodology used to analyse service business connections. Section 4 provides a historical overview of the producer services sector in the southern part of the Dublin-Belfast corridor. Section 5 follows with a description of the geography of the advanced producer services sector using original data. Section 6 presents the results of the connectivity computations. The paper concludes with a discussion of what the results tell us about the conceptual Dublin-Belfast economic corridor and the idea of polycentricity in the light of the connectivity data.

Theoretical Background: Corridors and Polycentricity

Economic corridors

While a 'fundamental characteristic' of a corridor is that of *connection*, there are many different conceptions of corridors (Chapman et al., 2003, p.190). According to Priemus and Zonneveld (2003, p.172–173), three distinct but interrelated meanings of the 'corridor' concept can be distinguished: a) the corridor as an infrastructural axis, b) the corridor as an urbanisation axis and c) the corridor as an economic development axis. The corridor as an *infrastructural axis* can be defined in terms of a "bundle of infrastructure" that links two or more urban areas (Priemus and Zonneveld, 2003, p.167). The infrastructure is usually understood in terms of transport for people and goods via roads, rail, air connections, waterways etc. In this sense corridors are frequently studied as "transport corridors" (see also Bruinsma et al., 1997; Albrechts and Coppens, 2003; Rodrigue, 2004). However, a broader definition of infrastructure would include the likes of power lines and, importantly, ICT infrastructure (see Priemus and Zonneveld, 2003, p.167).

The second meaning, the corridor as an *urbanisation axis*, evokes the idea that the "bundle of infrastructure" functions as the basis for the direction of future urbanisation for residential and employment activities (Priemus and Zonneveld, 2003, p.173). Subsequently, such a corridor can be described in terms of a 'linear city region' (first proposed by Soria y Mata), ''necklace of beads' (Hall et al., 1966) or more recently as a 'sustainable development corridor' (Hall and Ward, 1998) referring to a 'string' of settlements along major transportation corridors.

The third and the least explored meaning of a corridor is that of the corridor as an *economic development axis*. Here, a relationship is supposed between major transport and infrastructural axes and opportunities for economic development (Priemus and Zonneveld, 2003, p.173; see also Bruinsma et al., 1997). This stems from an assumption that traffic and infrastructure are not only derived from economic processes, but to a high degree determine these processes as well (cf. Priemus and Zonneveld, 2003, p.173). Therefore, it is not surprising that in some European regional policy corners there is a firm belief that enhancing the level of connectivity would stimulate the economic performance of regions lagging behind (ibid., p. 169). More specifically, economic advantages of closely connected cities or city-regions are said to include greater agglomeration economies (through pooled assets, facilities, labour markets etc.), higher propensity for economic innovation and growth (through business networks, exchange of knowledge etc.), and generally increased competitiveness through synergies and complementarities between such city-regions (see Bailey and Turok, 2001; for a discussion). These advantages are closely associated with polycentric forms of economic organisation to which we now turn.

Polycentricity

The starting points of the POLYNET research project included the specification of a world city network (Taylor, 2001, 2004) and the recognition of world city regions (Scott, 2001). The former describes inter-city relations as the organizational structure of the global economy, viewing world cities as 'global service centres' connected as a single worldwide network. The latter treats world cities as more than centre-cores – they are viewed as more complex urban regions encompassing several cities so that they may be polycentric in structure. The POLYNET project combines these two research strategies by studying global mega-city regions[2] within a network of regions that is worldwide.

Building upon Sassen (1991), the world city network was specified as a network in which advanced business service firms play a crucial role in network formation. At the broader level, building upon Castells (1996), Polynet takes a strongly relational view of the city as a process characterized by the structural domination of the 'space of flows'. Castells contrasts the traditional concern for 'spaces of places' (e.g. countries) with contemporary transnational movements of people, goods, and especially, information, which he calls 'spaces of flows'. Cities through the offices of advanced producer firms are connected in a global network with different intensities – 'intensities of flows' (Hoyler and Pain, 2002, p. 4). This space of flows is today found at a range of different geographical scales up to and including the global scale. Cities within networks and as city-regions are the critical hubs and nodes of the space of flows. The POLYNET project aims to describe the flows through measures of inter-city relations. These measures estimate the intra-firm information flows between offices of firms and are derived from the office network of firms.

Polycentricity can be defined in various ways and different definitions are used at different scales of analysis. It is sometimes conceived of as a set of connected cities where one of the main advantages for businesses lies in the economies of scale associated with serving the combined market from one location while

---

[2]   A 'mega-city region' is here interpreted as a large-scale 'networked urban region' or 'multi-core metropolis' (Hall, 1999, pp. 18-19). A functional definition of such mega-city region would imply that its constituent parts display linkages in terms of commuting to work, education, shopping, entertainment and culture, and services (*ibid.*, p.7).

avoiding the diseconomies associated with monocentric urban patterns (Bailey and Turok, 2001; Hague and Kirk, 2003; Kloosterman and Lambregts, 2001; Kloosterman and Musterd, 2001). In the context of the quantitative exercise the POLYNET research group defined a polycentric region as *an intensely connected set of urban centres of approximately equal connectivity.*

From this point of view, connectivity of urban centres along a 'corridor' can be seen as a form of polycentricity. In the case of the Dublin-Belfast Corridor, this would imply 'intense connections' along the axis Dublin-Drogheda-Dundalk-Newry-Belfast, with each of the urban centres displaying approximately 'equal connectivity'. This connectivity has been measured using the methodology described below.

Methodology[3]

Network interlock analysis

The analysis of the regional urban networks follows the methodology applied by the Global and World Cities (GaWC) research group (Taylor, 2001; Taylor 2004). This group used interlocking network analysis. This treats advanced producer service firms with a presence in more than one city as agents that, through their daily activity, interlock cities to form a network. Interlocking network analysis estimates city connectivities and inter-city linkages from the office networks of these multi-location firms. These office networks indicate flows of information generated between the various offices of individual firms. The methodology estimates these flows and these estimates are aggregated to calculate the links and connectivities that are the output of the quantitative exercise. The POLYNET project involved a unique exercise whereby the GaWC methodology designed for measuring global city networks was, for the first time, implemented at a city-regional scale. Much of the analysis presented below could be seen as experimental.

Interlocking network analysis involves the construction of a service value matrix, V, defined by n cities and m service firms. Each cell in the matrix is a service value, v_{ij}, that indicates the importance of city i to firm j. For the purposes of the POLYNET study this *importance* was defined by the size of an office and its functions and is presented as simple integers ranging from 0 to 3. The assumption is that the more important the office the more connections there are with other offices in a firms network and the greater the flow of information generated through the city. The matrix is interpreted as follows: vertically each column indicates the service values of a firm across a set of urban centres, i.e. the firm's locational strategy for servicing its customers; and horizontally each row indicates the services available within a city for a set of firms, i.e. the city's service mix across firms.

---

[3]   For a more extensive discussion of methodological issues see van Egeraat and Sokol (2005).

The basic relational element for each pair of cities derived from the matrix is:[4]

$$r_{ab,j} = v_{aj} \cdot v_{bj} \qquad (1)$$

This is the elemental interlock link which defines the relation between two cities a and b in terms of one firm j. These elemental interlock links are aggregated to derive a city interlock link:

$$r_{ab} = \sum_{j} r_{ab,j} \qquad (2)$$

Aggregating these interlocks for a single city, a, produces *interlock or nodal connectivity*, N_a:

$$N_a = \sum_{i} r_{ai} \quad \text{where } a \neq i \qquad (3)$$

This is a measure of the overall importance of a city within the network. In our research, for comparative purposes, this will be expressed as a proportion of the city with the highest interlock connectivity, N_h. For city a, this is given as:

$$C_a = N_a / N_h \qquad (4)$$

The biggest task in the methodology is the creation of the service value matrix. For this we first needed to select a set of cities. Secondly we needed to identify a set of producer service firms. Finally, we needed to derive service values that show the importance of each office to the service office network of each firm.

Selection of urban centres for coding

The GaWC group used interlocking network analysis for studying inter-city relations at the global scale. The POLYNET international research group had to adapt the methodology to the mega-city-regional scale. Rather than focussing only on global connectivity, the POLYNET project aimed to investigate connectivity at the global, European, national and city-regional scale. We needed to define servicing strategies at these four scales. For this we needed to create four matrices and select four sets of urban centres that were important for understanding connectivities at the different scales.

In the case of the Dublin mega-city region, the selection of urban centres for defining the *city-regional* servicing strategy was largely determined by the limited number of sizeable urban centres. The region was pragmatically defined at the start of the research project as the area stretching from Wicklow to Dundalk, along the Dublin-Belfast Corridor. The principal selection criterion was the number of jobs

---

[4] The equations are taken from Taylor (2001).

per urban centre (a proxy for the size of services sector activity). After Dublin, the region has no more than eight urban centres with more than 4,000 jobs (Bray, Drogheda, Dundalk, Naas, Navan, Newbridge, Maynooth/Leixlip/Celbridge and Wicklow). Four of these urban centres outside Dublin (Drogheda, Dundalk and Naas and Newbridge) are larger (in terms of jobs) than the other urban centres. However, from a polycentric mega-city region perspective all urban centres outside Dublin are very small. There was therefore little reason to select one urban centre over another. Hence all were selected.

Table 9.1   Cities used to Define Servicing Strategy

City-regional	National	European	Global
Dublin	Dublin	London	London
Balbriggan	Limerick Shannon	Paris	New York
Bray	Cork	Milan	Hong Kong
Drogheda	Galway	Madrid	Paris
Dundalk	Waterford	Amsterdam	Tokyo
Naas/Newbridge	Athlone	Frankfurt	Singapore
Navan	Drogheda	Brussels	Chicago
Mayn./Celbr./Leixlip	Dundalk	Zurich	Milan
Wicklow	Sligo	Stockholm	Los Angeles
	Wexford	Prague	Toronto
	Belfast	Dublin	Madrid
	Newry	Barcelona	Amsterdam
	Derry	Mocow	Sydney
		Istanbul	Frankfurt
		Vienna	Brussels
		Warsaw	Sao Paulo
		Lisbon	San Francisco
		Copenhagen	Mexico City
		Budapest	Zurich
		Hamburg	Taipei
		Munich	Mumbai
		Duesseldorf	Jakarta
		Berlin	Buenos Aires
		Rome	Melbourne
		Athens	Miami

We chose to regard Naas and Newbridge as a single centre because of established official development policy as well as their obvious propinquity. Finally we decided to include Balbriggan for heuristic reasons. In terms of numbers of jobs this town is far smaller than the other urban centres. It is, however, regarded with great interest as a key growth centre in the Regional Planning Guidelines (RPG Project Office, 2004). Furthermore, it is the largest settlement closest to Dublin on the conceptual Dublin-Belfast Corridor. The complete list of regional urban centres is presented in Table 9.1.

For defining the *national* connectivities of the regional cities 10 national urban centres were selected largely, but not exclusively, on the basis of population size (see Table 9.1). An additional perspective on the north-south linkage was included by adding the two largest cities in Northern Ireland - Belfast and Derry - as well as the main Northern Irish town on the Dundalk-Belfast corridor – Newry. The selection of cities for analysis on the *European* and *global* scales was based upon previous GaWC analyses of global connectivities (Taylor 2004). For the POLYNET study, the top 25 European cities were used to define European servicing strategies and connectivities for the urban centres in our region and the top 25 world cities were chosen to define global connectivities.

Selection of firms for coding

The next task was to select a set of firms. The POLYNET international research group focused on a particular set of service firms in the mega-city region - 'advanced producer service firms' (Sassen, 1991). Following the GaWC research group, one of the basic premises of the study is that these firms are one of the main agents in the production and configuration of city networks at various spatial scales (Taylor, 2004). For POLYNET advanced producer service firms were defined as comprising the following sectors: accountancy, advertising, banking/finance, insurance, law and management consultancy, design consultancies (architecture, civil engineering, planning), and advanced logistics services.

We started by creating a comprehensive inventory of service firms in these sectors for each of the selected urban centres. This inventory was compiled mainly on the basis of directories of sectoral representative/regulatory bodies. The fact that many firms have operations in more than one urban centre makes it difficult to talk in terms of numbers of *firms* and percentages of *firms*. If we treat all offices of a firm in Dublin as one single office, then we counted nearly 3000 offices of advanced producer service firms.

Subsequently, we identified the local or single-city firms in this comprehensive universe so the research could proceed with non-local or multi-location firms only. *Local* is defined as the urban centre's immediate hinterland area but clearly not constituting a regional strategy. The local firms were identified using information from sectoral directories and interviews with representatives of sectoral associations.

This action resulted in a final inventory of 728 'non-local' firms (see Table 9.2). The small amount of multi-location advanced producer service firms in the centres outside Dublin meant that some centres were left with very few firms, particularly in the case of Maynooth/Celbridge/Leixlip (4), Balbriggan (5) and Wicklow (5). Most of the firms left in the urban centres outside Dublin were branches of banking or insurance firms.

Table 9.2   Multi-location Firms in the Dublin Mega-City Region

	Account.	Advertising	Bank/Fin**	Design	Insurance	Law	Logistics	Man. Con.	Total
Dublin	22	23	303	73	89	53	50	32	645
Balbriggan			4			1			5
Bray	1		5		1	1			8
Drogheda	1		5	1	5	1			13
Dundalk	2		7	2	2	6	2		21
Navan			5	1	2				8
Maynooth			3			1			4
Naas	1		8	1	3	4	2		19
Wicklow			4		1				5
Total									728

*   Different companies of one group are counted as one firm.
**   Funds are not counted as firms. Fund managers and trustees are counted as firms.
       List of banking/finance firms can include a very small number of local firms.

From this list of multi-location firms we needed to select firms for detailed coding. The original aim was to select a minimum of 20 firms per urban centre and, given the complexity of development of the services sectors in Dublin, 160 firms in Dublin (20 firms in each of the eight sectors). However, nearly all the case study urban centres had less than 20 non-local firms while Dublin had far more than 160 firms. For this reason a *sample* was taken from the non-local firms with offices in Dublin. Subsequently, we completed the matrix by adding all non-local firms with a presence in the case study urban centres outside Dublin that had not yet been included in the matrix on the basis of a firm's presence in Dublin. For Dublin, the aim was to select, for each sector, a cross section of firms covering the various market scopes (global, European, national and city-regional), although with a deliberate bias towards the more highly networked firms.

The resulting data matrix contains 183 firms operating through 253 offices. Virtually all firms (170) in the matrix have an office in the capital. The numbers of firms in the other urban centres range from 4 in Maynooth to 20 in Dundalk. All sectors are fairly evenly represented. The average number of firms per sector is 23. The matrix contains a higher than average number of law firms while the number of advertising firms is slightly below average (see Table 9.3). The breakdown of the non-local firms by sector and urban centre will be discussed in more detail in the section on the geography of advanced producer services later in this chapter.

Table 9.3   Firms in the Matrix Broken Down by Sector

Accountancy	Advertising	Bank/Finn.	Design	Insurance	Law	Logistics	Man. Con.	Total
23	18	21	22	23	34	22	20	183

Coding (service values).

To define service values only two types of information were gathered: firstly, indications of size of a presence in a city (e.g. number of practitioners or partners working in an office), and secondly any indications that an office carries out extra-local functions for the firm (e.g. headquarters, research). This information was converted into a common data metric. The coding of information to create service values used four integers:

0: indicates that the firm has no presence in the urban centre at all.
1: indicates a sub-office of some sort, perhaps a law office without a partner or a minor representative office of a bank.
2: specifies a typical, standard office for a given firm. All cities in which a firm is present are initially scored 2.
3: indicates a superior office of some sort: it will usually have some extra-location functions or level of management which means it services other city offices (e.g. national, regional, or headquarters).

The final product was four matrices with cells containing numbers ranging from 0 to 3 indicating service values of offices of firms in cities functioning at four different scales of service provision. These matrices formed the input to all analysis.

Historical Development of Business Services in the Dublin Mega-City Region

Ireland has been a relative latecomer in terms of economic development (O'Malley, 1989) and the rapid expansion, diversification and specialisation of services industries experienced by many developed economies in the post-war period (Daniels, 1985) happened much later in Ireland. It was not until the economic up-turn in the 1960s that Ireland experienced a steady growth in services sector employment. Still, by 1971 the share of services sector employment (excluding building and construction) in total employment was low by international standards – 43.5 per cent (Bannon, 1979).

Much of the growth in the services sector was concentrated in (what was then) the East region, which approximately corresponds to the Dublin mega-city region.[5] In 1971 this region accounted for 47.2 per cent of all service jobs in the state. However, 88 per cent of these jobs in the East region were concentrated in Dublin (Drudy and Walker, 1996). Dublin's position was even more dominant if we consider the location of office jobs. Almost 60 per cent of all office jobs in 1971 were located in the East Region and 82 per cent of these jobs were located in the Dublin Metropolitan Area. Furthermore, the city centre increasingly housed most of the higher level office and control/headquarter functions in the state while the offices in the urban centres outside Dublin mainly provided services on a population basis, for example branches of local banks (Bannon, 1979).

After the economic downturn of 1973 and throughout the 1980s the services sector in Ireland grew steadily. Its share of total employment increased to 51 per cent in 1981 and 59 per cent in 1991 (Drudy and Walker, 1996). Between 1971 and 1991 services sector employment in the East Region grew by 51 per cent. Services sector employment in Dublin grew by 41 per cent, notably in insurance, finance and business services and professional services. Until the end of the 1980s office jobs in Dublin were still very much concentrated in the city centre although some office development had taken place in the southern suburbs (MacLaran and O'Connell, 2001).

In the following decade Ireland experienced unprecedented economic growth and made the leap to a fully-fledged service economy. Between 1991 and 2002 employment in the national services sector increase by 67.2 per cent and the sector now accounts for 69 per cent of total employment (Bannon, 2004). The services sector now accounts for 78 per cent of employment in the East Region. There is a considerable difference between the constituent regions with a figure of 67 per cent for the Mid-East region and 82 per cent for Dublin.

Again, much of the increase in producer services concentrated in Dublin. Important growth sectors in Dublin included insurance, finance and business services and professional services (Drudy and Walker, 1996). This was partly

---

[5]   The East Region is an old region consisting of the present Mid-East and Dublin NUTS II regions. It broadly corresponds with the Dublin mega-city region although it does not include Dundalk.

influenced by tax related incentives for the development and occupation of properties in designated urban renewal areas in central Dublin available since 1986 (Williams and MacLaran, 1996). Apart from this city-centre development, the second half of the 1990s witnessed a large-scale sub-urbanisation of office development, particularly to the south and west of the city (McLaran and O'Connell, 2001; Bertz, 2002). At the same time, the case study urban centres outside Dublin remained largely untouched by large-scale producer service activity. Interviews with local government representatives in urban centres outside Dublin provide very little evidence of substantial producer service investment projects in the pipeline. Similarly, the extensive office developments planned for Dublin give little reason to believe that Dublin's dominant position will diminish in the near future (McLaran, 2004).

Geography of Advanced Producer Services in the Dublin Mega-City Region

Based on the inventory of multi-location firms constructed for the study, Table 9.2 presents the geographical and sectoral breakdown of the multi-location advanced producer service firms in the selected urban centres of the Dublin Mega-City Region. The situation is graphically presented in Figure 9.1. As discussed, the fact that many firms have operations in more than one urban centre makes it difficult to provide an analysis in terms of numbers of *firms* and percentages of *firms*. If we treat all offices of a firm in Dublin as one single office, then the region contains 700 non-local *offices*. About ninety per cent of these are located in Dublin. Some of the urban centres outside Dublin, notably Maynooth/Celbridge/Leixlip, Balbriggan and Wicklow, have only a handful of non-local producer service firms. In reality the dominance of Dublin is far greater than these figures suggest. Many firms, notably in banking/finance and insurance, have multiple offices in Dublin and the employment and functionality of the Dublin offices far outstrips that of the offices in urban centres outside Dublin.

The advanced producer services sector is very underdeveloped in the urban centres outside Dublin. Apart from branches of bank and insurance companies, the number of sizeable firms can be counted on one hand – notably Generali in Navan (a branch of an international insurance company involved in internationally traded services) and Allied Irish Bank that operates a 24-hour customer support centre in Naas. None of the urban centres outside Dublin have advertising or management consultancy firms. Virtually all multi-location accountancy and law firms in the urban centres outside Dublin are very small two-office firms, employing very few accountants/solicitors and serving a very small geographic mark.

Any comparison of the sectoral distribution of multi-location firms in each of the individual urban centres (see Table 9.2 and Figure 9.1) has to be interpreted with care because of the small number of firms in some of the urban centres. One of the clearest observations is that banking and finance is the strongest sector in all the urban centres outside Dublin. In nearly all cases this involves branches of national/international banks. The advertising and management consultancy sectors are not represented outside Dublin. Drogheda has a relatively strong representation of non-local firms in the insurance sector with five branches of national/international insurance companies. Dundalk and Naas/Newbridge have the broadest mix of services. In Dundalk the law (6 multi-location firms) and combined design/logistics (4 multi-location firms) sectors are relatively strongly represented. Finally, Naas/Newbridge has a relatively high number of law firms (4 multi-location firms).

In Dublin, banking and finance is by far the largest sector with 47 per cent of the non-local firms. Other well-represented sectors include insurance (14 per cent), design (11 per cent) and logistics (8 per cent). Advertising and management consultancy account for a relatively small proportion of non-local firms in Dublin.

Regional Servicing Strategies of Firms, Linkages and Connectivities

A first inspection of the matrix suggested that firms in the individual sectors have different regional servicing strategies although all sectors are characterized by the concentration of regional (and national) control/organisation functions in Dublin. All advertising and management consultancy firms and virtually all design consultancy firms service the region from a single office in Dublin. This Dublin office often services the entire national market, particularly in the advertising and management consultancy sectors. Similarly, all but four logistics firms service the region from one office in Dublin.

All the larger accountancy and law firms in the matrix service the region from one office in Dublin. In the law sector this Dublin office often services the entire country. A handful of small indigenous accountancy firms and a substantial number of small law firms operate two offices in the region but this generally reflects family related or other incidental issues, rather than a deliberate and considered regional servicing strategy.

Banking firms can operate extensive regional office networks. Eight of the banking firms in the matrix operate a total of 48 offices in the selected urban centres (counting all Dublin offices as one office). In all these cases the offices in the urban centres outside Dublin operate as branches of the head-offices in Dublin. Other banks service the mega-city region (as well as national and even international markets) from one office in Dublin. In the insurance sector one can discern two main regional servicing strategies. One group of firms services the region from two offices, with the Dublin offices functioning as the main office. Another group of firms services the region (or the national/international markets) from a single Dublin office.

We will now consider what these servicing strategies mean for potential intra-firm information flow. The service data matrix is used to calculate the interlock connectivity of the selected urban centres at four spatial scales using equation (3) as described in the methodology section.[6] For comparative purposes, the urban centre with the highest connectivity is scored unity and other regional urban centres are recoded as proportions of this highest score using equation (4). The output of this exercise is presented in Table 9.4. The results inform us about how well connected an urban centre is to other centres in terms of intra-firm information and knowledge flows. By using four matrices containing cities at four different scales, the results inform us about the importance of an urban centre within a network at those different scales.

Table 9.4   Connectivity Scores at Regional, National, European and Global Scale

Regional				National		
Dublin	290	1.00		Dublin	1103	1.00
Naas/Newbridge	178	0.61		Naas/Newbridge	316	0.29
Dundalk	155	0.53		Dundalk	302	0.27
Drogheda	125	0.43		Drogheda	221	0.20
Navan	91	0.31		Bray	174	0.16
Bray	90	0.31		Navan	159	0.14
Wicklow	77	0.27		Wicklow	140	0.13
Mayn./Celb./Leix.	62	0.21		Mayn./Celb./Leix.	97	0.09
Balbriggan	52	0.18		Balbriggan	84	0.08

European				Global		
Dublin	7232	1.00		Dublin	7881	1.00
Naas/Newbridge	291	0.04		Naas/Newbridge	217	0.03
Dundalk	255	0.04		Dundalk	205	0.03
Drogheda	216	0.03		Drogheda	178	0.02
Navan	187	0.03		Navan	142	0.02
Bray	101	0.01		Bray	92	0.01
Wicklow	57	0.01		Wicklow	42	0.01
Mayn./Celb./Leix.	51	0.01		Mayn./Celb./Leix.	41	0.01
Balbriggan	36	0.00		Balbriggan	40	0.01

When considering the results it is important to remember that, due to the extremely low numbers of firms in the urban centres outside Dublin, a difference of one or two firms can have a strong effect on the proportional scores of individual urban centres. We now first discuss connectivity of the urban centres at the *city-regional* level. Dublin is clearly the most strongly connected urban centre at this scale of

---

[6]   We acknowledge the input of the GaWC research group in the actual computation of the connectivity measures.

service provision. Naas/Newbridge, Dundalk and Drogheda have the highest level of connectivity after Dublin, with levels ranging between 61 and 43 per cent of the Dublin level. The other urban centres have very low regional connectivity levels with the score of Balbriggan dropping below a fifth of the Dublin score.

Table 9.5 'Primacy' Rankings: Ratios between First and Second Urban Centre

City-region connectivities			Global connectivities		
Rank	Cities	Ratio	Rank	Cities	Ratio
8	Dusseldorf/Cologne	0.99	8	Amsterdam/Rotterdam	0.68
7	Brussels/Antwerp	0.94	7	Dusseldorf/Cologne	0.58
6	Amsterdam/Rotterdam	0.91	6	Zurich/Basel	0.41
5	Zurich/Basel	0.80	5	Brussels/Antwerp	0.38
2=	Paris/Rouen	0.61	4	Paris/Rouen	0.37
2=	**Dublin/Naas Newbridge**	**0.61**	3	London/Reading	0.23
2=	Frankfurt/Weisbaden	0.61	2	Frankfurt/Wesibaden	0.12
1	London/Reading	0.52	1	**Dublin/Naas Newbridge**	**0.03**

Source: *Polynet Action 1.1, Summary Report (forthcoming).*

Although these figures might not directly inform us about polycentricity in the Dublin mega-city region, they can be used to measure the opposite of polycentricity, primacy. The ratio between connectivity scores of the second and first ranked urban centres represents what might be called connection primacy – the lower the ratio, the greater the primacy. From Table 9.5 we learn that at the regional scale of service provision the Dublin region has a primacy of 0.61. On its own this figure is hard to interpret. For this reason Table 9.5 compares the figure with primacy figures for the seven other mega-city regions in north-west Europe. Clearly, compared to the other regions, the connectivity gap between Dublin and the second best connected centre (Naas) is very large. Only London has a lower ratio (greater primacy) on a regional scale.

The overall regional connectivity of an urban centre can be disaggregated into its links with each other regional centre. Using equation (2) we first calculate the city interlock links between pairs of urban centres (Table 9.6). For comparative purposes the pair of urban centres in the Dublin mega-city-region with the largest city interlock link - the prime link - is scored unity and the values of all other links are computed as proportions of the prime link (Table 9.7). The regional interconnectivity is graphically presented in Figure 6, using all links above 0.2 (20 per cent of the strongest link). The prime link in the region is between Dublin and Naas/Newbridge. Two other pairs of cities have a city-interlock link of between 0.6 and 0.8 (proportion of the prime link) – Dublin-Dundalk and Dublin-Drogheda. All other pairs of cities have city interlock links of 0.3 or below. The only inter-city links not involving Dublin, and reaching the 0.20 level, are between Naas-Dundalk and Naas-Drogheda. Balbriggan has no linkages with other urban centres that reach the 0.2 cut-off. Dublin is clearly the urban centre with the strongest regional links. The graph indicates primacy at the regional level. All major intra-regional links are with Dublin and the links between pairs of cities not involving Dublin tend to be very weak.

Table 9.6   City Interlock Links between Pairs of Cities – Absolute

	Dublin	Balbrig.	Bray	Drogheda	Dundalk	Navan	Maynooth	Naas	Wicklow
Dublin	0	12	23	49	59	23	18	77	21
Balbrig.	12	0	5	4	12	4	4	7	4
Bray	23	5	0	11	13	11	6	15	6
Drogheda	49	4	11	0	13	12	6	19	11
Dundalk	59	12	13	13	0	13	7	22	8
Navan	23	4	11	12	13	0	6	15	7
Mayn./C./L.	18	4	6	6	7	6	0	9	6
Naas/Newbr.	77	7	15	19	22	15	9	0	14
Wicklow	21	4	6	11	8	7	6	14	0

Source: *Calculations based on data obtained from company web sites.*

Up to this point the discussion focussed on connectivity at the city-regional scale of service provision. We will now put our attention to the other three scales. Referring back to Table 9.4 we can see that the primacy of Dublin increases at the *national scale*. The connectivity gap between Dublin and the second most connected urban centre at this scale already exceeds 70 percentage points. Only Naas and Dundalk have a national connectivity score exceeding 20 per cent of the Dublin score. The ranking of individual urban centres does not change. If the connectivity of the urban centres outside Dublin is low at the regional and national scale, it is trivial at the European and global scale. None of the urban centres outside Dublin has a connectivity level higher than four per cent of the Dublin level at either the European or global scale. At a global scale of service provision, the Dublin region has by far the largest global connectivity gap and greatest primacy (highest ranking in Table 9.5) of all mega-city regions in the study.

Table 9.7   City Interlock Links between Pairs of Cities – as a Proportion of the Prime Link (Dublin-Naas/Newbridge = 77)

	Dublin	Balbrig.	Bray	Drogheda	Dundalk	Navan	Maynooth	Naas	Wicklow
Dublin	0.00	0.16	0.30	0.64	0.77	0.30	0.23	1.00	0.27
Balbrig.	0.16	0.00	0.06	0.05	0.16	0.05	0.05	0.09	0.05
Bray	0.30	0.06	0.00	0.14	0.17	0.14	0.08	0.19	0.08
Drogheda	0.64	0.05	0.14	0.00	0.17	0.16	0.08	0.25	0.14
Dundalk	0.77	0.16	0.17	0.17	0.00	0.17	0.09	0.29	0.10
Navan	0.30	0.05	0.14	0.16	0.17	0.00	0.08	0.19	0.09
Mayn./C./L.	0.23	0.05	0.08	0.08	0.09	0.08	0.00	0.12	0.08
Naas/Newbr.	1.00	0.09	0.19	0.25	0.29	0.19	0.12	0.00	0.18
Wicklow	0.27	0.05	0.08	0.14	0.10	0.09	0.08	0.18	0.00

Source: *Calculations based on data obtained from company web sites.*

A comparison of the rankings across the four geographical scales is of little interest given the small differences in the rankings of individual urban centres outside Dublin and the small number of firms in these urban centres. What the comparison does show is that the connectivity ratios decrease with scale. This means that Dublin dominates even more at the global scale than it does at the regional scale. Urban centres outside Dublin are able to share to some degree in regional service provision in a way they are unable to do globally.

We will now shift our attention to include the northern section of the *Dublin-Belfast corridor*. The service value matrix was constructed around the set of the nine selected urban centres in the Republic of Ireland. However, the matrix does contain data on two other urban centres on the corridor – Belfast and Newry. These centres were included to define national connectivities of the nine case-study centres (see section 2). The matrix only contains service values for firms that are included on the basis of their presence in one of the nine selected centres. It does not include a complete sample of advanced producer service firms in Belfast and Newry. The matrix can therefore not be used to compute the overall regional connectivity of these urban centres. However, the data can provide some insight into the city interlock links between pairs of urban centres on both sides of the border.

Using equation (2) we computed the city-interlock link between pairs of urban centres on both sides of the border. Table 9.8 should be read in conjunction with Table 9.6. The two tables are not combined because the interlock links for the two urban centres north of the border were computed on the basis of incomplete samples. The table shows that Dublin-Belfast is by far the strongest link along the Dublin-Belfast corridor. The interlock link of 199 is much stronger than the second largest interlock link of 77 between Dublin and Naas. Furthermore, the figure underestimates the interlock link because of the incomplete nature of the Belfast sample. We can be more concrete about the links between Belfast and the other case-study urban centres since the matrix includes all multi-location advanced producer service firms in these other centres and thus captures all information flow between these urban centres and Belfast. These links tend to be very modest and often weaker than the links between pairs of urban centres south of the border.

Table 9.8   City Interlock Links* Involving Belfast and Newry – Absolute

	Dublin	Balbrig.	Bray	Drogheda	Dundalk	Navan	Maynooth	Naas	Wicklow
Belfast	199	8	11	12	19	8	8	21	8
Newry	24	4	6	5	28	5	5	12	5

*City interlock links are computed on the basis of an incomplete sample of firms for Belfast and Newry (see text)

Source: *Calculations based on data obtained from company web sites.*

The interlock links between Newry and urban centres south of the border are generally among the weakest of all links in the study. The only exception is Newry's link with nearby Dundalk. Although still relatively weak, the Dundalk-Newry link is the second strongest link involving Dundalk, after the Dundalk-Dublin link. The figure for the Newry-Dublin link is difficult to interpret because of the incomplete nature of the sample for Newry. The available data suggest that the regional interconnectivity picture for the entire corridor is strongly dominated by a single link. The dominance of this prime link between Belfast and Dublin is even greater than the dominance of the prime link (between Dublin and Naas/Newbridge) identified in the earlier analysis of the southern part of the corridor. Fewer links would reach the 0.2 cut-off level for inclusion in Figure 9.6.

Conclusions

The notion of a Dublin-Belfast economic corridor suggests the existence of linkages of some sort between the constituent urban nodes. This paper considers intra-firm information-flow between urban centres. The analysis adopts most the conceptual framework guiding the POLYNET research project – a study into polycentric urban regions. A polycentric region can be conceived of as *an intensely connected set of cities of approximately equal connectivity*. The office network of advanced producer service firms was used to compute linkage and connectivity measures that can serve as a proxy for the knowledge flows between urban centres.

What do the results of the analysis tell us about the presence of information flows and polycentricity in the southern part of the Dublin-Belfast Corridor? It was shown that apart from Dublin, none of the urban centres in the region has a substantial multi-location advanced producer services sector. This suggests that the *intensity* of the flows between the urban centres is very small. What about the *pattern* of the information flows? The analyses of network connectivity at the various levels and urban interconnectivity at the regional-level all point to the opposite of polycentricity – a high level of connection primacy. The region has one of the highest primacy rankings at the regional scale and by far the highest primacy ranking at the global scale of all regions studied in the POLYNET project. The regional interconnectivity data suggest that the strongest regional information links are with Dublin, with relatively weak direct flows between the urban centres outside Dublin. The incomplete cross-border data suggest a stronger city interlock link between Belfast and Dublin. On the other hand, both Belfast and Newry have very weak interlock links with other centres south of the border.

When considering these results one has to take account of one of the main limitations of the study. The study aimed to capture the functional connections between urban centres based on the intra-firm flows of information. The connectivity data measure estimates of the potential knowledge flows between cities. However, the data still only *suggest* the existence of knowledge flows. The presence of a head-office in Dublin and a branch office in Navan might well involve knowledge flow and functional connectivity between the two centres. But does the presence of bank or insurance branches in Navan and Drogheda necessarily involve knowledge flow between these two centres. Or do the flows (if any) between these regional centres pass through the head-offices in Dublin? These questions require further study. Later work carried out in the context of the POLYNET research project suggests that Dublin functions as a regional and national hub-city with very little information flowing directly between the branch-offices of firms located in the smaller urban centres. If anything, the data presented in this chapter overestimate polycentricity in the region.

A similar observation can be made on the measurement of the connectivity along the Dublin-Belfast Corridor. Again, the connectivity measures only *suggest* the existence of knowledge flows. Advance producer service firms may have offices in both Dublin and Belfast. But to what extent does the information flow between operations in the two cities or is it routed via a superior office, possibly in London? This cannot be detected from the data set. Therefore, the advancement of any firmer conclusions on the information flows between the two cities (and other urban centres along the corridor) and on potential economic benefits this may have (if any) would require further study.

While some would argue that Dublin-Belfast economic corridor "was already here" (see University of Ulster, 2002, p.26), clearly there remains much to be explored and debated. The corridor can be seen as both a "desirable and necessary concept" (*ibid.*, p.26) potentially contributing to both competitiveness and more balanced development (see also Brady and Williams, 2002). However, as Priemus and Zonneveld (2003, p.176) argued, corridors comprise the arena "within which an attempt must be made to arrive at an integration of a multitude of social interests". As such corridors represent a "major challenge for spatial governance" (de Vries and Priemus, 2003) where integration of policies on infrastructure, urbanisation and economic development should be sought (Priemus and Zonneveld, 2003). Within the particular cross-border context of the Dublin-Belfast Corridor, the need for such an integrated approach is even more compelling.

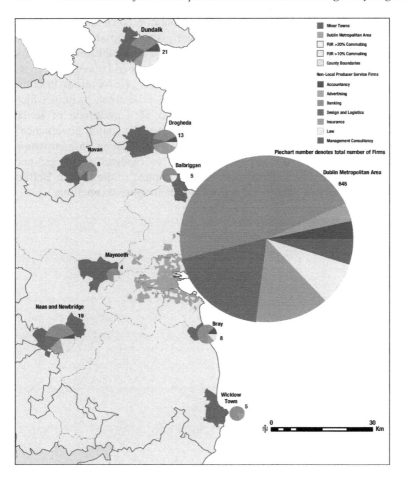

Figure 9.1   Distribution of Non-Local Producer Service Firms

References

Albrechts, L. and Coppens, T. (2003), Megacorridors: striking a balance between the space of flows and the space of places, *Journal of Transport Geography*, Vol. 11, No. 3, pp. 215–224.

Bailey, N. and Turok, I. (2001), Central Scotland as a Polycentric Urban Region: Useful Planning Concept or Chimera, *Urban Studies*, Vol. 38, Issue 4, pp. 697–715.

Bannon, M. (1973), *Office Location in Ireland: the Role of Central Dublin* (Dublin: An Foras Forbartha).

————, (1979), Office Concentration in Dublin and its Consequences for Regional Development. In, Daniels P. (ed.), *Spatial Patterns of Office Growth and Location* (Chichester: John Willey).

————, (2004), Service Activity Concentration in Dublin and its Implications for National Urban Policy and the Regional Development of the Country. Paper presented at the *Urban Institute Ireland Seminar Series* 3 June 3004 (Dublin: University College Dublin).

Bertz, S. (2002), The Growth in Office Take-up in Dublin's Suburbs: a Product of occupiers' Changing Locational Criteria? *Journal of Irish Urban Studies*, Vol. 1, Issue 2, pp. 55–77.

Brady, N.J. and Williams, B. (2002), *Metropolitan Corridors – Planning for the Future*. Faculty of the Built Environment, Dublin Institute of Technology (DIT) Spring 2002.

Bruinsma, F.R., Rienstra, S.A. and Rietveld, P. (1997), Economic Impacts of the Constrution of a Transport Corridor: A Multi-level and Multi-approach Case Study for the Construction of the A1 Highway in the Netherlands, *Regional Studies* Vol. 31, No. 4, pp.391–402.

Chapman, D., Pratt, D., Larkham, P. and Dickins, I. (2003), Concepts and definitions of corridors: evidence from England's Midlands *Journal of Transport Geography* Vol. 11, No. 3, pp. 179–191.

Daniels, P. (1985), *Service Industries: A Geographical Appraisal* (London and New York: Methuen).

Davoudi, S. (2002), Polycentricity – Modelling or Determining Reality, *Town and Country Planning*, April 2002, pp. 114–117.

Drudy, P. and Walker, L. (1996), Dublin in a Regional Context. In: Drudy, P and Maclaran, A. (eds.), *Dublin Economic and Social Trends* Vol. 2, pp. 7–20.

Egeraat, C. van and Sokol, M. (2005), Polycentricity in the Dublin Mega-City-Region: a Quantitative Analysis of Service Firm Connections. UII working paper series No. 1 (Dublin: Urban Institute Ireland).

Hall, P. et al. (Economic Associates Ltd.) (1966), *A New Town for Mid-Wales* (Her Majesty's Stationary Office, London).

Hall, P. and Ward, C. (1998), *Sociable Cities* (Wiley, Chicester).

Hall, P. (1999), Planning for the Mega-City: A New Eastern Asian Urban Form? In: Brotchie, J.F., Batty, M., Blakely, E., Hall, P. and Newton, P. (eds.) *Cities in Competition* pp.3–36 (Melbourne: Longman Australia).

Hague, C. and Kirk, K. (2003), *Polycentricity Scoping Study* (London: Office of the Deputy Prime Minister).

Hoyler, M. and Pain, K (2002), *London and Frankfurt as World Cities: Changing Local-Global Relations* (GaWC Research Bulletin 62).

Institute of Public Administration (IPA) (2003), *Administration Yearbook and Diary* (Dublin: IPA).

Kloosterman, R and Musterd, S. (2001), *The Polycentric Urban Region: Towards a Research Agenda, Urban Studies* Vol. 38, Issue 4, pp. 623–633.

Kloosterman, R. and Lambregts, B. (2001), Clustering of Economic Activities in Polycentric Urban Regions: The Case of the Randstad, *Urban Studies* Vol. 38, Issue 4, pp. 717–732.

MacLaran, A. and O'Connell, R. (2001), The Changing Geography of Office Development in Dublin. In: Drudy, P and Maclaran, A. (eds.*), Dublin Economic and Social Trends* Vol. 3, pp. 25–37.

MacLaran, A. (2004), Negotiating Urban Space: from Frying Pan of Congestion to Fire of Suburbanisation. Whither Planning? *Paper presented at the Urban Institute Ireland Seminar Series* 29 March 2004 (University College Dublin, Dublin).

O'Malley, E. (1989), *Industry and Economic Development: The Challenge for the Latecomer* (Dublin: Gill and Macmillen).

Priemus, H. and Zonneveld, W. (2003), What are corridors and what are the issues? Introduction to special issue: the governance of corridors. *Journal of Transport Geography* Vol. 11, No. 3, pp. 167–177.

RPG Project Office – Greater Dublin Area (2004); Regional Planning Guidelines Greater Dublin Area 2004–2016. Dublin: Dublin Regional Authority and Mid East Regional Authority. Rodrigue, J.P. (2004), Freight, gateways and mega-urban regions: the logistical integration of the Bostwash corridor, *Tijdschrift voor Economishe en Sociale Geografie* Vol. 95, No. 2, pp. 147–161.

Taylor, P. (2001), *Specification of the World City Network*, Geographical Analysis 33 pp. 181–94.

———, (2004), *World City Network: a Global Urban Analysis* (Routledge).

University of Ulster (2002), *Partnership, Prosperity and Place: A Report on the 2nd Annual Planning Conference run by the University of Ulster in association with other Irish Universities and the Harvard Graduate School of Design.* The School of the Built Environment, University of Ulster, September 2002.

Vries, J. de and Priemus, H. (2003), Megacorridors in north-west Europe: issues for transnational spatial governance. *Journal of Transport Geography* Vol. 11, No. 3, pp. 225–233.

Williams, B. and MacLaran, A. (1996), Incentive Areas for Urban Renewal. In: Drudy, P. and Maclaran, A. (eds), *Dublin Economic and Social Trends* Vol. 2, pp. 43–46.

Chapter 10

Housing Growth, Land Delivery and Sustainable Urban Management

Mark Scott, Niamh Moore, Declan Redmond and Menelaos Gkartzios
School of Geography, Planning and Environmental Policy,
University College, Dublin

Introduction

The background to this chapter is the increasing difficulty that is being experienced in addressing the issue of managing settlement growth in Ireland within the context of sustainable development. Ireland is now an urban society and cities in the Republic of Ireland have been transformed by the economic growth of the 1990s and the so-called 'Celtic Tiger', and in Northern Ireland by the economic 'spin-offs' of the peace process and increased political stability (Moore and Scott, 2005). While the success of the Irish economy has been well-documented (see for example, Breathnach, 1998; Clinch et al., 2002; Walsh, 2000), much less international attention has been given to the impact of economic growth on patterns of urban development.

Recent years have witnessed considerable progress in Ireland in developing environmental and spatial policy frameworks, including 'Sustainable Development – A Strategy for Ireland' (DOE, 1997), the 'National Spatial Strategy' (DOELG, 2002) and in Northern Ireland, the 'Regional Development Strategy' (DRD, 2001). In relation to the built environment and managing settlements, a number of core aspirations can be identified, including: reducing dependency on car travel and encouraging sustainable modes of transport; integrating land-use planning and transportation policy; encouraging efficient settlement patterns that minimize land-take and urban sprawl; emphasizing compact urban form; and increasing urban densities and brownfield development. However, in contrast to this policy direction, evidence would suggest that the emerging geography of Ireland displays distinctly unsustainable characteristics, such as urban sprawl and metropolitan decentralisation, an increase in the spatial separation of home and workplace, persistent urban-generated rural housing, and increased traffic congestion. This chapter outlines the key challenges to managing rapid settlement growth within a framework of sustainable urban management. Focusing on the Dublin city-region, the chapter evaluates housing supply and spatial trends to identify the emerging geography of settlement. The chapter then considers a series of policy barriers to achieving more sustainable patterns of urban development. In particular, it will focus on three components of the city-region – the inner city, edge-of-city, and the urban-rural fringe. The final part of the chapter reflects on the steps necessary to ensure the translation of well-intentioned rhetoric into real change.

Sustainable Urban Management

In an international context, the concept of sustainable development has emerged as *the* central and unifying theme of a new environmental agenda for public policy (Counsell, 1998). There is now a growing realisation that much of the sustainability debate has an urban accent as the world's cities are the major consumers of national resources and the major producers of pollution and waste. Any credible strategy to address these problems has to respond to the urban pressures on the environment (McEldowney et al., 2003). Therefore, as Breheny (1992) suggests, if cities can be designed and managed in such a way that resource use and pollution are reduced, then a major contribution to the solution of the global problem can be achieved. Increasingly urban management is characterized by resource protection approaches which emphasize the concept of capacity in two senses – environmental capacity, the ability of the environment to accommodate development without damage; and urban capacity, generally applied to accommodating development within existing urban areas (Counsell, 1999).

From an urban planning perspective, much of the interest in planning for the city-region surrounds the issue of sustainable cities and urban form. In particular, a key theme in both the literature and policy has been the focus on the apparently inexorable rise in the demand for car travel and the contribution that certain urban forms and land-use relationships can make to reducing energy consumption and emissions, harmful to both local environmental and global ecological conditions. Furthermore, even if the environmental consequences of increased car mobility can be limited, issues associated with traffic congestion and its impact on quality of life will remain problematic. As Banister (1999) suggests, although some of the growth in car dependency can be attributed to the acquisition of cars by individuals, it also reflects the distribution of functional opportunities which have become more dispersed throughout the city-region. The post-war period has been characterized by trends in which both land-use and travel patterns have reinforced each other to produce an increasingly mobile society. Rapid growth in car ownership has permitted more dispersed and complex patterns of urban development; these land-use patterns in turn require longer journeys for most daily activities and have become increasingly difficult to serve by energy-efficient modes of transport (Owens, 1992). It is the increased spatial separation of homes and workplaces, shops and schools that causes travel distances to rise particularly in low-density, sprawling cities.

Rapid decentralisation has been a deep-seated feature of urban growth in most western countries in the post-1945 period. Land-use trends alongside the opportunities afforded by past road construction efforts and the mass availability of private cars has led to the breaking of traditional relationships between home, work and leisure opportunities (Vigar, 2002). Urban sprawl has resulted from increasingly affluent householders and commercial investors exercising their locational choices in a free market, aided by the availability of good quality transport infrastructure and relatively cheap private transport (McEldowney et al., 2005). As identified by Banister (1998), transport has been seen as a principal permissive factor in the development of suburban housing and in redirecting development pressures away from the city centre. This dynamic is reinforced by the development of out-of-town and edge-of-town growth in retail, business and leisure services at motorway intersections and along bypasses.

Within this context, the compact city and urban consolidation is now widely espoused as a counter strategy to urban decentralisation and inner city decline (de Roo and Miller, 2000). The compact city model is supported for a number of reasons which relate to sustainable urban management and include: conservation of the countryside; less need to travel by car, thus reduced fuel emissions; support for public transport and walking and cycling; improved access to services and facilities; more efficient utility and infrastructure provision; and revitalisation and regeneration of inner urban areas (Burton, 2003). Policy prescription has increasingly favoured a compact city approach to sustainable urban management to address the physical separation of daily activities and the resultant dependency on the private car. Recently in Ireland, following trends in mainland Europe, the notion of a dense and compact city with mixed-use neighbourhoods has gained a high political currency. The Commission of the European Communities' Green Paper on the Urban Environment (1990, p.60) strongly advocates a 'compact city' solution to mounting environmental problems, proposing that "strategies which emphasize mixed use and denser development are more likely to result in people living close to work places and the services they require from everyday life". Since the Green Paper, European, national and local policy and discussion documents have repeated a dual theme: greater densities and mixing of land uses will significantly contribute to emissions and energy consumption reductions via shorter and possibly less frequent intra urban car-based trips, and will raise the vitality and viability of urban areas. In the Republic of Ireland these sentiments have been enthusiastically embraced by planners and translated into formal guidance through the National Spatial Strategy (DOELG, 2002), Planning Guidelines on Residential Density (DOELG, 1999) and the Regional Planning Guidelines for the Greater Dublin Area (Atkins and Associates et al., 2004), with an emphasis on increasing residential densities in the urban core and along key transport corridors. Similarly, Northern Ireland's Regional Development Strategy (DRD, 2001) has placed a greater emphasis on directing new development towards existing built-up areas, suggesting (in theory) a shift from greenfield development to one of urban consolidation, brownfield regeneration and increasing residential densities.

Although acceptance of the virtues of the compact city approach and urban consolidation is now widespread among the policy community, it is unclear if this policy direction is matched by emerging settlement patterns. In the case of Ireland, the rhetoric of sustainability has been embraced in a raft of spatial and urban policy initiatives. However, major questions arise in terms of translating policy objectives into implementation, relating to, for example, housing and land supply, the ability of the planning system to effectively direct development to desired locations, and the delivery of infrastructure.

Housing Supply

The recent report on housing in the Republic by the National Economic and Social Council (2004) concludes that the housing system is operating in a dynamic but unbalanced way. By this they are referring broadly to the extraordinarily rapid increases in new housing supply over the past decade but also to spatial and social imbalances in such supply. Figure 10.1 illustrates the rapid growth in housing supply from the early 1990s to the present. The period from 1994 to 2004 has seen approximately a 200 per cent increase in new house-building which has been driven almost wholly by the rise in private house-building.

While national housing supply has increased substantially over the past decade, one of the more arresting aspects of this boom has been the changing spatial pattern of new house-building. This is best seen in the Eastern region and Figure 10.2 depicts the changing pattern of building in the Dublin Region, the Mid-East Region and the Rest of Leinster. While all areas have seen very large increases in supply, what is particularly noticeable is the very rapid increases in both the Mid-East and Rest of Leinster. In proportionate terms the Dublin region has seen its share of new house-building decrease from 56 per cent in 1994 to an average of 42 per cent in recent years. Indeed, in the Dublin region, only Fingal County has seen large increases in supply on the northern fringe of the city in recent years, with supply in the core of the city being relatively static over the decade. The Mid-East region has seen its share of new supply increase from 20 per cent to 25 per cent over the same period while the Rest of Leinster has seen its share grow from 24 per cent to an average of 36 per cent in recent years. These figures illustrate the push of new housing supply into areas well beyond the administrative boundaries of Dublin and into areas up to 80km from the city centre, generating a large and very complex commuter belt.

Settlement Trends

To examine the spatial distribution of new housing in more detail, this section examines recent residential spatial trends in the Dublin city-region to consider the extent that residential growth has been occurring in line with spatial policy objectives. Firstly, recent demographic changes in the city-region and in individual local authority areas will be outlined. Secondly, house-building activity will be considered, and finally travel-to-work commuting patterns will be highlighted. In addition to considering trends within established administrative boundaries (local authority level, County Dublin and the Greater Dublin Area), trends in the wider city-region will be outlined, to capture trends in the increasingly extended commuter belt for Dublin, encompassing most of the province of Leinster (Figure 10.3). The intention is to use the province of Leinster as a case study area in an effort to study urban-rural relationships in the wider periphery of Dublin, rather than define a specific area that relates to these relationships from the beginning. We have chosen the region of Leinster because it is the greatest geographically defined area that includes Dublin City, significantly more extended than the commonly used GDA region. In our approach the Leinster Province works as a sample for studying relations between Dublin city and its rural hinterland rather than an area that exclusively relates to such phenomena.

Demographic Changes

Whereas counties Kildare, Kilkenny, Meath, Wicklow and Dublin increased their population between 1986 and 1991, the remainder of Leinster experienced population decline during this period. However, since 1991, this has been dramatically altered as all counties, except the somewhat remote County Longford, have experienced significant growth. In particular, counties Meath, Kildare and Wicklow, all within easy commuting distance of Dublin, grew significantly faster than both the national rate of growth (8 per cent) after 1996 and that of Co. Dublin (6.1 per cent), illustrated in Figure 10.4.

To obtain a comprehensive spatial analysis of the recent demographic changes in the city-region, population levels from the 2002 Census have been analysed from the Electoral Division[1] scale and read into Geographical Information System (GIS) maps. The most dramatic increases of population (3 times or more than the national rate of growth) have taken place in rural areas north and south of the existing built-up area, in the mid-eastern counties of Meath, Kildare, Offaly, Westmeath and Laois, and along the eastern coastline of Counties Louth, Wicklow and Wexford. Outside these counties, most areas in the city-region grew less than the national average or even decreased their population (Figure 10.5).

---

[1]   The term Electoral Division was changed on 24 June 1996 (Section 23 of the Local Government Act, 1994) from District Electoral Division. There are 3,440 Electoral Divisions in the State.

The maps below illustrate spatial changes for two counties within the Dublin-Belfast corridor that have experienced significant levels of population change outside Co. Dublin (Louth and Meath). Co. Louth (Figure 10.6) increased its population by 10.5 per cent from 1996 to 2002 with higher increases in the southern parts of the county, outside Drogheda. The spatial distribution of growth demonstrates that the rural environs of Dundalk and Drogheda experienced higher increases of population than their urban areas. For example, Dundalk town increased its population by 4.5 per cent whereas the adjacent rural areas increased two times more than the town itself. Similarly the urban area of Drogheda increased its population by 3.8 per cent, while some of the rural areas around Drogheda increased their population by almost 50 per cent. This may be because the existing built-up areas were already at full capacity and the rural environs provided an ideal location for expansion, or it may be due to changing residential preferences among the general population.

Another county forming part of the Dublin-Belfast corridor, County Meath (Figure 10.7), increased its population more than any other county in the GDA, almost three times more than the national average (22.1 per cent). Major population increases took place close to the boundary with Fingal local authority area (Co. Dublin) and particularly in Ratoath (82.1 per cent population increase). Population growth has also been recorded around towns like Drogheda (i.e. in Julianstown), Navan, Kells and Trim. In all cases the population of these urban areas increased at a lower rate than their surroundings, except in the case of Trim where the town itself showed a significant decrease of population (-16.8 per cent), while its rural surroundings increased their population by 39.7 per cent. Despite the high levels of population increases in the county as a whole, 21 EDs (22.8 per cent of 92 EDs) decreased their population or remained stable, exhibiting a considerably unequal redistribution of population in Co. Meath away from small towns and villages and towards the rural environs of larger towns particularly along the road and rail transport (i.e. Enfield).

House-building Activity

Housing activity also provides a useful indicator to examine current patterns of development in the case study area. Figure 10.8 shows absolute numbers of private house completions in the city-region (excluding Local Authority and voluntary/non profit houses). County Dublin, as expected, has had the highest housing completions followed by the adjacent counties and then the outer counties. Outside of Co. Dublin, Co. Meath had the strongest residential growth in the GDA in 2003, followed by Co. Kildare (with 3,519 and 2,824 completions respectively). Significantly, Co. Meath increased its private house completions by 163 per cent in only 5 years (1999–2003) whereas the corresponding figure for Co. Dublin was 37 per cent.

Figure 10.9, which considers density of occupied dwellings built between two different periods during 1991 and 2002, highlights an emerging pattern of expansion and sprawl in the city region. Significant increases of new houses outside Dublin took place in counties Louth (throughout the whole county but especially around Drogheda and Dundalk), Kildare and Wexford. In Co. Meath many new houses after 1996 were built in the south-east part of the county (Dunshaughlin, Ashbourne, Dunboyne and Ratoath) and also in the rural environs of Navan, Kells and Trim, in line with population increases in these areas during the same period. Interestingly Co. Wicklow had distinctively less new houses built after 1996, as a result of both its stricter planning policy related to its outstanding landscape quality, and physical restrictions, such as the Dublin-Wicklow mountain range which forms the NE-SW spine of the county.

Travel-to-Work Commuting Patterns

All of this has been facilitated by the development of a close relationship between commuting patterns and urban sprawl. For people living in the rural fringe of towns and work in urban areas, commuting is probably the most important trip of the day. Car ownership in the Republic of Ireland has grown rapidly in line with the economic performance, placing Ireland amongst the most car-dependent societies in Europe. There were almost 1.2 million private cars in the country in 1998 and car ownership exceeded 50 cars per 100 persons for the first time in the same year (Goodbody Economic Consultants, 2000). The rising level of car ownership has led to an increasing reliance on the private motor vehicle as the preferred mode of transport (Clinch et al., 2002).

Indeed, according to the 2002 census, the private car is the most popular mode of transport in the city-region. The majority of people in the city-region (and particularly in a zone surrounding Co. Dublin in counties Kildare, Meath and Wicklow) are commuting to work, school or college by car, either as the driver or passenger. The use of public modes of transport (bus and train) accounts for less than 30 per cent of the people living in the city-region. Much higher percentages of people using public transport can be seen in areas along efficient public transport corridors such as the DART. Cycling and walking seem to be the least popular ways of daily commuting to work, restricted as expected to the most urbanized areas in the city-region, for instance in inner Dublin city, Drogheda, Dundalk and Kilkenny (Figure 10.10).

For the first time, long-distance commuting has also begun to characterize the GDA and other urban areas like Waterford and Wexford (Gkartzios and Scott, 2005). These are areas that significantly increased their population during the 1996–2002 period. Yet in contrast to the aspirational nature of government policy, long-distance commuting has led to further congestion, increased travel time to work, rising frustrations and stress, and increased fuel and associated pollution (Clinch et al., 2002).

Policy Barriers

Having reviewed the available evidence regarding the patterns of urban growth in the Dublin city-region, it would appear that spatial trends run counter to spatial planning policy objectives. Empirical evidence suggests that the critical issue at present in Ireland is narrowing the gap between policy development and implementation at a range of scales. This section selectively focuses on policy challenges related to land supply and housing provision within three components of the city-region: (1) inner urban areas; (2) edge-of-city development; and (3) the urban-rural fringe.

Inner-Urban Consolidation

Of prime importance in an Irish context, and given public concern over dramatic urban sprawl and the emergence of an almost continuous line of development along the eastern seaboard, is how existing urban cores may be consolidated. This is a European problem, with the Expert Group on the Urban Environment (2001, p. 3) arguing that:

> The better management of land resources is essential for sustainability and for improving the quality of life in cities and towns .... The re-use of urban brownfields and the more efficient use of infrastructure are ways of 'retro-fitting' existing areas of sprawl and preventing further outward expansion.

All the recent policy documents and most noticeably the National Spatial Strategy (NSS) aspire to, and strongly emphasize, the promotion of brownfield regeneration as a key policy component. The NSS argues for a strengthening of existing policies of urban consolidation to halt the further development of a large urban conurbation on the eastern seaboard. A policy of containment is called for, the integration of effective land use and public transport policies is promoted, and the potential for brownfields to contribute to intensification and compaction is made explicit. The document argues that within the Dublin Metropolitan area 'a systematic and comprehensive audit of all vacant, derelict and underused land (should be undertaken) to establish its capacity to accommodate housing and other suitable uses'. A practical prescription to ensure consolidation of the Greater Dublin Area and other large urban centres within Ireland is given: 'the efficient use of land by consolidating existing settlements, focusing in particular on development capacity within central urban areas through re-use of under-utilized land and buildings as a priority'. But although this suggests that brownfield regeneration has the potential to become a cornerstone of future spatial development, it is evident that this is being thwarted by major barriers.

One of the most critical barriers to success at present in Ireland is the lack of any formal research about the extent of brownfields, and the small number of individuals with limited resources trying to plug the information gap with little support. There is currently no up-to-date and comprehensive survey in Ireland of the number of former industrial sites. In contrast to the perception of some academics and policymakers, the Environmental Protection Agency (EPA) estimate that even after the large urban regeneration projects that were completed through the 1990s, between 2,000 and 2,400 potentially contaminated sites remain, mostly located in Dublin and Cork (CLARINET, 2002). These include former gasworks, closed mines, dockyards, landfills, fertiliser plants, railyards, old petrol depots and stations. This emphasis on contamination as a characteristic of 'brownfields' has resulted in the identification of 487 sites previously used for hazardous activities in the Republic of Ireland through the National Hazardous Waste Management Plan, and gives some indication of the potential effect that brownfields may have on ground and surface water resources. This number is not large in comparison to other countries, but until the figures compiled by Brogan et al. (1999) are up-dated and clarified, the true extent of the problem and the potential that these areas may provide for environmental restoration will remain unknown. One of the primary difficulties is that this issue falls between many stools, encompassing a broad range of aspects from waste management, to groundwater protection, pollution control, planning and development and both human and ecological health. Policy integration rather than a sectoral approach is critical to providing a comprehensive framework for redevelopment across a range of discrete yet interconnected territorial scales, but given the policy ownership boundaries that exist between government departments in Ireland, it will require a centralized initiative to facilitate inter-agency and cross-policy co-operation.

Compounding the lack of integration, one of the major difficulties in moving towards consolidation of the city-region is the existence of weak policy instruments. In the Republic of Ireland, the primary legislation dealing with brownfield sites is the Derelict Sites Act introduced to address the issue of blight in urban cores. This legislation compels local authorities in urban areas to keep a register of all derelict sites, including the location of the property, the name and address of the owner and details of any action that the local authority has taken regarding the site. If the owner of a site does not engage in improvement, the local authority is empowered to fine them 3 per cent of the market value of the site per annum until such time as the necessary changes are made. The legislation also grants the local authorities power to buy derelict sites or dangerous land in their areas, either by agreement with the owner or compulsorily. However, this legislation has proved highly ineffective as it has only provided a framework within which local authorities may act without compelling them to do so, unlike in Northern Ireland where all local authorities are working to achieve set targets for development on brownfield land. In the Republic, private landowners have avoided penalties under the Derelict Sites Act by erecting a palisade fence and thereby 'tidying' the site, even though it may remain vacant or under-utilized. The punitive nature of the legislation has been totally ineffective due to lack of enforcement and the management of the Derelict Sites Register. Many of the large and more obviously derelict sites throughout urban areas have not been entered on this list because of the poor procedures utilized to manage the database. It is also totally ineffective in determining whether a site is contaminated, as there is no indication of the characteristics of that place. Organisations such as the Dublin Docklands Development Authority (2003, p. 58) have criticized the narrow definition used in the Act which 'does not provide an accurate indication of the widespread nature of under-utilized sites'. Although the National Spatial Strategy has compelled local authorities to use this legislation to solve the problem of brownfields and to undertake a comprehensive and rigorous audit of derelict land, more resources should be allocated to local government to undertake this analysis and prioritize brownfields as future growth centres. By late 2004, Dublin City Council, with minimal resources, had already identified 27.7 hecates of brownfield in the north inner city and rezoned it in an attempt to encourage redevelopment, but by their own admission the lack of resources has meant that their approach is neither entirely comprehensive nor totally accurate.

Finally and perhaps of greatest concern to developers, who after all will be the core group to deliver consolidation, is the lack of clarity regarding liability for derelict, and particularly contaminated, sites. Internationally this has been a major stumbling block to regeneration as a number of questions, including who pays for the clean up of contaminated sites, how clean is clean, and who is responsible for these sites once they have been de-contaminated, are left unanswered. Whether the polluter or new owner bears responsibility for any future liability from historical contamination is a critical issue, particularly given that the national media and politicians are increasingly referring to the emergence of a litigation culture in Ireland. Potential investors in brownfield areas may be unwilling to accept the risk that they could become liable for future compensation claims, and therefore the public sector may need to intervene with protection mechanisms similar to the US Superfund programme. Beyond the national level, European Commission directives and guidelines are of little use in this regard given that they do not cover contamination retrospectively. Apart from the end user taking a claim against a particular developer, there is also the employer liability that may arise from the remediation of a contaminated site. McIntyre (2003) argues that Section 2 of the Health, Safety and Welfare at Work Act, 1989 could potentially include a development site where personal injury claims may emerge. There are also constitutional difficulties (McIntyre, 2003) as the Irish Parliament cannot declare an act to be an infringement of law retrospectively. Therefore if a landowner created a brownfield but the action was not illegal at the time, then they bear no responsibility for the contamination. It is therefore virtually impossible to legally assign liability for historically contaminated land in Ireland. It would seem that because of legal and constitutional difficulties in this jurisdiction, 'responsibility [for regulating liability] is ultimately likely to pass to the public sector, perhaps explaining the Irish authorities' lack of resolve to tackle this problem' (McIntyre, 2003, p 117).

However, although the above remain critical issues in terms of promoting consolidation, their resolution alone will not guarantee success. A dual approach to future development is necessary. Even if brownfield sites are identified and brought to market their attractiveness vis-à-vis greenfield sites may become a further stumbling block to redevelopment. It is thus essential that for brownfield regeneration to effectively contribute to land delivery in any city-region a simultaneous consideration of edge-city growth must be undertaken and a complimentary suite of policy instruments delivered, as discussed in the following section.

Edge City Development: Policy and Practice

Implicit in the notion of a spatial planning framework for the Dublin-Belfast corridor is the fairly simple idea that land use development should adhere to the parameters of the relevant spatial plans. Dealing with the spatial planning frameworks for the Dublin region, and in particular for development at the edge of the city and beyond, spatial planning policy is now relatively well developed. Core principles in these spatial plans include adherence to a hierarchy of settlement and development patterns with an emphasis on the need for the integration of land use and transportation. With respect to the planning of the edge city, the Regional Planning Guidelines for the Greater Dublin Area call for a policy of urban consolidation in the metropolitan area (extent of the built up area) of Dublin with development to be focused as far as possible on public transport routes. Outside of the metropolitan area, in what is termed the hinterland, development is to be focused on a series of primary and secondary development centres (Atkins and Associates et al., 2004). The National Spatial Strategy (NSS) essentially reiterates these policies and calls for the consolidation of the Greater Dublin Area (DOELG, 2002).

As shown in Table 10.1, the NSS sets out a series of tests which should in future be used in determining the location of housing in urban areas and are thus important for future development patterns. While these tests are inevitably general, the emphasis is very much on sustainability, integration and the maximisation of existing urban land and associated services. The NSS and the regional guidelines further emphasize the need to develop and consolidate existing urban areas before deciding to develop greenfield sites. This sequential approach to development, if actually implemented, would have profound consequences for the planning and development of edge cities, as it would in theory seek to locate a substantial amount of new development within the existing metropolitan area and avoid fragmented development at and beyond the edge.

Table 10.1 Housing Location Tests for Urban Areas

Tests	Evaluation Considerations
The Asset Test	Are there existing community resources, such as schools etc. with spare capacity?
The Carrying Capacity Test	Is the environmental setting capable of absorbing development in terms of drainage etc.?
The Transport Test	Is there potential for reinforcing usage of public transport, walking, cycling etc?
The Economic Development Test	Is there potential to ensure integration between the location of housing and employment?
The Character Test	Will the proposal reinforce a sense of place and character
The Community Test	Will the proposal reinforce the integrity and vitality if the local community and services that can be provided?
The Integration Test	Will the proposal aid an integrated approach to catering for the housing needs of all sections of society?

Source: *DOELG, 2002, p103.*

However, the long term success of any kind of regional planning framework is predicated on development patterns complying at least in large part with the parameters of the spatial plan. However, as the research presented in this chapter demonstrates, the pattern of development in the GDA reflects to some extent a laissez faire pattern of development, with little linkage to the Regional Guidelines or the transportation plans of the Dublin Transportation Office. In the past decade the pace, scale and location of development on the edge of Dublin and beyond have created dispersed and complex patterns of land use with even more complex ramifications with respect to transportation and commuting (Williams and Shiels, 2002; MacLaran and Killen, 2002). In very broad terms, the emergence of the edge city has been dominated by two patterns of development. First, around the M50 motorway there has developed large scale commercial and industrial development around the edge of Dublin. Second, as a consequence of the massive escalation of house prices and the attendant crisis of access and affordability, a dispersed pattern of housing development has occurred not only in what is termed the hinterland of the GDA, but also well beyond into what have been termed the outer Leinster counties. Relatively low levels of supply in the Dublin local authorities have resulted in residential development leapfrogging to towns and villages up to 90km around Dublin, resulting in what can only be described as unsustainable spatial development and commuting patterns (Williams et al., 2002). The economic costs, still less the social and environmental costs, of this approach to development have not been calculated. Apart from the obvious costs with respect to commuting, there are clear costs associated with providing new transport and social infrastructure in the many towns and villages where new residential estates have mushroomed over the past decade. Ironically, these costs are being incurred at the same time as there has been significant population loss, and potential under utilisation of services, in many of the older areas of Dublin city.

Thus, while policy is fairly well developed, it is also clear that spatial planning frameworks seem to be more often honoured in their breach than their compliance. This is particularly the case in the Greater Dublin Area and the Eastern area generally, where the scale and location of development has at best been only loosely correlated with existing spatial plans. The Regional Planning Guidelines for the Greater Dublin Region, for example, have been breached on several occasions and development proposals continue to emerge which contravene the guidelines. In theory, local development plans and development control decisions are meant to 'have regard' to the strategic guidelines for Dublin (Atkins and Associates et al., 2004). However, as a result of a recent court case testing the guidelines, it seems that having regard to the guidelines can mean as little as being familiar with the front cover of the report, thus opening up the possibility, perhaps even probability, that the guidelines can be breached at will. Key infrastructure planners, such as the Dublin Transportation Office, have argued as follows:

> ... the use of the term 'have regard to' instead of 'shall comply with' in the Planning and Development Act, 2000 when addressing the relationship between Development Plans and Regional Planning Guidelines has effectively meant that the latter can be virtually ignored. This in turn will have severe economic/quality of life consequences in the medium/long term future' (Dublin Transportation Office, 2003).

This disconnect between the regional planning guidelines and local development plans and development control decisions is sometimes defended on the grounds that local authorities need flexibility and that the guidelines are after all, merely indicative. As a defence this is quite flimsy. It is possible to achieve a relationship between regional guidelines and local development patterns while still retaining some local flexibility. The current system, however, allows local development patterns to contravene the regional guidelines with relative ease. This policy failure is perhaps symptomatic of a general lack of political will when it comes to achieving planning goals and would lead one to be pessimistic about achieving the goals of sustainable urban management outlined earlier.

The Urban-Rural Fringe

Although the Dublin-Belfast axis is the most urbanized and densely populated part of the island, a significant rural component exists along and nearby the corridor – some of which is under considerable pressure from urban growth, while other areas display characteristics of more peripheral rural communities such as in south Armagh, the Mournes and the Cooley Peninsula in Louth. Planning policy throughout Europe has tended to address urban and rural issues as separate policy arenas (Davoudi and Stead, 2002) however, taking a holistic approach to housing provision and land supply in the Dublin-Belfast corridor clearly encompasses an integrated perspective of urban and rural planning dimensions.

The proliferation of dispersed single dwellings in the countryside has been an issue for many years, but the scale and pace of recent years appears to be intensifying, particularly in accessible rural areas in close proximity to urban centres. For example, analysis undertaken during the preparation of the National Spatial Strategy suggested that between 1996-1999 over one in three new houses built in Ireland have been one-off housing in the open countryside, and highlighted that the issue of single applications for housing in rural areas has become a major concern for most local planning authorities (Spatial Planning Unit, 2001). Commentators such as Aalen (1997) and McGrath (1998) have argued that the planning system is unable to respond effectively to rural settlement growth. In a critique of rural planning, both commentators suggested policy has been driven by the priorities of a few individuals, an intense localism, and the predominance of incremental decision-making. Similarly, Gallent et al. (2003) classified rural planning in Ireland as a *laissez-faire* regime, suggesting that: 'the tradition of a more relaxed approach to regulation, and what many see as the underperformance in planning is merely an expression of Irish attitudes towards government intervention' (p. 90).

Although dispersed housing in the countryside is often portrayed as a singular issue among many commentators and in the national media, clearly differences exist between different types of rural areas. For example, the drivers of settlement change and rural community context varies considerably between rural areas in close proximity to Dublin and those in remote, sparsely populated rural areas in the west of Ireland. A positive development in the National Spatial Strategy was the adoption of a differentiated rural policy, and this was reflected in its approach for housing in the countryside. Encouragingly, the Strategy called for different responses to managing dispersed rural settlement between rural areas under strong urban influences and rural areas that are either characterized by a strong agricultural base, structurally weak rural areas and areas with distinctive settlement patterns, reflecting the contrasting development pressures that exist in the countryside. This was further developed in the NSS with a distinction made between urban and rural generated housing in rural areas, defined as (p. 106):

- Urban-generated rural housing: development driven by urban centres, with housing sought in rural areas by people living and working in urban areas, including second homes;
- Rural-generated housing: housing needed in rural areas within the established rural community by people working in rural areas or in nearby urban areas who

are an intrinsic part of the rural community by way of background or employment.

In general, the National Spatial Strategy outlined that development driven by urban areas (including urban-generated rural housing) should take place within built up areas on land identified in the development plan process and that rural-generated housing needs should be accommodated in the areas where they arise. These themes have been further addressed in the recent Planning Guidelines for Sustainable Rural Housing (DEHLG, 2005). However, these guidelines appear to suggest a more relaxed approach to managing rural housing, including in those areas accessible to urban centres. In summary, the guidelines outline that (p. 1):

• People who are part of and contribute to the rural community will get planning permission in all rural areas, including those under strong urban-based pressures, subject to the normal rules in relation to good planning (related to site layout and design);
• Anyone wishing to build a house in rural areas suffering persistent and substantial population decline will be accommodated, subject to good planning practice in siting and design.

Implementation of these guidelines is the responsibility of local authorities. However, there are major questions regarding the impacts, costs and benefits of translating these guidelines into development plan policies and development control decision-making. For example, it may be possible that implementation of the rural housing guidelines in rural areas accessible to urban centres, could further reinforce trends towards increasingly dispersed city-regions, and undermining policies aimed at promoting urban consolidation.

Policy Implications

As suggested above, Ireland and, in particular, the Dublin city region, has experienced rapid residential change characterized by urban sprawl and residential preferences for living in accessible rural areas in close proximity to urban centres. To address this emerging geography of Ireland and gaps in the provision of policy, the late 1990s and early 2000s have witnessed a clear attempt by policy-makers to influence patterns of development to achieve more sustainable goals. This has included a comprehensive review and consolidation of planning legislation, the publication of a national sustainable development strategy and a national spatial strategy, the emergence of regional planning guidelines, and central government planning guidelines relating to both urban density and rural housing. On paper (at least) this policy formulation is impressive, and represents a major step forward in the development of the planning policy framework for the Republic of Ireland. However, major questions can be identified in relation to the *effectiveness* of this policy framework to *deliver* more sustainable patterns of regional and spatial development:

- **How can we effectively implement spatial strategies?** Currently, a number of weaknesses can be identified in relation to implementing existing spatial plans and policies, diminishing the ability of policy-makers to influence change processes. Firstly, there is an absence of effective mechanisms for ensuring that national and regional spatial goals are translated into statutory local authority development plans; a significant gap in policy implementation – for example, the recent County Meath Development Plan failed to comply with regional planning guidelines for the Greater Dublin Area, an action that was successfully upheld in court. Secondly, an intense localism within Irish politics often constrains attempts to formulate strategic policies, clearly illustrated with the policy process driving the rural housing planning guidelines. Related to this, spatial planning and urban policy currently lacks a political champion that could provide much needed drive, vision and political leadership. And thirdly, there is a clear need to explore innovative and imaginative policy instruments. Traditional regulatory approaches to managing urban spatial change have been less than successful in securing more sustainable patterns of urban development. Although policy prescription increasingly favours a sustainable urban development agenda, the emerging geography of Ireland displays distinctly unsustainable trends, suggesting a gap between policy intentions and actual outcomes. In this context, market-based instruments for policy implementation and addressing the current 'disconnect' between spatial plans and public investment programmes may offer some potential to address the 'implementation gap'. Furthermore, a clear need exists to develop evidence-based approaches to policy-making to address the gap between policy intentions and outcomes. For example, although policy-makers increasingly favour introducing higher residential densities in urban areas, evidence from the Greater Dublin Area, suggests that consumers continue to express a preference for lower density residential areas. In this regard, research to examine consumer residential decision-making would allow policy-makers to develop appropriate policy responses.
- **How can we avoid policy fragmentation and develop holistic approaches to sustainable urban management?** In assessing urban change processes, a number of inter-related drivers of change can be identified including, the perceived benefits of rural living, push factors away from the metropolitan core, the perceived attractiveness of urban living environments, house prices and the availability of appropriate housing, housing supply, and land and infrastructure delivery. Any response to addressing these factors involves not only land-use regulation and settlement strategies, but also initiatives to address, for example, improving urban design and the quality of the urban living environment, housing affordability and supply, and the integration of transport and land-use planning, which are currently fragmented in formulation

and delivery. In addition, policy-makers should also recognize the importance of not only ensuring more sustainable future patterns of development, but also improving the sustainability of those areas that experienced rapid urban growth during the 1990s. For example, although policies for developing compact cities and increasing urban density in future developments are important, the rapid housing development and urban growth in the 1990s was characterized by low-density, edge of city development and rural settlement growth. Many of these areas lack key 'community infrastructure' such as schools and childcare facilities, as well as being dependent on the private car for transport. Addressing the problems caused by recent urban-generated development in rural areas must also provide a key departure point for policy development, in addition to aspirational policies for future city development.

- **What are the implications of the Dublin-Belfast corridor on existing patterns of urban growth?** At present, the Dublin city-region is increasingly characterized by urban sprawl and decentralized and dispersed patterns of residential development. These urban growth processes are likely to be further reinforced with enhanced investment in transport infrastructure in the Dublin-Belfast corridor. Without careful management, the corridor could emerge as a linear suburb between the twin poles of Dublin and Belfast, leading to the increased spatial separation of functional activities and longer-distance commuting. The future geography of employment is likely to be characterized by two contradictory trends: firstly, the increased concentration of key business and service functions within Dublin and Belfast; and secondly, the suburbanisation of offices and retail driven by investment in road infrastructure. Both trends may lead to increasingly complex commuting and travel patterns along the corridor.

- **What is the optimum balance in housing supply between urban and rural areas along the Dublin-Belfast corridor?** Both the NSS and RDS give a clear policy steer that primacy is to be given to the main urban centres (gateways and hubs) in order to support the achievement of 'critical mass'. The optimal housing balance between towns, villages and dispersed small settlements is predicated on ensuring that the growth potential of the principal urban centres for employment and services is not undermined (see Greer and Murray, 2003, for a discussion relating to Northern Ireland). Therefore a clear relationship emerges between housing supply and land delivery in both urban and rural areas. For designated gateways, hubs and development centres to develop the necessary critical mass for services and employment, it is likely that restrictive rural settlement policies will be required to facilitate the growth of larger settlements in the hierarchy. For example, if a designated gateway such as Dundalk, with a current population of 32,000, is to develop into a key node with a major expansion of residential development, what types of rural settlement policy would be required in the remainder of Louth to achieve the required scale of development? In this regard, the recent Planning Guidelines for Rural Housing may undermine wider policy objectives for the Dublin-

Belfast corridor, and indeed, the emerging policy framework in the Dublin city-region perhaps presents 'mixed-signals'. On the one hand, national and regional spatial strategies propose that residential development in the rural hinterland of Dublin should be concentrated in identified towns and service villages. On the other hand, the rural housing guidelines along with county development plans suggest a more permissive approach to dispersed housing in the countryside, including areas in close proximity to urban centres. Dispersed rural housing in proximity to the Dublin-Belfast corridor may present a significant challenge to achieving critical mass in key development nodes and in promoting more sustainable patterns of development. However, household consumer and lifestyle choice throughout Europe has increasingly displayed trends of counter urbanisation and urban-rural migration (Gkartzios and Scott, 2005).

- **How can we develop effective governance structures at a metropolitan and city-region scale?** Related to both policy implementation and integrative policy-making, lies the challenge of developing effective governance mechanisms, and the need to broker connections between cities and their rural hinterlands. Regional governance remains poorly developed in the Republic of Ireland, with limited responsibilities for the State's Regional Authorities. A recent opportunity has emerged following the publication of the National Spatial Strategy, whereby Regional Authorities have been involved in developing regional planning guidelines. In the case of the Greater Dublin Area, though, the administrative area (the Dublin and Mid-Eastern Regional Authorities) does not correspond to the emerging functional area of the city-region, which has extended far beyond even the regional administrative boundaries. Although it is possible to present a strong case for devolving powers and finance to a regional structure that addresses the functional urban area of Dublin, the scope for enhancing regional governance may be limited for two reasons: firstly, given an absence of regional identity in Ireland generally, and the intense localism that characterizes Irish politics, it is unlikely that regional level governance would capture the public imagination; and secondly, an enhanced administrative structure for the Dublin city region would be viewed politically as an alternative power-base to national politics, and unlikely to gain the necessary political support. In this context, addressing the institutional capacity and connectivity of the existing administrative structures should remain a priority, through establishing regional networks of politicians and key stakeholders.

Conclusion

Although policy prescription currently advocates a compact city approach for urban cores and concentrated development in key settlements in the hinterland, empirical evidence suggests that deconcentrated and decentralized spatial patterns are emerging. Recent population growth has taken place, in general, outside city administrative boundaries and into the surrounding counties instead. This population growth has been accommodated in edge-of-city growth, and in smaller towns and rural areas in close proximity to Dublin city, leading to urban sprawl and increasingly dispersed settlement patterns at a city-region scale. Evidence also suggests that a significant commuter belt exist well beyond the immediate suburbs of Dublin. In particular, the mid-eastern counties of the Greater Dublin Area have become significant residential targets with increasing private house completions. These trends are consistent with notions of counter urbanisation and metropolitan dispersal. In particular, the housing pressure in Dublin suggests a displaced-urbanisation (drawing on Mitchell's classification, 2004) whereby people migrate to rural areas and small towns outside of the metropolitan area simply because it is cheaper to buy or build a house there. On the other hand, preferences for rural living in Ireland suggest the existence of an Irish rural idyll, which fit closely with ex-urbanisation and/or anti-urbanisation trends.

Urban sprawl and dispersed patterns of settlement growth with long distance commuting are now established components of the settlement structure of the Dublin city-region. This presents a considerable challenge to policy-makers, suggesting the importance of not only ensuring more sustainable future patterns of development, but also improving the sustainability of those areas that experienced rapid urban growth during the 1990s. Although policies for developing compact cities and increasing urban density are important, the rapid housing development and urban growth in the 1990s was characterized by low-density, edge-of-city development and rural settlement growth. Addressing issues related to the deficit of physical and community infrastructure in these areas, the 'greening' of transport, particularly commuting patterns, and developing effective urban and regional governance should provide key themes for urban and spatial policy.

Within the context of the Dublin-Belfast corridor concept, a polycentric urban system implies the development of dynamic 'nodes' (in the spatial organisation of society and the economy), which are connected with one another via physical transport infrastructure and communication links as well as economic ties (and certain division of labour patterns and political and cultural communication links (Kratke, 2001). At the EU-wide level the European Spatial Development Perspective (ESDP) advocates the creation of several 'dynamic zones of global economic integration, well distributed throughout the EU territory and comprising of a network of internationally accessible metropolitan regions and their hinterlands' (Committee for Spatial Planning, 1999). At a regional scale, the ESDP places considerable emphasis on the creation of networks of cooperation between urban centres to develop functional complements which may be the only possibility for achieving viable markets and maintaining economic institutions and services.

The polycentric concept has been criticized for being too vague and underdeveloped (Atkinson, 2001), as naïve in terms of levels of intra-urban cooperation rather than increased competition (Kratke, 2001), and dominated by a rationale of economic competitiveness at the expense of social cohesion and environmental concerns (Richardson and Jensen, 2000). However, the concept may provide a useful framework, or at least provide a starting point, for questioning the future shape of development along the Dublin-Belfast corridor, particularly in terms of land supply and housing provision. For example, key questions include:

- To what extent is it possible to further consolidate urban development in designated gateways and hubs?
- What are the interrelationships *between* development nodes and urban and rural areas?
- What linkages exist between problems at different spatial scales and what challenges does this present for territorial governance, including the cross-border dimension?
- How can planning policy be more effectively implemented particularly vis-à-vis the delivery of planned residential development?
- Therefore, in terms of land management and housing supply, a polycentric framework enables a more realistic scale of analysis and action that reflects existing housing and labour markets, travel-to-work patterns and retail and leisure activities.

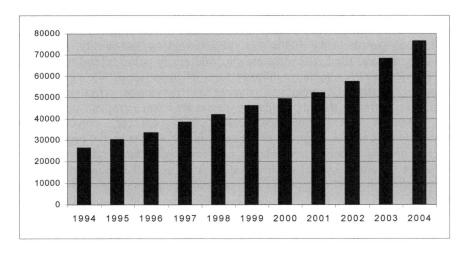

Figure 10.1   Total House Completions in the Republic of Ireland

Source: *Department of the Environment, Heritage and Local Government (2004)*

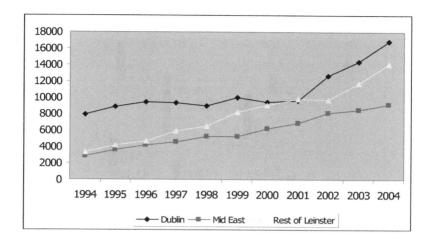

Figure 10.2   New House-building in the Eastern Region

Source: *Department of the Environment, Heritage and Local Government (2004)*

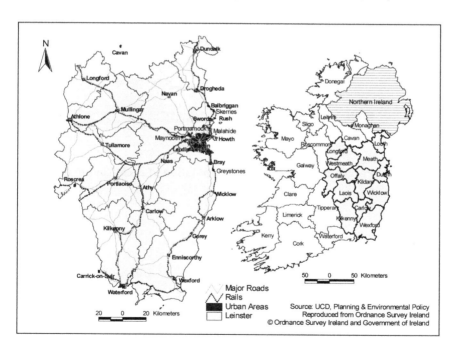

Figure 10.3   Leinster Map

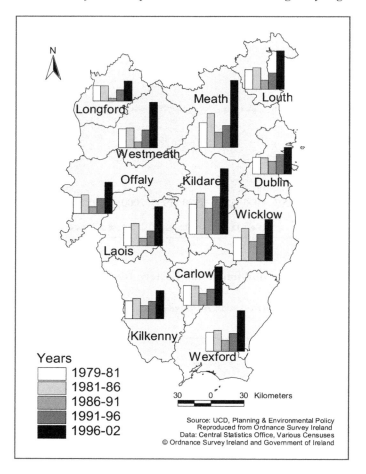

Figure 10.4   Percentage Change in the Population of each County of Leinster

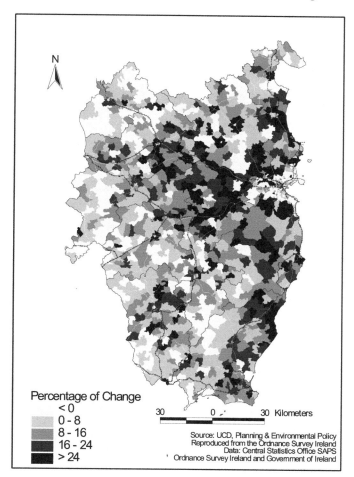

Figure 10.5   Percentage Change of Population in the Electoral Divisions of Leinster

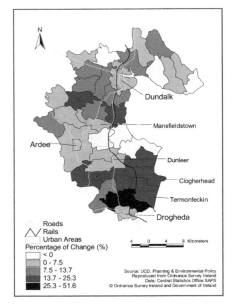

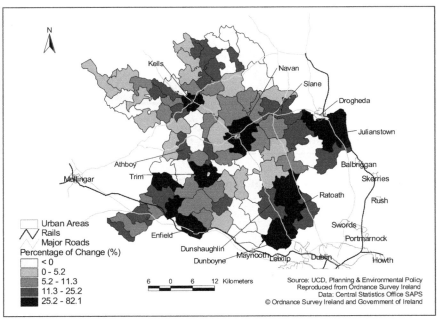

**Figures 10.6 and 10.7   Population Change 1996–2002 in Louth (above) and
Meath**

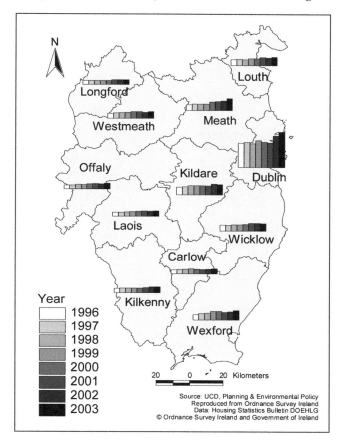

Figure 10.8   Private House Completions by County in Leinster 1996–2003

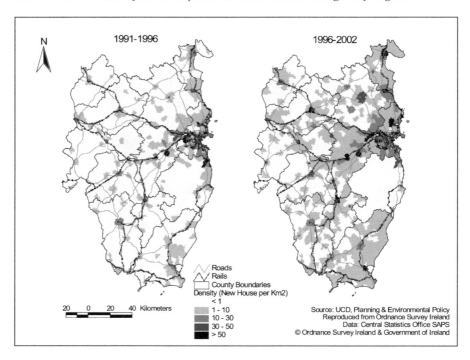

Figure 10.9   Density of Occupied Houses Built Between 1991 and 2002

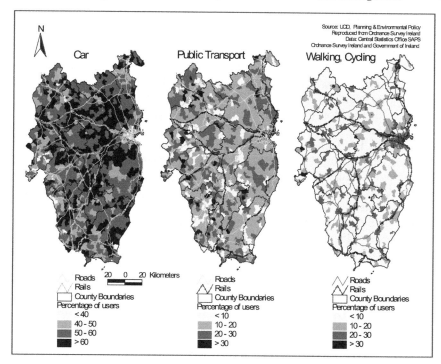

Figure 10.10 **Percentage of People Travelling to Work, School and College by Mode of Transport, 2002**

References

Aalen, F. (1997), 'The challenge of change' in Aalen, F, Whelan, K. and Stout, M. (eds), *Atlas of the Irish rural landscape* (Cork University Press, Cork).

Atkins and Associates et al. (2004), *Regional Planning Guidelines for the Greater Dublin Area* (Dublin Regional Authority, Dublin).

Atkinson, R. (2001), The Emerging 'Urban Agenda' and the European Spatial Development Perspective: Towards an EU Urban Policy?, *European Planning Studies* 9, 385–406.

Banister, D. (1998), *Transport Policy and the Environment*, E & FN Spoon, London.

———, (1999), 'Planning more to travel less: land use and transport' *Town Planning Review* 70, 313–338.

Breathnach, P. (1998), 'Exploring the 'Celtic Tiger' Phenomenon: causes and consequences of Ireland's economic miracle' *European Urban and Regional Studies* 5, 305–316.

Breheny, M. (1992), 'The Contradictions of the Compact City: A Review'. In Breheny, M. (ed.) *Sustainable Development and Urban Form* (Pion Limited, London).

Brogan, J. et al. (1999), 'Ireland' in Ferguson, C.C. and Kasamas, H. (eds), *Risk Assessment for Contaminated Sites in Europe Vol. 2, Policy Frameworks* (LQM Press, Nottingham).

Burton, E. (2003), 'Housing for an Urban Renaissance: Implications for Social Equity' *Housing Studies* 18, 537–562.

Clarinet (2002), Brownfields and Redevelopment of Urban Areas: A report from the Contaminated Land Rehabilitation Network for Environmental Technologies. Federal Environment Agency, Austria.

Clinch, P., Convery, F. and Walsh, B. (2002), *After the Celtic Tiger, challenges ahead* (O'Brien Press, Dublin).

Commission of the European Communities (1990), *Green Paper on the Urban Environment* (CEC, Brussels).

Committee for Spatial Planning (1999), *European Spatial Development Perspective: Towards a balanced and sustainable development of the territory of the EU* (CEC, Luxembourg).

Counsell, D. (1998), 'Sustainable development and structure plans in England and Wales: a review of current practice' *Journal of Environmental Planning and Management* 41 (2), 177–194.

———, (1999), 'Making sustainable development operational' *Town and Country Planning* 68 (4), 131–133.

CSO (Central Statistics Office) (1979–2002), Small Area Population Statistics (SAPS) (Stationery Office, Dublin).

CSP (Committee for Spatial Planning) (1999), *European Spatial Development Perspective: Towards a balanced and sustainable development of the territory of the EU* (CEC, Luxembourg).

Davoudi, S. and Stead, D. (2002), 'Urban-Rural Relationships: An Introduction and Brief History' *Built Environment* 28, 269–277.

DEHLG (Department of the Environment, Heritage and Local Government) (2005), *Sustainable Rural Housing, Guidelines for Planning Authorities*.(Stationery Office, Dublin).

DOE (Department of the Environment) (1997), *Sustainable Development: A Strategy for Ireland* (Stationery Office, Dublin).

DOEHLG (Department of the Environment, Heritage and Local Government) DEHLG (Department of the Environment, Heritage and Local Government) (1994–2004), *Housing Statistics Bulletin* (Stationery Office, Dublin).

DOELG (Department of Environment and Local Government) (1999), *Residential Density: Guidelines for Planning Authorities* (Stationery Office, Dublin).

———, (2002), *The National Spatial Strategy 2002-2020: People, Places and Potential* (Stationery Office, Dublin).

DRD (Department of Regional Development) (2001), *Shaping our Future – Regional Development Strategy for Northern Ireland 2025* (DRD, Belfast).

Dublin Docklands Development Authority (2003), *Dublin Docklands Area Master Plan* (DDDA, Dublin).

Dublin Transportation Office (2003), *Submission on Property Rights to All-Party Oireachtas Committee on the Constitution* (All-Party Oireachtas Committee on the Constitution, Dublin).

Expert Group on the Urban Environment (2001), *Towards more sustainable urban land use* (Eurocities, Brussels).

Gallent, N., Shucksmith, M. and Tewdwr-Jones, M. (2003), *Housing in the European countryside, rural pressure and policy in Western Europe* (Routledge, London).

Gkartzios, M. and Scott. M. (2005), Urban-generated rural housing and evidence of counterurbanisation in the Dublin city-region, in Moore, N. and Scott, M. (eds) (2005), *Renewing Urban Communities: Environment, Citizenship and Sustainability in Ireland* (Ashgate, Aldershot).

Goodbody Economic Consultants, Department of Regional and Urban Planning (UCD) and The Faculty of the Built Environment (UWE) (2000), *The Role of Dublin in Europe*, A Report Prepared for the Spatial Planning Unit (Department of Environment and Local Government, Dublin).

Greer, J. and Murray (2003), 'Rethinking Rural Planning and Development in Northern Ireland'. In (eds) Greer, J. and Murray, M. *Rural Development and Planning in Northern Ireland* (IPA, Dublin).

Kratke, S. (2001), 'Strengthening the Polycentric Urban System in Europe: Conclusions from the ESDP' *European Planning Studies* 9, 106–116.

MacLaran, A. and Killen, J. (2002), 'The suburbanisation of office development in Dublin and its transport implications' *Journal of Irish Urban Studies*, 1, 21–36.

McEldowney, M., Ryley, T., Scott, M. and Smyth, A. (2005), *'Integrating land-use planning and transportation in Belfast: a new policy agenda for sustainable development?, Journal of Environmental Planning and Management 48 (4), 507–526.*

McEldowney, M., Scott, M. and Smyth, A. (2003), 'Integrating land-use planning and transportation: policy formulation in the Belfast Metropolitan Area' *Irish Geography* 36, 112–126.

McGrath, B. (1998),'Environmental sustainability and rural settlement growth in Ireland' *Town Planning Review* 3, 227–290.

McIntyre, O. (2003), 'Problems of liability for historical land contamination under Irish law', *Irish Planning and Environmental Law Journal* 10 (4), 112–118.

Mitchell, C.J.A. (2004), 'Making sense of counterurbanization' *Journal of Rural Studies* 20, 15–34.

Moore, N. and Scott, M. (eds) (2005), *Renewing Urban Communities: Environment, Citizenship and Sustainability in Ireland* (Ashgate, Aldershot).

Owens, S. (1992), 'Energy, Environmental Sustainability and Land Use Planning'. In Breheny, M. (ed.) *Sustainable Development and Urban Form* (Pion Limited, London).

Richardson, T. and Jensen, O. (2000), 'Discourses of Mobility and Polycentric Development: A Contested View of European Spatial Planning', *European Planning Studies* 8, 503–520.

de Roo, G.D. and Miller, D. (2000), *Compact Cities and Sustainable Urban Development* (Ashgate, Aldershot).

Spatial Planning Unit (2001), *Rural and urban roles – Irish spatial perspectives* (Dublin, DOELG).

Vigar, G. (2002), *The Politics of Mobility: Transport, the Environment and Mobility* (Spon Press, London).

Walsh, J. (2000), 'Dynamic Regional Development in the EU Periphery: Ireland in the 1990s'. In Shaw, D., Roberts, P. and J. Walsh (eds), *Regional Planning and Development in Europe* (Ashgate, Aldershot).

Williams, B. and Shiels, P. (2002), 'The Expansion of Dublin and the Policy Implications of Dispersal', *Journal of Irish Urban Studies* 1, 1–20.

Williams, B., Shiels, P. and Hughes, B. (2002), *Housing Supply and Urban Development Issues in the Greater Dublin Area* (Society of Chartered Surveyors, Dublin).

Chapter 11

Urban Design Principles and Local Environments in the Dublin-Belfast Corridor

Philip Geoghegan
University College, Dublin

Introduction

Even if the policy and tactical issues raised in previous chapters, such as transportation, land use and land delivery were solved, it is still possible that the resulting environment would be unattractive, due to inappropriate design on the ground. The improved speed and convenience of transportation connections to metropolitan destinations is likely to have an early and lasting impact on those settlements in the corridor. In particular, it might suburbanize their style.

Might the hundred-mile corridor landscape become a vast, uniform, suburban ribbon? Or, alternatively, could it become a succession of unique places, each one rooted in its own *genus loci*?

In this chapter we describe and characterize typical and distinctive settlement form and structure, ('morphology'), and then exemplify the changes, which are already having an impact on some of those settlements. We propose the need for pro-active development guidelines, intended to produce sustainable development, which would benefit in particular the less-developed, weaker rural areas adjacent to the corridor.

Responding to the Landscape

The visual impact of development within the corridor will have a lot to do with the 'urban edge', or (in other words), the impact of new buildings on the surrounding landscape and views from it. The edge currently is often formless, ragged, naked, obtrusive and overscaled. See *Figure 11.1, Example of the Urban Edge,* for a characteristic case. New settlements 'sit' badly in relationship to surrounding vegetation and topography. The boundaries of land use zones are usually conceived from the scale of a planning diagram downwards, rather from the small scale of the hedgerows, woodlands, walls, streams and topographical inflections upwards. Landscape architects should be playing a far more powerful role in the basic land use zoning.

The language of urban form and the imagery of building design in the corridor have been copied from the universal suburbia of the towns and cities, with repetitive villas, evenly spaced with common orientation, along straight, parallel roads of uniform width. Such 'estates' have nothing to do with any particular locality. See *Fig. 11.2 Example of the Suburban Style.*

Responding to the Diversity and Quality of Historic Settlement Form

Study of settlement morphologies, (the characterisation of their form and structure), is an analytical tool to establish the essential qualities and distinctiveness of a place. This information can be incorporated as an essential part of a future plan for a settlement. The morphological studies in County Louth and Fingal County show the desirability of gentle, sensitive growth in smaller settlements, and also indicate that this has become something of a luxury in the face of growing pressure for development in these corridor counties. Planning authorities have already embraced growth projections and policies which will accept a level of growth not experienced for over a century, and the pattern of growth has nothing to do with the distinctive qualities of the villages and towns concerned. The examples below offer some insight into the diversity of form and structure of the historic settlements and underline the importance of protecting their distinctive qualities whilst providing a framework for growth in the next decades.

In 1999, Louth County Council commissioned and published guidelines for development in towns, villages and the countryside. This demonstrated within a small county the rich diversity of settlement form, and allowed two observations to be made, firstly that the distinctive form should be protected, and consolidated; and secondly that new development around the periphery should recognize and reflect the particular morphology of the settlement, to maintain the local distinctiveness of place. The examples that follow in this section are extracted from the publication.

Whitestown, near Greenore on the Cooley peninsula, is a remarkable survival of an almost complete *'clachán' settlement,* with a fascinating distribution of space and building form. Simple themes and variations combine to produce a rich and consistent language for the settlement. Whilst an exact replication might be unfeasible in extending the settlement, the future layout should be informed by the unique historic pattern.

Carlingford, also on the Cooley peninsula is *a mediaeval Borough* with a tight urban structure deriving from its constricted size as a walled town, which contained its Main Street and market square. The tight plan and spectacular landscape surround suggests that incremental expansion would work if the pattern was continued in street form, or by distinguishing new areas by separation from the historic core – a greenway separation, perhaps. See *Figure 11.3, Mediaeval Street in Carlingford and Figure 11.4, New Dwellings in Carlingford.*

Baltray and Queensborough are two settlements close to each other, but with very different forms. Baltray is made up of small fishermen's cottages, mainly single storey with smallholding at the rear for growing vegetables. Queensborough is a *landlord estate village.* It has simply a long terrace with a diversity of houses, yet with a consistent treatment of boundaries together with a frontage line to the road, which creates a distinctive pattern. Enlargement would be achieved simply by elongation of the same pattern. See *Figure 11.5 Baltray and Figure 11.6, Queensborough.*

Collon is another estate village, this time created by an industrialist with cotton, linen and flax mills, and housing for six hundred employees. It is a *crossroads village,* improved in the late eighteenth and early nineteenth century to give a strong urban quality and, in its provision of social facilities, a model village quality. The traffic reduction with the extension of the M1 is an opportunity for regeneration of the centre and consolidation of its form.

Termonfeckin is the archetypical *Arcadian ideal landlord village* of individual houses in dispersed plots set in a landscape of trees, valley and river. The village is a landscape experience and a lesson in creating shelter in an exposed coastal area. There is a strong case for continuing the dominant landscape themes. See *Figure 11.8, Termonfeckin.*

There are many villages of comparable size and diversity of character within a few miles of the motorway in County Louth. The dilemma is how to succeed with development and expansion without compromising their distinctive qualities. By adding suburban forms, (such as standard terraced houses to Termonfeckin or semi-detached houses or bungalows to Carlingford), erosion of local distinctiveness is certain to arise.

However, the reality of a recently growing tidal wave of metropolis-induced development was bound to shake the complacency with which urban design work had previously progressed. Substantial housing estate applications made it seem that delicate attempts to maintain the structure and form of historic settlements were out of step with what was actually happening.

New Principles and the Compact Neighbourhood

In the cases just mentioned, it was preferable to expand the settlement on the basis of its historic form. In other cases, however, it was additionally necessary to envisage a completely new approach. Our experiences with Louth and Fingal suggested that there were two alternative approaches to settlement development; (a) the protection and consolidation of the existing settlement, and (b) the differentiation and innovation of the extended growth of secondary centres. See *Figure 11.9, Long Term Growth of Prosperous.*

As for the villages, it was seen that local distinctiveness should continue to be a major criterion, to maintain their attraction for both existing residents and new arrivals.

We (ICON Urban Design,) were asked to prepare the design and development guidelines for Fingal County Council. We also prepared case studies applying the guidelines to the towns of Balbriggan, Swords, Skerries, Rush and Lusk. It became clear to us that the planned growth around these towns was so large that a policy of consolidation would be insufficient. This growth would be more akin to a separate neighbourhood than an incremental extension. In response to this, compact/sustainable neighbourhood ideas were developed, accepting the change in scale implied by increasing densities beyond those already existing in the town.

Lusk is an attractive village in Fingal, now served by the new motorway and the railway. It is in the heart of Fingal commuter land. Lusk village has maintained a rural scale in its centre with many remaining traditional village houses surrounding the exceptional landmark Round Tower, with a mediaeval church tower nearby. However, designation of housing zones completely encircles the village in a doughnut shape of about 300 metres width, the completed development of which will increase the population to the scale of a town.

We concluded that newly-zoned lands could not reasonably 'consolidate' the village form and should be treated as a 'new town', suggesting that this is a new development phase in the urban morphology, distinct but well-connected. It should be seen as a mixed use neighbourhood. Our aim was to avoid high densities yet to achieve urban rather than village scale in an identifiable new band around the existing village. This could be seen as a way of strengthening the sense of place by protecting the core and differentiating the new scale of development. We tried to connect to the village through route systems and recognition of the powerful landmark centre in the layout, allowing the meandering forms of the village streets to influence the shaping of the route system in the scheme, and generating a new urban edge.

Balbriggan is a corridor town in Fingal, coastal in location, with a railway station and two miles from the motorway. There is extensive land rezoning between motorway and town. In this instance it was possible to emulate the existing grid pattern of streets, comfortably extending the connectivity of the town and its extension area within an overall layout form. Here, the distributor roads become main avenues with relatively high density, three and four storey frontages. Thus the town is extended by emulating its morphological structure whilst providing for new standards of housing and open space.

The population of **Manorhamilton** is no more than 1,000, but its form as a 17th century plantation settlement is compact and town-like. In common with most Irish settlements, its twentieth century growth has been an untidy sprawl along the main routes. The task was to consolidate a compact core whilst maintaining the town's powerful relationship with its surrounding landscape. These are seen to be the determining factors for a major new phase in the development of the town.

Prosperous is located at the edge of the fastest growing part of County Kildare, a village with strong attraction for young people working away from home, which has already grown substantially in the last twenty years, and is under continual pressure for further growth. As with most of the earlier examples, the plan is structured in two sections - 'Strengthening the existing structure and fabric', and 'Dealing with growth'- with the intention that the growth will serve as catalyst for sensitive protection of the historic core of the village.

The Millennium Business Park outside Naas on the motorway is within five miles of Prosperous, and it could be argued that growth would cater for people employed there. Thus, it was considered realistic to plan for long term growth, allowing for a strategic urban design approach, which would see Prosperous evolve from Village to a small Town in an incremental way by developing mixed use neighbourhoods around the edge. This also allowed for the integrated development of an open space greenway, which will serve existing as well as new development. Whilst the densities overall of the proposal are comparable with existing densities in the village, the form is manipulated to produce higher density housing areas with exceptionally good access to green recreational areas.

A Cautionary Tale

By way of conclusion, we will present a cautionary tale for those who may be sceptical about the need for guidelines, or indeed for any planning control at all. Dunleer, in County Louth, was originally a station on the Dublin-Belfast line and more recently, benefited from the privilege of not just one, but two access roads to the M1. This has made Dunleer a hot competitor among settlements along the corridor for development, not relating to its local needs but responding to the opportunity for exploitative development with easy access to Drogheda and Dundalk, and further afield to Dublin and Belfast. An Taisce started the ball rolling in Dunleer, in June 1999, when the local association sought help from UCD to produce a truly local area plan: that is, one generated in response to local demand. But the conflicting aspirations of sustainable development versus exploitative development of the corridor location took over and mired the work in controversy.

The Council then appointed independent consultants to make a Local Area Plan. The Council failed to agree on adoption of the Plan, however, and in 2003 asked its own planners to prepare a new Plan. Whereas the projected population growth in the second, plan was limited to (an already substantial) six year growth of 130 per cent to 2,300 persons, the third plan envisaged a population expansion to 5,292, despite its assertion that *"....... it is not the intention that Dunleer should develop solely as a dormitory town based on commuting to Dublin"*. By any standards, the growth was promoted at such a pace and scale as to overwhelm the present village structure. There was totally inadequate management and no design guidance on how to deliver a balanced community in that period. In addition to the increased housing provision there was a huge proposed increase of space between

Dunleer and the motorway with designation of 'industrial and employment generating uses'. Substantial opposition to this Plan resulted in a final outcome which was that the Council rejected the Council-prepared Plan and reverted to the earlier previous one.

Whilst this Dunleer Local Area Plan story is a simplification of a long, drawn out saga, with many steps and stages, it serves to show how powerful the forces for exploitative development have become along the corridor, and also how strong is the countervailing demand to protect both landscape and the characteristic urban form.

Guidelines on Changes to Settlement Form

A key conclusion to this chapter is the need to prepare planning and design guidelines, which should be a vehicle for communication and concensus-building between local planning authorities, local communities, builders and investors at a very local level. We argue that corridor development should not be only a large-scale and abstract affair, but equally a sensitive, detailed and local affair. The main points about design briefing are set out below.

- **Consolidation of Settlements**. There is a clear case for giving priority in time and phasing to the process of consolidating existing settlements. The prevalence of suburban sprawl around settlements in both Louth and Fingal is evident to all. Consolidation implies greater efficiency in the use of land within the actual boundaries of towns and villages, with adequate recognition of the connectivity of the settlement with its surrounding landscape.
- **Long Term Vision to allow for growth potential within a unified settlement structure.** Plans for consolidation of settlements are likely to follow the established morphology, albeit in an evolutionary way. A long term vision is more likely to deal with substantial growth and different lifestyle aspirations, including more private and public open space. Thus a change in form and structure may generate new morphological patterns to deal with different house-types and open space requirements. We used the expression 'a new urbanity' in the Fingal Guidelines to convey the fresh urban design approaches needed.
- **Sustainable Increases in Density.** The strongest case for increases in housing density would seem to be the demographic trends in Ireland, where household size is decreasing and the rate of household formation is increasing. Smaller households may be better suited to apartments and may have less need for private open space. Efficiency in the use of land is also a strong factor in the justification of higher densities.

    Our own exploration of densities in the quoted studies showed a rapidly declining benefit as densities were increased beyond a certain point. Open space and parking requirements used up more land as density rose, and this conspired to push the number of storeys upwards so as to meet density targets. Underground car parks and solid waste storage can lead to improved ground level environmental quality, but these measures are resisted by developers on cost grounds.

- **Better Localisation of Services** in small settlements, and promotion of small settlements as service areas off the motorway. Settlements such as Dunleer have an excellent opportunity to combine their growth with better services, patronized to some degree from the motorway.

- **Improvement of Accessibility to High Amenity Areas** from settlements close to the motorway. The location of high amenity areas in the corridor is strongly, though not exclusively, focussed around the centre of the corridor and along the coast. Increased accessibility will inevitably put new burdens on the protection and management of these areas as recreational resources for the settlements. There is a case for creating inter-regional country parks. This would show the continuity of the natural setting, and facilitate the creation of elegant 'urban edges'.

This chapter argues that design and development guidelines can promote the protection of settlement morphology and surrounding landscape, as well as integration between historic forms and new mixed use neighbourhoods. Sustainable development guidelines offer an opportunity to strengthen the identity of each settlement by providing an appropriate vocabulary. Flexible and adaptable, this promotes good urban environmental quality and socially successful places to live.

Figure 11.1   Example of the Urban Edge

Figure 11.2   Example of Suburban Style

Figure 11.3   Mediaeval Street in Carlingford

Figure 11.4   New Dwellings in Carlingford

Figure 11.5   Sketch of Baltray Fishing Village with mainly single storey cottages, originally all thatched

Figure 11.6   View of Queensborough across Boyne Estuary

Figure 11.7   Sketch of Carlingford

Figure 11.8   Termonfeckin – a designed village under a canopy of trees

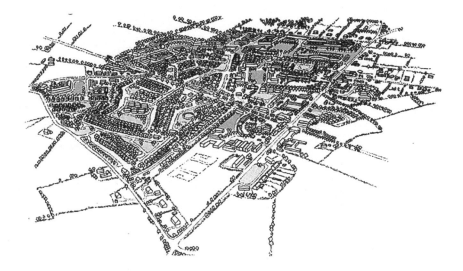

Figure 11.9   Prosperous, Co. Kildare – Image of the Long Term Growth Plan

Figure 11.10   Whitestown, Street View

References

ICON Architecture and Urban Design (2000), *Building Sensitively and Sustainably in County Louth* (Louth County Council, Dundalk).
————, Residential Development Guidelines (Draft) (2002) (Fingal County Council, Swords).

Chapter 12

Housing Markets and Cross-Border Integration

Chris Paris
University of Ulster

Introduction

This chapter explores some changes in the structure of cities, regions and housing systems on this island, in terms of population movement and housing development. My interest in this issue developed during a pilot study of changing structures of housing provision in the border counties. Paris and Robson (2001) set out to make sense of rapid changes which were easily noted by the most casual visitor: a building boom was under way where there had been little or no development for twenty years. Our pilot study concluded that it was only possible to understand changes in housing provision in the borders by situating a local study within an analysis of housing and urban-regional change in the whole island, and by reviewing housing and planning systems in the two jurisdictions. This chapter is a development of that earlier work, but with a focus on the topic of the 'Dublin Belfast corridor'. I review previous research on housing in the border counties and introduce new census analysis and interview data. This is put into a context of changing planning regimes and urban systems in the two jurisdictions, especially the Northern Ireland Regional Development Strategy (RDS) and the Republic's National Spatial Strategy (NSS).

Housing in The Border Counties

Earlier work by Paris and Robson (2001) on the changing housing situation in the border counties argued that de-militarization of the border had been followed by rapid changes in local housing markets. In contrast to the long bleak years of economic decline associated with conflict and the militarized border, there has been substantial inward investment on both sides of the border since the mid-1990s. The image of the border region changed from that of a depressed and militarized region with structural economic and social problems, to one of growing prosperity, de-militarized, with rapid growth in private housing investment. There were signs of increasing cross-border urban development, especially in the northwest, where Derry was overflowing into Co. Donegal and into the Dublin-Belfast corridor.

These changes are especially striking in new housing estates blossoming adjacent to the now-hidden sites of former military checkpoints. Those stark icons of a heavily militarized border have been replaced by new homes on all of the roads out of Derry, especially towards Muff, Killea or Bridgend in Co. Donegal. As a visitor moves nearer to the border along those same roads, passing many disused petrol stations on the way, new housing can be seen in the border 'villages' just inside Co. Donegal, although these expanding settlements are functionally suburbs with no connection to a 'rural' economy. The back gardens of many homes in these estates mark out the line of the border. Other new one-off detached homes are scattered along just about every road in the border zone beside Derry. These developments during the last five years have resulted in some of the fastest-growing electoral districts in the Republic of Ireland being located immediately across the border from Derry in Co. Donegal. The turnaround in the fortunes of the border villages has been dramatic, as a local journalist noted:

> Twenty years ago border villages such as Bridgend, Burt, Burnfoot, Muff, Killea, Carrigans and St Johnston were dying on their feet. Shops were closing, petrol stations lying abandoned, emigration was rife and in places like Burt, where the GAA was the social cement holding the community together, there were days when team mentors had trouble fielding a side such was the dearth of young men in the area. How that has changed … there have been huge housing developments bringing life back to the villages … the Elaghbeg Business Park in Bridgend, is testimony to the thriving local economy and is now home to a number of great home-grown businesses. Shops on the border have reopened and refurbished to look bigger and better than before for the deluge of customers … Today the border villages are a hive of activity. Just visit at any time, night or day. Thousands of cars pass through them daily, many availing of the first class petrol stations on offer. And on Lotto night, just join the queue. City centre Dublin could hardly be busier. Right along the border, new businesses are opening, from hairdressers to warehousing. Even Muff has a Chinese restaurant – a sure sign of economic well-being. The feel-good factor has changed the social landscape totally. (Anon. 2003: 14).

Even allowing for the hyperbole – nightlife in Muff and Killea may *occasionally* be less lively than in central Dublin – the local newspaper was reporting real changes in the Derry-Donegal border zone, most especially on the Donegal side. The author's evidence may have been anecdotal and impressionistic rather than data-based, but the article nicely illustrated local awareness of the spectacular change since the de-militarization of the border. As recently as five or six years ago, it was commonplace for motorists from the Republic to come to Northern Ireland for their cheaper petrol, but sweeping changes in exchange rates and growing differentials in fuel tax have put many Northern garage owners out of business (those, that is, who haven't had a bob each way by owning petrol stations on both sides of the border!) Some garages have been re-invented as car-washes, fast food outlets and/or shops, but many are simply mothballed, awaiting the next swing of the wheel of cross-border economic fortune.

Cheaper building land in Donegal – at the start of the boom, anyway – and a more permissive planning system, also fuelled the growth of Derry's suburbs across the border into Co. Donegal. The rapid growth of new housing estates on the Donegal side of the border has not been without one or two problems: not everything is always rosy, or, at least, not *smelling* of roses:

> Liquid sewage is threatening the health of some ... residents as it flows daily down the street of their new housing development. Children at play are being put at risk of disease in ... as filthy wastewater flows from a manhole due to an apparent blockage of the sewage system. The stench is worst in the evenings, particularly in warm weather, according to residents. But little has been done to rectify the disgusting problem and their frustration has bubbled to breaking point as they claim that neither Donegal County Council nor the developer will admit responsibility. (Cullen, 2003: 11).

Our pilot study of changing local housing systems in the border counties was put into a context of wider changes within the two jurisdictions. We focused on the impact of widespread metropolitan de-concentration, private sector housing booms and re-structuring of social housing systems (Paris and Robson 2001). We argued that there was both continuity and change within the border region with increasing market inter-relations between the two jurisdictions but continued differences in terms of legal and administrative structures. This paper develops the earlier analysis through a review of recent population and housing trends, deriving from analysis of official government housing statistics from both two jurisdictions and recently released census data.

For this chapter, I have set out to examine whether there is any discernible Dublin-Belfast 'corridor effect' on urban development. There clearly is a 'corridor' in terms of transport network between Dublin and Belfast: but is it a *development zone* or simply a *route between places* that are growing more generally? We explore evidence about processes of change in the next section of this chapter, which examines the issue of metropolitan de-concentration. Analysis of census data indicates strong population growth in *all* Dublin's outer commuter belt, without any distinctive concentration in the Dublin-Belfast corridor. Spatial population trends in Northern Ireland do not indicate any distinctive Belfast-Dublin component. It is argued, therefore, that there has been metropolitan de-concentration outwards *generally* from Dublin and Belfast with no particular emphasis on the corridor. This raises the question: 'what corridor?'

The next section of this chapter takes up the issue of changing systems of housing provision in Northern Ireland and the Republic. This section is based largely on official government housing statistics, but it also makes use of some recent census data. It is not possible at the time of writing to undertake comprehensive comparative analysis of changing tenure patterns, as the Central Statistics Office in the Republic had not released its census housing volume. Even so, housing construction data and data on sales of social housing together provide a basis for an analysis of the changing overall shape of the two housing systems. We can identify increasing private sector dominance, with some convergence in terms of the level of social housing provision. There are clear similarities in house price trends and it is argued that the increased rate of house price growth in Northern Ireland since the mid-1990s owes more to the boom in the Republic than the often-proclaimed impact of the so-called 'peace process' in Northern Ireland. There are grounds for arguing that private sector elements of the two housing systems are converging more rapidly than state and voluntary sectors, as the latter continue to be more constrained by political and administrative differences. This section also considers the finding of qualitative research designed to assess the changing significance of the border as a barrier between two housing systems. Paris and Robson (2001) conducted a series of semi-structured interviews with estate agents and public officials, primarily planners and housing managers, on both sides of the border during 1999 and 2000. These interviews highlighted the widespread incidence of new housing development throughout the border region, especially in the Northwest and the Dublin-Belfast corridor, and indicated that considerable cross-border investment activity was happening both by households for their own use and by investors. Further interviews were conducted with planning officials in June 2003 to examine whether there had been any significant changes since our first round of interviews. Planning officers in both jurisdictions reported extremely high volumes of work, with ever-increasing demand for new house building, and they saw few if any significant barriers to cross-border housing development.

Metropolitan De-concentration: What 'Corridor'?

Paris and Robson (2001) argued that it was useful to conceptualize urban development in both jurisdictions of Ireland as 'metropolitan de-concentration' taking the form of widespread low density suburban growth, both with new housing estates in formerly more tranquil locations and also with a high proportion of detached dwellings in the countryside. This argument was based on an analysis of government housing statistics that showed the spread of new housing construction ever further from metropolitan cores of Belfast and Dublin. The idea of metropolitan de-concentration is consistent with the notion of 'counter-urbanisation' (see, for example, Breheny 1995; Champion et al 1998) as well as analyses in the Northern Ireland Regional Development Strategy and the National Spatial Strategy in the Republic. We prefer the term 'metropolitan de-concentration' to identify low density spreading as an emergent urban and/or metropolitan form rather than a movement towards non-urban living.

Urban-Regional Change in the Two Jurisdictions

The publication of data from recent censuses in Northern Ireland (2001) and the Republic (2002) provides an opportunity to test the metropolitan de-concentration thesis. The postponement of the census in the Republic means that comparative data do not exist for precisely the same time period. Even so, my interest is in overall trends and broad orders of magnitude; the data are perfectly satisfactory for that level of analysis and are set out in a comparative fashion wherever possible.

We have developed an ad hoc regionalisation of the island of Ireland, partly following Horner (1993), but adapted in line with the availability of published data in the two jurisdictions and using census spatial categories for the first cut analysis. This comprises the regions identified in Table 12.1, within which the same logic is used to differentiate broad spatial zones. The regions as much as possible comprise units of approximately the same population size/share, *mutadis mutandis* the different scale of the two jurisdictions and the existence of more second tier cities within the Republic.

We identify three broad zones for each of the two dominant metropolitan regions. Firstly, the metropolitan cores comprising the cities of Dublin and Belfast, respectively contained 14 per cent and 18 per cent of the population of their jurisdiction in 1991. Secondly, inner metropolitan zones in both jurisdictions each had around 15 per cent of the population of the jurisdiction. Thirdly, outer metropolitan regions comprised 34 per cent of the population of Northern Ireland and, separated into Mid East and 'rest of Leinster', comprising around 21 per cent of the population of the Republic. We excluded Co. Louth from the 'rest of Leinster' for analytical purposes, as part of our focus is on the borders, and we have placed Louth within that category for other ongoing analyses. In any case, as is discussed below, this categorisation makes little if any difference to the analysis.

Given the small overall size of Northern Ireland, a large proportion of its physical area can be considered as Belfast's commuting zone. By way of contrast, a much larger share of the Republic's territory is clearly at present outside Dublin's commuter belt, both in less densely populated areas in the far west, south and northwest, or within the ambit of Horner's (1993) 'embryo city-regions'. Our fourth regional category comprises these secondary urban regions: Derry in Northern Ireland and the quartet of Cork, Limerick, Galway and Waterford in the Republic. For convenience, our analysis used data aggregated at the district council level for Derry and we combined each of the four Irish cities with their eponymous county (the use of city and county aggregates generates some boundary effects but they are trivial at the national level). The four Irish city regions together comprised around 24 per cent of the national population in 1991 whereas Derry only accounted for 6 per cent of the Northern Ireland population – this highlights the relative dominance of Belfast within the Northern Ireland space economy.

Our other regional categories are the 'border' zones in the two jurisdictions and the remainder, comprising the north coast in Northern Ireland and mainly midlands and western counties of the Republic. The border region was defined for convenience in the first cut analysis in terms of district council aggregates in Northern Ireland and counties in the Republic: accounting for about 10 per cent of the population of the Republic in 1991 but 20 per cent in Northern Ireland. Others may prefer different regional categories, but our categorisation makes sense functionally and in terms of available data.

Table 12.1 sets out data on regional population change in the two jurisdictions. Overall population increased by about 7 per cent in Northern Ireland and 11 per cent in the Republic. The availability of a 1996 census in the Republic, unlike Northern Ireland, shows that population growth increased most strongly after 1996: from under 3 per cent between 1991 and 1996 to 8 per cent between 1996 and 2002. Official estimates of annual population change suggest that there was no equivalent sharp increase in Northern Ireland.

Despite different overall rates of population growth, data in Table 12.1 show that regional population trends in the two jurisdictions were remarkably similar during the 1990s and confirm the metropolitan de-concentration thesis.

The population of the metropolitan city cores was static or falling. The Belfast City population fell by about 5,000 persons, or nearly 2 per cent overall between 1991 and 2001. The recorded population of Dublin City increased slightly between 1996 and 2002, but the percentage increase of 0.7 per cent was way below any other part of Leinster. The population of inner metropolitan areas in both metropolitan regions grew slightly. When net population change in the city and inner metropolitan zones of Dublin and Belfast is combined, both exhibited net declining share of about 1 per cent of the national population.

By way of contrast, net population growth was very strong in outer metropolitan regions, especially west of Dublin City where the Mid East region experienced overall growth of 27 per cent between 1991 and 2002. Population growth was especially strong between 1996 and 2002: counties Kildare and Meath both grew by over 21 per cent. Strong growth was also evident in other regional cities, especially Derry, which grew above the Northern Ireland average. The four regional cities in the Republic together held their own within the national hierarchy, with Galway's growth consistently the strongest throughout the 1990s.

Although time and space preclude extensive analysis here, our preliminary analysis shows that the population of central areas of regional cities also tended to be static or falling: implying that population moved out to new suburbs or detached homes in outer commuting rings. The population of Cork City, for example, fell by 3 per cent between 1996 and 2002 whereas Cork County grew by nearly 11 per cent. The 2002 census records similar processes of urban 'unpacking' at almost every spatial scale, right down to very small towns and villages in the countryside: de-concentration is going on *everywhere*!

Table 12.1   Regional Population Change, Northern Ireland & Republic of Ireland 1991–2001/2

Region	Census population (000)		Population change		Regional share of population change
NI regions[1]	1991	2001	Actual (000)	Percent	
Belfast City	279.2	277.4	-1.8	-0.6	-1.7
Inner Metro[2]	239.4	260.5	21.1	8.8	19.6
Outer Metro[3]	528.6	578.0	49.4	9.3	46.0
City of Derry	95.4	105.1	9.7	10.2	9.0
North Coast[4]	119.0	131.6	12.6	10.6	11.7
Other borders[5]	316.1	332.7	16.6	5.3	15.5
NI total	*1,577.8*	*1,685.3*	*107.4*	*6.8*	*100*
Republic regions[6]	**1991**	**(2002)**			
Dublin City	478.4	495.1	16.7	3.5	4.3
Inner metro[6]	546.9	627.5	80.6	14.7	20.6
Mid East[7]	325.3	412.7	87.4	26.9	22.3
Rest of Leinster[8]	419.6	468.3	48.7	11.6	12.4
City regions[9]	844.3	934.1	89.9	10.6	23.0
Borders[10]	348.2	374.2	26.0	7.5	6.6
Rest of state	563.0	605.4	42.4	7.5	10.8
Republic total	*3,525.7*	*3,917.3*	*391.6*	*11.1*	*100*

Sources: *Northern Ireland census 1991 & 2001: Republic of Ireland census 1991 and 2002.*

Notes:
[1]Carrickfergus, Castlereagh, Newtownabbey and North Down. [2]Antrim, Ards, Ballymena, Banbridge, Cookstown, Craigavon, Down, Larne, Lisburn and Magherafelt. [3]Ballymoney, Coleraine, Limavady, Moyle. [4]Armagh, Dungannon, Fermanagh, Newry & Mourne, Omagh and Strabane. [5]Source: Irish censuses 1991 & 2002. [6]Dun Laoghaire-Rathdown, Fingal and South Dublin. [7]Kildare, Meath, Wicklow. [8]Excluding Co. Louth (now in Border RA) and Co. Sligo (counted within Rest of state). [9]Cork, Limerick Galway and Waterford (cities and counties). [10]Including County Sligo (formally within Borders RA).

Table 12.1 shows strong population growth along the north coast of Northern Ireland, but a lower rate of population growth in the border districts, on both sides of the border. This is partly consistent with new housing developments, although the rate of new building in both areas of Northern Ireland, on a proportional basis, is higher than the rate of population growth. That largely reflects falling average household size and thus more households per 1,000 of the population. The higher rate of new house building in the Northern Ireland border districts and north coast is partly explained by differential rates of household formation, with a younger population in the west and south of Northern Ireland, and also by the growth of second homes in coastal and areas and around the Fermanagh lakes. In population terms, though, it is clear from Table 12.1 that the rate of population growth in both parts of the border region was below the average rate of population growth within the respective jurisdictions. Finally, Table 12.1 shows that the rate of population growth in other parts of the Republic was similar to that of the border region: well below the national average.

Implications for the Dublin-Belfast Corridor

What does this analysis imply for the Dublin-Belfast corridor? Firstly, it suggests that any observable growth in the corridor is part of a wider process of metropolitan expansion rather than any distinctive focus of growth in itself. Indeed, the strongest population growth in the Republic was to the west rather than north of Dublin. Outer metropolitan regions in both jurisdictions gained as metropolitan cores lost population in relative terms. There were many variations within the inner two zones of Dublin: Fingal exhibited very strong growth between 1996 and 2002 (17 per cent), South Dublin (9.7 per cent) was also above the national average but Dun Laoghaire-Rathdown was stagnant at only 0.7 per cent. There were also strong variations within the mid east between 1996 and 2002, with Kildare and Meath over 21 per cent but Wicklow lagging somewhat at 11.7 per cent. Within the rest of Leinster, the populations of Westmeath (13.8 per cent), Wexford (11.7 per cent) and Laoighis (10.9 per cent) all grew faster than Louth (10.5 per cent). Indeed, most growth in Co. Lough was in southern part of the county, in and around Drogheda, with 17–18 per cent population growth between 1996 and 2002, compared to around 7 per cent in Dundalk (urban and rural) and Ardee rural. In similar vein, the growth of population in Newry and Mourne district was below that of other regional councils. For example, the population of Ards increased by 25 per cent between 1981 and 2001 and Carrickfergus and Lisburn grew by over 30 per cent. Banbridge, however, which is next in line from Newry and Mourne on 'the corridor', grew strongly (40 per cent between 1981 and 2001).

Rates of population increase were lower outside the main rings of rapid growth extending from Belfast and Dublin. A quick overview of household change, also by regions, confirms that there is little variation between the rates of regional population and household change. This is not surprising. The overall evidence so far, therefore, cautions against any belief that there has been a distinctive growth corridor between Dublin and Belfast. What appears to have been happening is that waves of outward development from the two metropolitan cores are beginning to coalescence near the border. But this metropolitan de-concentration is happening more strongly to the west of Dublin and all round the horseshoe-shaped motorway network in and to the NW and SE of Belfast.

Geographers who are still prepared to take note of physical elements of urban-regional landscapes might also pay regard to the barrier of the Wicklow mountains which constrain Dublin to the south and southeast, as well as the ring of mountains around Belfast City, and Lough Neagh to its west. (Of course, such barriers are partly social as well as physical through the implementation of planning policies to restrict development: witness new homes on steep mountain sides in Hong Kong or estates running across once beautiful hillsides in Letterkenny). Commuting traffic from around the Belfast regional motorway system, with ever-increasing distances to travel, routinely grinds to a crawl on Belfast's Westlink. There is no point referring to any specific road blockage in Dublin: despite greatly improved motorways and trunk roads, the city seems to be one large traffic jam verging on the edge of gridlock.

Changing Demography: Changing Places

Recently released census data, particularly for the Republic, allow us to take this analysis a little further. Table 12.2 shows a typology of areas based upon different combinations of demographic change. We have used a conventional measure of the concentration of change: location quotients. Location quotients show the variation between changes in particular localities measured against the average for that phenomenon throughout the whole area (i.e. the rate of change within the sub-region divided by the rate of change for the whole region). If the rate of change in area X is the same as for the region or country as a whole, the location quotient (LQ) is 1. Areas with very high incidence of the phenomenon in question will have LQs of 2 or more; conversely, areas with a low incidence have LQs below 1.

On that basis, it is possible to identify distinctively different kinds of area based on systematic variations in terms of natural increase and relative rates of migration gain and/or loss. We have so far only undertaken preliminary analysis for data in the Republic, and on the basis of simple cross-tabulations, but believe that this is worth exploring more generally and systematically using multi-variate analysis. Four distinctive kinds of area can be identified on the basis of our first cut analysis.

- Areas of high natural increase (excess of births over deaths).
- Areas of very low levels of natural increase (excess of deaths over births).
- Areas with high levels of net migration gain.
- Areas with net migration loss or relatively low levels of net gain

The first kind of area, which we could term 'breeding grounds', are residential inner metropolitan South Dublin and Fingal and the surging population growth zone in Counties Kildare, Meath and Wicklow. Birth rates are very high, especially in the Mid East with its high proportion of young households: often first time home purchasers in new suburban estates. Natural increase is very strong in these areas, though rates of net in-migration vary enormously between inner metropolitan and outer urban examples. Death rates in the 'breeding grounds' are very low, especially when compared to the second kind of area, characterized by low levels of natural increase.

Table 12.2   Republic of Ireland Typology of Components of Population Change, 1996–2002

County/City	Average annual rate per 1,000 of average population			
	Births	**Deaths**	**Natural increase**	**Net migration (est.)**
1. 'Breeding grounds': highest levels of natural increase				
South Dublin	17.4	3.6	13.8	1.5
Fingal	16.6	4.2	12.4	13.7
Kildare	17.7	5.4	12.3	20.0
Meath	14.9	6.1	8.8	24.4
Wicklow	15.9	7.7	8.1	10.3
2. 'Ageing grounds': lowest levels of natural increase				
Leitrim	11.4	13.5	-2.1	7.0
Roscommon	10.2	11.2	-1.0	6.7
Mayo	12.5	11.7	0.7	7.9
Kerry	12.3	10.4	2.0	6.1
Sligo	12.9	10.2	2.8	4.1
3. 'Migration magnets': highest levels of net migration gain				
Meath	14.9	6.1	8.8	24.4
Kildare	17.7	5.4	12.3	20.0
Galway City	13.4	5.4	8.1	15.0
Westmeath	15.5	8.9	6.5	14.9
Wexford	14.8	8.5	6.2	12.1
4. 'Net migration losers': net migration loss or lowest levels of migration gain.				
Cork City	13.2	10.1	3.2	-8.3
DunLaoghaire-Rathdown	13.6	7.8	5.9	-4.7
Limerick City	16.6	10.4	6.2	0.1
Waterford City	13.7	9.7	4.0	0.5
Dublin City	13.7	9.7	4.0	0.5
State	14.3	8.2	6.1	6.8

Source: *Republic of Ireland census 2002*

Areas of low or even negative natural increase, which we might term 'ageing grounds', are typically in the west of Ireland. Counties Leitrim, Roscommon, Mayo, Kerry and Sligo had very low birth rates, high death rates and, in the first two cases, negative natural increase with a surplus of deaths over births. Net migration gain was around or slightly below the national average. Although they did not feature in the top five listed in Table 12.2, some inner city areas also exhibit a low rate of natural increase, especially Cork City, as well as the inner areas smaller towns including Cavan and Monaghan.

The third type of area in this typology, the 'migration magnets', had the highest net migration gain between 1996 and 2002. Like the first category, these were mainly ex-urban Dublin or suburban zones of other metropolitan cores but also Galway City. Our fourth type of area comprises 'migration losers': mainly metropolitan cores, especially Cork, inner Dublin and Limerick. Natural increase tended to be low and in some cases there was a very high net migration outflow.

These relations are explored in another way in Table 12.3, which ranks LQs for all counties and cities on the basis of relative shares of net population change between 1996 and 2002. Areas with high LQs were sites of above average concentration of population growth. Table 12.3 highlights the very high concentration of net population growth, in relative terms, in the Dublin metropolitan region. The rank placing of Co. Louth is of significance here: firmly among the second tier of net gainers, but not near the level of top ranking Meath, Kildare and Fingal. The bottom ranking places were primarily inner metropolitan cores (Cork and inner Dublin) and 'rural' counties in the BMW zone (Borders, Midland and West, that is, not the Bavarian Motor Company.) There are many minor boundary effects on the typologies in Tables 12.2 and 12.3 and fine-tuning of spatial units of aggregation, with multi-variate analysis may generate different typologies. These tables together, however, usefully demonstrate the impact of population growth and movement urban-regional systems at the national level.

Implications for Planning and Housing Markets

We have already argued that there was no identifiable Dublin-Belfast 'corridor' effect as such on urban development. But we can go further: the rapid outward growth of Irish cities, often at low densities, stands in sharp contrast to the aspirations and objectives of the recent turn in spatial planning in both jurisdictions. The aspiration in the Northern Ireland RDS to achieve 60 per cent of new development on brownfield sites implies an *extraordinary* reversal of previous trends. So, too, does the aspiration in the NSS to achieve more compact and 'sustainable' future urban development.

Recent trends may not be irreversible. We know that cities and regions are dynamic and that net migration outcomes always represent the residual of many larger flows. Past patterns of development, therefore, might not be repeated. What is clear, however, is that the main tendency in Irish urban development in the 1990s was metropolitan de-concentration: suburbanisation and scattered low-density urban forms. If citizens had wanted more compact cities and living forms, then development on this island might have been rather different in the 1990s. The proposed strategies in the Republic and Northern Ireland aim to counter the dominant urban-regional development trends of the last 10 years. This may prove difficult to accomplish and will generate new forms of political mobilisation opposing attempts to increase urban densities. The proposed policies may result in reduced housing land supply and house price inflation, thus generating even more problems for first home buyers.

Housing Market Booms

The 1990s building boom, of course, was not restricted to the borders but has been a noted feature of the Republic's Celtic Tiger economy. Demand for new housing surged through a combination of economic growth, population growth and faster increase in households numbers (see Table 12.4) Population growth in the Republic was also fuelled by a shift from net out-migration in the late 1980s to high levels of net in-migration, especially after 1995. Total population growth in the Republic between 1991 and 2002 amounted to some 391,000 persons: more than treble the 1991 population of Cork City. The 2002 census estimated net immigration of 153,000 between 1996 and 2002. Natural increase and net in-migration together resulted in total population growth of more than in 290,000 in the Republic between 1996 and 2002 alone. By way of contrast, the Northern Ireland census indicated net out-migration from Northern Ireland of around 4,000 between 1991 and 2001, thus generating slower overall population growth than the Republic (some of this net out-migration may have included migrants to the Republic.)

Growth in the number of households was much more rapid than population growth in both jurisdictions, especially in the Republic where the number of households increased by over 26 per cent between 1991 and 2002. Even with its slower overall population growth, Northern Ireland had household growth of over 18 per cent. Surging growth in the number of households, together with the booming economy, strong employment growth, demand for second homes and falling levels of unemployment, especially in the Republic, resulted in massive increases in private house building in the 1990s. Private starts in the Republic grew from around 16,000 a year in the late 1980s to over 50,000 in 2002 (see Table 12.6) There was slower growth in house building in Northern Ireland, but private starts still grew from around 6,000 to over 10,000 a year in the same period.

Despite greatly increased production, house prices grew strongly in the 1990s especially in the Republic where new and second hand home prices doubled between 1994 and 1998. Despite a dip in 2001, house prices doubled again between 1998 and 2002. The strongest house price growth was in Dublin, but prices increased throughout the country for all types of dwellings. House price increases were steady rather than spectacular in Northern Ireland, though the rate of increase accelerated after 1996, especially in Belfast. Many commentators have related Northern Ireland house price growth to the 'peace process', but I am sure it is more a secondary effect of the boom in the Republic.

**Table 12.3 Republic of Ireland, Shares of Population Change 1996–2002:
Location Quotients**

County or City	Regional Authority	Functional region	LQ
Meath	Mid-East	Dublin metro region	2.8
Kildare	Mid-East	Dublin metro region	2.7
Fingal	Dublin	Dublin metro region	2.1
Galway City	West	Other metro region (core)	1.9
Westmeath	Midland	Dublin metro region	1.7
Wicklow	Mid-East	Dublin metro region	1.5
Wexford	South-East	Outer Dublin metro region	1.5
Laoighis	Midland	Outer Dublin metro region	1.4
Carlow	South-East	Outer Dublin metro region	1.3
Louth	Border	Outer Dublin metro region	1.3
Cork County	South-West	Other metro region (suburbs)	1.3
South Dublin	Dublin	Dublin metro region	1.2
Clare	Mid-West	BMW (& other metro suburbs)	1.2
Waterford County	South-East	Other metro region (suburbs)	1.2
Galway County	West	Other metro region (suburbs)	1.1
Offaly	Midland	BMW non-metro	1.0
Limerick County	Mid-West	Other metro region (suburbs)	0.9
Cavan	Border	BMW non-metro	0.8
Kilkenny	South-East	South non-metro	0.8
Mayo	West	BMW non-metro	0.7
Tipperary North	Mid-West	BMW non-metro	0.7
Donegal	Border	BMW non-metro	0.7
Kerry	South-West	BMW non-metro	0.6
Tipperary South	South-East	South non-metro	0.6
Waterford City	South-East	Other metro region (core)	0.6
Limerick City	Mid-West	Other metro region (core)	0.5
Sligo	Border	BMW non-metro	0.5
Monaghan	Border	BMW non-metro	0.4
Roscommon	West	BMW non-metro	0.4
Leitrim	Border	BMW non-metro	0.4
Longford	Midland	BMW non-metro	0.4
Dublin City	Dublin	Dublin metro region (core)	0.3
Dun Laoghaire-Rathdown	Dublin	Dublin metro region (core)	0.1
Cork City	South-West	Other metro region (core)	-0.4

Source: *Republic of Ireland Census 2002*

Changing Social Housing Sectors

The rate of new social housing construction was much less than in the booming private housing sector (see Table 12.6). I estimate that around 420,000 private dwellings were constructed in the Republic between 1991 and 2002 (including second homes and holiday lets) but only 38,000 additional council dwellings were constructed or acquired, amounting to about 8 per cent of all new dwelling units. The ratio of new social housing to private housing was higher in Northern Ireland: around 20 per cent of the total of about 102,000 dwellings constructed between 1991 and 2002.

Table 12.4   Persons and Households, Northern Ireland and Republic of Ireland 1991-2002

	1991	2001/2	Change 1991-2001/2	
	(000)		Actual	Percent
All persons: Republic of Ireland	3,525.7	3,917.3	391.6	11.1
All persons: Northern Ireland	1,577.8	1,685.3	107.4	6.8
Persons not in households: Republic of Ireland	92.7	107.7	15.0	16.2
Persons not in households: Northern Ireland	23.3	24.3	1.0	4.1
Persons in households: Republic of Ireland	3,433.0	3,791.3	358.3	10.4
Persons in households: Northern Ireland	1,554.5	1,661.7	96.4	18.2
Households: Republic of Ireland	1,019.7	1,288.0	268.2	26.3
Households: Northern Ireland	530.4	626.7	96.3	18.2
Average household size: Republic of Ireland	3.37	2.94	n.a.	n.a.
Average household size: Northern Ireland	2.93	2.65	n.a.	n.a.

Sources: *1991 census in Northern Ireland & the Republic; 2001 census in Northern Ireland and 2002 census in the Republic.*

The overall stock of social housing changed much more significantly in Northern Ireland than in the Republic, because Housing Executive sales greatly exceeded new construction by the Housing Executive and housing associations combined. The effect was to reduce the absolute size of the social housing sector by over 30,000 dwellings, reducing its share from 29 per cent of households in 1991 to 19 per cent in 2001. Home ownership increased from 62 per cent of households to 70 per cent in 2001.

Table 12.5 shows how these changes worked out in the border counties. The social housing stock fell in all of the Northern border district council areas, with net sales from 12 per cent of the 1991 Housing Executive stock in Derry to over 28 per cent in Armagh and Newry and Mourne. The volume of sales to tenants was much lower in the Republic border counties, so that the council stock increased, albeit not as fast as rates of new private sector construction. The net effect was to reduce the level of social housing on the northern side of the border, bringing it nearer to the lower level in the Republic, and substantially reducing the overall level of social housing in the border region.

Changing Regional Tenure Distributions

Irish housing systems became more 'private' during the 1990s as a result of the combination of the private building boom, the sale of public housing and weak growth of other social housing. As the overall housing stock in both jurisdictions became more dominated by home ownership, there was also a change in the regional distribution of social housing.

Table 12.6 shows net changes in the housing stocks in the two jurisdictions and changing regional distributions of the housing stock. It includes a calculation of the net change in the social housing sectors, based on data on new housing construction, disaggregated by sectors, and on sales of Housing Executive in Northern Ireland and council dwellings in the Republic. The measure of net 'private gain' is relatively crude, as it cannot include other social housing in the Republic. Even so, the orders of magnitude are sufficiently great to identify real variations.

Firstly, social housing in Northern Ireland became more concentrated in metropolitan areas. Housing Executive sales were stronger outside Belfast and Derry, but social housing construction, after 1999 almost exclusively by housing associations, was concentrated in Belfast. Thus the overall housing system became more 'private', but this was even more marked in the outer metropolitan area and border districts (apart from Derry). Sales of Housing Executive dwellings picked up in the late 1990s in areas of previously low sales, including Belfast and Derry, and the relative balance would change between regions if sales continued at those rates. The likely introduction of a sales scheme for housing associations following the 2003 Northern Ireland Housing Order may also affect this picture.

There was less socio-spatial change in social housing provision in the Republic in the 1990s, with it's a smaller, spatially more concentrated council sector. Sales continued, but with modest overall little growth social supply. The table shows that Dublin experienced most sales during the 1990s, but that was because the very high level of sales in the late 1980s in other parts of the Republic took longer to get through the system in Dublin.

Table 12.5   Social Housing Stock, Border Counties and Districts, 1991–2002/3

		Changes to social stock 1991-2002	
Republic of Ireland	**Council stock 1991**	**Actual**	**% 1991 stock**
Co. Cavan	784	643	82
Co. Donegal	2290	1650	72
Co. Leitrim	472	332	70
Co. Louth	2746	303	11
Co. Monaghan	795	344	43
Border Counties	7087	3272	46
RoI total	*98929*	*13727*	*14*
Northern Ireland	**NIHE Stock 1991**	**Actual**	**% 1991 HE stock**
Armagh	4013	-1124	-28
Derry	12365	-1533	-12
Dungannon	3574	-891	-25
Fermanagh	4096	-1068	-26
Newry & Mourne	7380	-2143	-29
Omagh	3476	-747	-21
Strabane	4090	-807	-20
Border districts	38994	-8313	-21
NI total	*160674*	*-27480*	*-17*

Sources: *Northern Ireland censuses 1991 and 2001; Republic of Ireland census 1991 and 2002; government annual housing statistics in both jurisdictions.*

Secondly, Table 12.6 shows that the pattern of new building echoed population change during the 1990s. This is not surprising, but a close inspection of data sets on house building and population change shows that some areas, notably North Donegal, had high rates of new building but little or no recorded net population increase. A high proportion of construction in such areas has been for second homes and holiday accommodation (stimulated in some coastal towns, such as Bundoran, by tax breaks encourage the construction of holiday accommodation).

The strongest rates of new private construction, relative to the 1991 population, were in outer metropolitan areas of Dublin and Belfast, with correspondingly lower rates of building in core and inner metropolitan areas. In absolute terms, however, there was a higher level of construction in Dublin core and inner metro, though their shares fell in the 1990s and appeared set to continue to fall. The volume of new private construction in the city regions in both jurisdictions tended to match their overall population share in 1991.

Only 4 per cent of new housing construction in Northern Ireland the 1990s was within Belfast City, despite the much-publicised apartment boom of the late 1990s. Belfast and the inner metropolitan area contained 37 per cent of the 1991 housing stock, but had only 19 per cent of new housing starts in the 1990s. By way of contrast, the 'other borders' only contained 18 per cent of the 1991 stock but had 24 per cent of starts between 1990 and 2001/2. The outer metropolitan zone, approximating to the wider Belfast metropolitan labour market, contained around 39 per cent of new construction compared to 33 per cent of the 1991 stock.

These developments suggest that there has been an increase in commuting or an outward movement of jobs, or elements of both. The impact of these developments on the border region varied in proportion to distance from metropolitan cores, but appears to be moving outward since the late 1990s on both sides of the border; there was a surge of new private housing starts in Dungannon after 1996 and County Louth completions increased significantly throughout the period.

Implications for the Dublin-Belfast corridor

With regard to the Dublin-Belfast corridor and the border counties, therefore, the evidence in Table 12.6 is mixed. It shows that the growth in new private housing construction was much stronger on the northern side of the border. The borders generally were areas of growing private housing construction, but growth on the Republic side border counties was less rapid than adjacent outer metropolitan zones, especially in comparison to the rest of Leinster. Again, therefore, there is limited evidence of a 'corridor' effect in terms of new private housing construction. Although 'other borders' in Northern Ireland did have high levels of new housing construction, so too did the North Coast and outer metropolitan areas.

Footnotes to Table 12.6 (on next page)

Notes:

1. Private gain in NI = private starts + NIHE sales – (all social starts). No data on subsequent sales of ex–NIHE dwellings or demolitions &/or conversions. Private gain in Republic = private starts + council sales – (council starts & acquisitions). (No data on demolitions/conversions subsequent sales of ex-council dwellings or demolitions &/or conversions).
2. 1991 stock based on Irish census vol. 10 Housing table 26A: permanent private housing units only, thus lower than total households.

Table 12.6 Housing Stock Change, Northern Ireland and the Republic of Ireland 1991–2002

	1991 stock		Stock change 1991 to 2001 (Northern Ireland)/2002 (Republic of Ireland)									
			Private starts		Social starts		Social sales		Net social change		'Private gain'[1]	
	(000)	%	(000)	%	(000)	%	(000)	%	(000)	%	(000)	%
Northern Ireland												
Belfast City	117.3	21	3.6	4	6.4	31	7.8	15	-1.4	4	5.0	5
Inner metro	91.9	16	12.0	15	1.7	8	5.6	11	-3.9	12	15.9	15
Outer metro	185.2	33	32.1	39	5.4	26	18.1	34	-12.7	39	44.8	39
North Coast	42.4	7	10.0	12	0.9	4	5.0	9	-4.1	13	14.1	12
City of Derry	29.7	5	4.4	5	2.8	14	4.4	8	-1.6	5	6.0	5
Other borders	102.6	18	19.4	24	3.3	16	12.2	23	-8.9	27	28.3	24
Total	*569.1*	*100*	*81.5*	*100*	*20.5*	*100*	*53.1*	*100*	*-32.6*	*100*	*114.1*	*100*
			Private starts		Council adds		Councils sales		Net council change		'Private gain'	
			(000)	%	(000)	%	(000)	%	(000)	%	(000)	%
Republic of Ireland[2]												
Dublin City	158.9	16	38.0	9	5.3	14	5.5	28	-0.2	-1	38.2	10
Inner metro	151.2	15	64.3	15	3.2	8	2.3	12	0.9	5	63.4	16
Mid east	88.9	9	49.2	12	3.7	10	1.1	6	2.6	14	46.6	12
Rest of Leinster	115.9	11	51.2	12	5.6	15	2.3	12	3.3	18	47.9	12
City regions	240.9	24	104.3	25	8.8	23	3.5	18	5.3	29	99.0	25
Borders	99.6	10	44.3	11	6.0	16	2.1	11	3.9	21	40.4	10
Rest of state	164.2	16	66.7	16	5.4	14	3.0	15	2.4	13	64.3	16
Total	*1,019.7*	*100*	*418.0*	*100*	*38.0*	*100*	*19.7*	*100*	*18.3*	*100*	*399.7*	*100*

Sources: *1991 stock – censuses in Northern Ireland and Republic of Ireland and government housing statistics in both jurisdiction*

Cross-Border Housing Market Integration

There is also evidence of growing cross-border housing market developments. We have already noted Derry's suburban extension into Co. Donegal. Our pilot study (Paris and Robson 2001) concluded that there are signs that the significance of the border as a barrier within housing markets was declining at an accelerating rate with considerable growth in cross-border purchase of second homes, extensive cross-border investment activity, especially in apartment and resort sub-markets. We suggested that outward extensions of the commuting zones of both Dublin and Belfast were coalescing within the Dublin-Belfast corridor and beginning to move westwards along either side of the border. We carried out a series of semi-structured interviews with government officials (planning officers and housing managers) and estate agents on both sides of the border during 1999/2000 and then again, but only with planning officers, in summer 2003. The aim was to assess their understanding of major trends in housing demand and supply in the border region.

During 1999/2000, the most significant trend in the housing market identified in the semi-structured interviews was increasing demand for new housing and increase in planning permission in the southern border counties. In Donegal alone, an increase of 300 per cent in planning applications was recorded by planning officials, with 'substantial' increases being noted in Monaghan. In the 'Northern' border counties there were considerable increases in the development of apartment buildings especially in Derry and Enniskillen with housing being the main focus of investment in Strabane, a town usually noted for its depressed state. One possible explanation for this could be the town's proximity to and gain from growth in the Donegal economy, in addition to a rapidly expanding professional sector in Derry. In Newry, at the other end of the border, housing prices increased 'dramatically'; this, according to a local estate agent, was influenced by growth in investment activity by both local and outside investors. Estate agents in Derry pointed to southern border villages such as Muff, Killea and Bridgend as catchment areas for an increasing Derry housing market. Interestingly, Derry was reported to have become an attractive area for speculation from outside investors, mainly from the Republic, in particular those seeking to become involved in the rental market. One estate agent estimated that 50 per cent of the total investment in some new projects came from investors based in the Republic.

Expanding development in counties Louth and Monaghan was considered by planners to be due in part to the increase in job opportunities associated with the introduction of multi-national corporations such as Xerox in Dundalk. As well, government officials and estate agents suggested that much growth was a result of more long-distance commuting. In Leitrim and in other border counties planners argued that growth was due to returning migrants, the potential offered by EU support for road and communication infrastructure, and competitive housing prices for Dublin commuters. Planning officials also reported an increase in the size of new houses, especially in Monaghan and Leitrim.

Conflicting views were revealed during the 1999/2000 interviews regarding the effect of the border on housing decisions by homebuyers, developers and builders. Many respondents felt that the border was no longer the contentious issue that it may have been before the Good Friday agreement. Planners and housing officials on both sides of the border were concerned with the practical and concrete matters before them in terms of planning applications and management of existing housing stock. Estate agents, on the other hand, were strongly aware of the potential for development of the changing political and economic conditions of the border, in particular during 2000 in the differences between the Irish punt and sterling. One Derry-based agent viewed the developments taking place on the Donegal side of the border as a logical extension of the city of Derry stretching into its natural hinterland. In this instance, both the developer and the builder were based in Derry and both had long records of activity on either side of the border.

The estate agents also considered in 1999/2000 that there was extensive and growing cross-border investment activity both by home owners and investors, especially in counties Donegal and Leitrim and the district council areas of Derry and Newry and Mourne. Estate agents operating in Donegal and Leitrim noted significant increases in incoming investment into housing, especially apartment and holiday homes. Much of this interest was considered to stem from the response to the possibility of a long-term solution to the political problems after the Good Friday Agreement:

Matters relating to second homes, retirement development and long-distance commuting on border housing systems were somewhat more problematic for all of officials involved in planning and housing. Whilst most agreed that the border was becoming less of a barrier, the question of second homes was a matter of concern for some, in particular Donegal County Council, and to a lesser extent the northern county of Fermanagh, especially the lakeland area (where new holiday/second home apartments were being marketed and managed by Belfast-based, rather than local estate agents). Second home developments, as well as resort developments, were having a much greater impact on Co. Donegal. Planners and estate agents suggested that most of the interest in second homes originated in Belfast, although, in this case much of the management of such developments remained firmly fixed within the local housing suppliers. Major national developers as well as local developers were active in this area of development.

On the northern side of the border, one Derry-based estate agent was principally involved during 2000 in the first home market and he was acutely aware of issues surrounding the levels of commuting from Donegal to Derry. But many of those on other parts of the border would not see such developments in quite the same way. After all, the Derry city boundary on the west bank of the river Foyle is the border with the county of Donegal in the Irish Republic. In some locations, major public housing estates are a mere few hundred yards from the border.

Many of the same issues were explored during the return interviews in summer 2003. We were struck by the continued intensity of the housing boom and the pressure that this put on local planning officials in both jurisdictions. As during the earlier round of interviews, we were also struck by the limited knowledge that local planners had of a range of issues, especially overall demographic trends in their areas of operation, and who were the main purchasers of newly constructed housing. Most responses to questions about in-migration, the growth of local population, the extent of retirement in-migration, whether there was a change in patterns of commuting, house price increases and the incidence of second home development were answered anecdotally or to the effect that 'we don't really know about that'.

Planners were very well aware, however, which parts of their areas were experiencing most growth: Cavan town; southern parts of Monaghan; the main towns in Donegal (especially Letterkenny), as well as coastal areas and the border zone adjacent to Derry; Dundalk hinterland, the coast and areas by the new motorway in Louth; 'everywhere' that there was zoned land in Derry; and so on. They were also well aware of the kinds of new dwellings being built: mainly large detached homes but an increasing amount of higher density homes in some areas, including both Cavan and Derry. They also knew who was doing most of the housing development in their areas and they held considered views about the effects of the border on local housing markets. There was universal agreement that the border did not present any significant barrier to house builders and developers. In particular, planners in Republic border counties reported increases in 'Northern' developers and builders operating in their areas. In Derry, as well, planners noted movement in both directions, with builders from the Republic operating locally and local builders going across the border.

Planners had much less grip on who was purchasing new houses in their areas and either admitted ignorance or resorted to anecdotal comments. One planner commented that Derry people were moving across the border to live but continued to send their children to school in Derry. There have been local newspaper reports about Derry residents who resent their children being denied places in local schools when children from families who had moved over the border were given places. Some households may operate strategic 'addresses' in Derry to retain Northern Ireland links for health, education and other services, as well as cheaper car registration: it would be interesting to find out how – and where - they filled in their census forms and where they are registered to vote!

The overall impression from the recent interviews with planners was of a group of officials with close working knowledge of specific parts of their local housing systems, who were in most cases carrying very heavy workloads. They considered that there would be strong continuing demands for housing development, that planning permission remained easier rather than harder to obtain, and that demand was not likely to ease during the foreseeable future. They expected demand to continue to be strongest in the areas where it had been concentrated in recent years and they had no expectation of significant changes in the availability of land or the volume of new building. They had mixed views on the desirability and likelihood of switching development to brownfield sites or to greater densities. Even those who favoured brownfield development over greenfield development considered that in practice it would be very hard to achieve a significant shift.

On the basis of these interviews, we remain convinced that there has been considerable integration of housing markets across the border. Many builders, developers and estate agents operate within both jurisdictions. Building materials suppliers sell in what is effectively a single market. Nobody is aware of any significant difficulties involved in obtaining mortgage finance: most lending institutions based in Northern Ireland do not lend for purchase across the border, but they have associates, alliances or colleagues across the border doing so.

The border is no longer a barrier to housing market activity, but it remains significant as a symbolic barrier and in terms of wider difficulties regarding closer cross-border integration of public administration and policies. There are still two different systems of public administration, especially concerning social housing provision and management. For example, very different systems operate for capital financing of new social housing projects within the two jurisdictions and there are different mechanisms for delivering subsidy to low income tenants of social and private landlords. Housing and related policies continued to reflect different national priorities. These developing and changing relationships suggest that it is easier for market forces and factors to transcend national boundaries than for nation states to overcome a barrier which was created in fear and anger and which may remain in existence so long as those emotions dominate public policy in this small corner of the world.

Conclusions

This chapter has argued that there is strong evidence of widespread metropolitan de-concentration throughout both Northern Ireland and the Republic of Ireland. Metropolitan de-concentration included the rapid expansion of Dublin and Belfast commuter zones as:

> ... the so-called "commuter belt" stretched and strained so much ... that it needed to be made of elastic, as gussets were stitched into towns and villages in its rounded compass to make way for new housing in every nook and cranny (IAVI 1999 *Property Survey*).

There were signs of 'hollowing out' of inner areas (especially Belfast) as well as some inner area regeneration and gentrification (Temple Bar and Docklands in Dublin; Laganside in Belfast) (Horner, 1999). There was also strong outward expansion of other cities as Derry spread over the border into Co. Donegal and

Galway, Cork, Limerick and Waterford spread out into former countryside. There was widespread building of detached 'rural' homes.

We have argued that there is little evidence for a Dublin-Belfast corridor effect as such, but that the corridor appears to be a zone where outward growth impulses from both metropolitan cores are coming together and will inevitably coalesce. Rapid population growth and internal migration, typically to new suburban zones, have had dramatic effects on different parts of the two jurisdictions. New housing developments, together with changes in social housing provision, have resulted in more 'private' housing systems in both jurisdictions, with some convergence in tenure patterns due to the higher volume of social housing sales in the north. We have also introduced qualitative data which support the contention that the two housing markets are increasingly integrated: this is consistent with the observed high degree of correlation between trends in house prices in the two jurisdictions, both of which have tracked interest rates.

I conclude with some preliminary responses to questions about the corridor and the capacity of the two planning systems to respond in a 'joined up' way. Firstly, many of the changes reported in this chapter occurred during a period when the two planning regimes on the island of Ireland were being subjected to reappraisal and proposed reforms. Dramatic changes have been signalled for planning regimes, with new urban and regional planning strategies. These are the subject of other chapters so have not been covered here in any depth. The policy shifts reflect concerns over metropolitan expansion, the costs of dispersed development (including service provision and road congestion) as well as concern over the environmental impacts and sustainability of low density dispersed development. Whether these new planning priorities reflect widely-held views and aspirations within the two jurisdictions remains to be seen. In particular, I will be fascinated to see whether, in practice, there will be strong support for the RDS' proposed target of 60 per cent of new housing on 'brownfield' sites and the move towards tighter control of new development.

How will the new planning regimes affect already-heated housing markets, especially Dublin and Belfast, especially in terms of land availability and house prices? Might we not be trying to restrict building in precisely the areas of most population growth and high housing demand? If so, is there not a great danger of pricing out lower income buyers and concentrating poorer households in a residualized social sector? How will changing planning regimes affect ongoing processes of change: can metropolitan de-concentration simply be stopped by administrative decree? Will 'preferable' patterns of new development arise spontaneously? Will gentrification push poor households out of the countryside? Will new social movements arise to oppose town cramming?

We already have a pretty good idea of the main 'winners and losers' in the housing booms of the 1990s (Clinch, Convery and Walsh, 2002; Drudy and Punch, 2002). Winners included investors and homeowners able to benefit from the rising tide of house prices (including tenant purchasers of discounted Housing Executive or council dwellings). Other beneficiaries included landowners, financiers, speculators, exchange professionals and developers. Beneficiaries in the Republic also included recipients of generous tax breaks under urban renewal, seaside resort and rural regeneration schemes. The main losers in the Republic have been first time buyers priced out of market, low income and unemployed tenants and others in housing need (Drudy & Punch, 2002). Housing policy in the Republic has attempted to cope with rapid shift from problems of low demand in the 1980s to managing the boom in the later 1990s; there have been many reports and much micro-management but according to Berry et al (2001) the impact of policy changes has been modest. There has not been anything like the same affordability problem in Northern Ireland to date, but the emphasis on brownfield development could fix that!

Finally, we have argued that there is evidence of significant convergence in at least major parts of the housing systems of Northern Ireland and the Republic, especially in terms of the operations of builders, developers, estate agents, home buyers and private rental investors. There has not been any equivalent cross-border integration in terms of social housing policy and provision. We have seen the development of a new social geography of Irish housing within changing urban regions during the 1990s, the emerging planning regimes may turn the present decade into one where *political* geography becomes even more interesting.

Acknowledgements

I should like to thank my colleague Dr Terry Robson for his excellent collaboration during the pilot study, in the re-working of findings of that study, and for undertaking the 2003 interviews of planning officials. This research has been supported by the Northern Ireland Housing Executive and the (then) Department of the Environment and Local Government and two University of Ulster Research Units of Assessment: Social Policy (1999-2000) and Built Environment (2003). None of these are responsible for any views expressed or errors contained in this chapter.

References

Anon (2003), Bordering on the brilliant 'Inishowen Shopper' Supplement to the *Derry Journal* p. 14, 23 May.

Berry, J. et al (2001), Government intervention and impact on the housing market in Greater Dublin *Housing Studies* 16:6, 755–770.

Breheny, M. (1995), Counter urbanisation and sustainable urban forms, in Brotchie, J., Blakely, E., Hall, P. and Newton, P., *Cities in competition:*

productive and sustainable cities for the 21ˢᵗ century pp 402–29 (Melbourne, Longman).

Champion, T. *Counterurbanization: the changing pace and nature of population concentration* (London, Edward Arnold).

Clinch, P, Convery, F and Walsh, B (2002), *After the Celtic Tiger* (Dublin, O'Brien Press).

Cullen, I. (2003), Liquid sewage flowing down the street, *Derry Journal* p11, 11 July.

Drudy, P. J. and Punch, M. (2002), Housing models and inequality: perspectives on recent Irish experience, *Housing Studies* 17:4, 657–672.

Horner, A. (1993), Dividing Ireland into geographical regions, *Geographical Viewpoint* 21, pp5–24.

———, (1999), Population dispersion and development in a changing city-region, in Killen, J and MacLaren, A. (eds), *Dublin: Contemporary Trends and Issues for the Twenty-First Century* (Dublin, Geographical Society of Ireland & Centre for Urban and Regional Studies, Trinity College).

Murray, G. (2003), Derry – an ideal business location, *Derry Journal* 1 August 2003.

Paris, C (ed.) (2001), *Housing in Northern Ireland, and comparisons with the Republic of Ireland*, Policy and Practice Series (Coventry, Chartered Institute of Housing).

Paris, C. and Robson, T. (2001), *Housing in the Border Counties* (Belfast, Northern Ireland Housing Executive).

Chapter 13

Sub-Regional Planning in Cross-Border City-Regions: The Case of North-West Ireland

Brendan Murtagh
Queens University, Belfast

Brian Kelly
Planning Consultant, Belfast

Introduction

This chapter examines the application of the European Spatial Development Perspective (ESDP) to cross-border planning in Ireland. It makes a conceptual connection between the ESDP and the National Spatial Strategy in the Republic of Ireland and the Regional Development Strategy in Northern Ireland. However, the chapter argues that the utility of the ESDP outside national growth corridors, (such as Dublin-Belfast) is limited and using experience in the North-West, it suggests that the city region offers a more locally relevant way to understand cross-border spatial dynamics in peripheral areas. We conclude by drawing out the implication for multi-scalar governance, infrastructure and regional planning in Ireland.

The European Spatial Development Perspective (ESDP), devolution and the preparation of national physical development plans for the Republic of Ireland and Northern Ireland have generated a new debate about the meaning of regionalism on the island (Greer and Murray, 2003). The establishment of North-South political and administrative structures has focused particular attention on potential growth corridors, border region planning and strategic cooperation in tourism and infrastructure. Both the National Spatial Strategy (NSS) (DELG, 2003) and the Regional Development Strategy (RDS) (DRD, 2001a) borrowed heavily from the language and practices of the ESDP (CEC, 1999). Decentralising development along the eastern seaboard and networking hubs, gateways and growth poles via key strategic transport corridors seem to suggest, in the Irish case at least, that the ESDP makes sense in national scale planning.

This chapter attempts to evaluate that assertion by drawing empirically in the North-West Cross-Border Region (NWCBR) and on the literature concerned with the changing nature of regionalism and how this is treated in official discourses on national scale planning in the ESDP. The shift of attention from localism in the 1980s to urban regions in the last decade reflects the restless search within advanced capitalist states to find the appropriate spatial scale to respond to industrial restructuring and the global flow of technology and knowledge (Murtagh, 2001). The first part of the chapter examines the origins of the ESDP and in particular it explores its approach to peripheral places as well as its more obvious benefits to the European core and the most developed metropolitan economies. The NSS and the RDS are then read within this context and connections are made between European concepts of space and national level planning in Ireland. The multi-scalar theme of the paper is taken forward with a case study of the NWCBR. Here, the paper finds conceptual value in Jones and McLeod's distinction between *regional spaces* and *spaces of regionalism*. The former draws primarily on the literature on regional development and institutional economics and sees regions and regional governance rooted in successful business clustering, institutional thickness and a distinctive stock of hard and soft infrastructure to support spatial competencies in the context of globalisation. Spaces of regionalism, on the other hand 'features the (re-)assertion of regional and natural claims to citizenship, insurgent forms of political mobilisation, democratic participation and cultural expression along side analogous shifts in territorial government' (Jones and MacLeod, 2003, p.5). The case study argues that the NSS in particular presents a conceptualisation of the North-West as a regional place rather than the spatial region articulated by local interests. The chapter concludes by arguing for a strong participatory basis to sub regional planning that can help to shape conceptions of place that match localized development imperatives. A city region spreading across the border clearly has important political implications but might be the only basis on which the North-West periphery can resist economic structuring, globalisation and the effects of inexorable European integration.

The European Spatial Development Perspective (ESDP)

Designing the ESDP

European regional policy has always had a concern for the uneven distribution of growth across member states (Murtagh and McKay, 2003). However, as global restructuring and economic change affected the efficiency of even the most complex urban agglomerations, the European Union (EU) took a closer interest in the organisation and interaction of its major towns and cities (Atkinson, 2001). *Europe 2000* (CEC, 1991) and *Europe 2000* + (CEC, 1994) looked at the future role of cities in creating economic and social cohesion and completing the internal market. In particular, *Europe 2000+* highlighted the role of spatial planning in urban restructuring and drew on cross-national initiatives such as that for the Baltic Sea Region. But the texts were more analytical than prescriptive, raising issues about border effects, urban and rural relations and the need to tackle the spatial concentrations of social exclusion at the urban and regional scale (Nadin and Shaw, 1996). The *Study Programme for European Spatial Planning (SPESP)* and the *European Spatial Planning Observatory Network (ESPON)* gave further intellectual weight to the development of cross-national European principles and in particular the information and methodological requirements for supra-scale development planning (Jensen and Richardson, 2001).

Vickerman (2000) pointed out that the ESDP also emerged from frustration that the Trans European Network (TENS), developed after Maastricht Treaty, had not produced the economic integration and efficiencies required to complete the internal market. In effect, the ESDP was designed to drill down TENS priorities to the national and regional scale. This was particularly the case where TENS removed barriers to communication and facilitated economic convergence and competition (Richardson and Jensen, 2000).

The ESDP was formally adopted by the EU in May 1999 and it established a non-binding statutory agreement by the member states on common objectives and concepts for the spatial development of Europe. Work began on the strategy in the early 1990s by the Committee for Spatial Development (CSD), which drew on leading planners and academics in each member state. The major principles and policy goals of the ESDP were established at Leipzig in 1994 and these in particular promoted the concepts of cohesion, sustainability and balanced competition (Faludi, 1997). The first draft was published in Noordwijk in June 1997 and the complete draft was discussed a year later under the United Kingdom presidency. The document discussed sixty policy options designed to achieve 3 overarching goals:

- A polycentric urban system;
- Equal access to infrastructure and knowledge; and
- Sustainable development, prudent management and protection of natural and cultural heritage (CEC, 1999).

A polycentric urban system was offered as the most balanced response to increasing economic and growth centralisation within Europe (Richardson and Jensen, 2001). Balance will be achieved through the creation of a number of dynamic, economically integrated areas distributed evenly across Europe and consisting of metropolitan and rural areas as well as towns and cities of different sizes (CEC, 1999). It also emphasized that smaller settlements in peripheral areas could function more effectively and at a *higher level* if they cooperate around mutually supportive but distinctive urban functions (Kratke, 2001). This sort of strategic networking was in particular offered as an alternative to mono-centric development that produced uneven economic opportunity, congestion and urban inefficiencies across the EU (Kloosterman and Musterd, 2000).

Implementing the ESDP

At the outset, the ESDP faced difficulties in integrating very different land ownership rights, planning traditions, building codes and laws (Faludi, 2000). The Perspective has its roots in French style comprehensive planning, which may be less appropriate for narrower British and Irish regulatory land use management approaches. For example, Davies (1998) pointed out that the control and development of land has different constitutional status across the EU and that strong vertical administration within and between member states makes it difficult to achieve the sort of integration envisaged by the ESDP.

The universalistic application of the ESDP to very different settlement geographies and cultures was also questioned by Groth (2000). Writing from a Scandinavian perspective, he argued that the ESDP is suited to sorting out high growth agglomerations rather than more dispersed and fractured urban landscapes. Copus (2001) pointed out that the notion of polycentricity would inevitably favour the stronger town or city in developing a network, creating a degree of internal competitiveness especially in border regions where integration is dulled by political, economic and administrative partition (Anderson and O'Dowd, 1999). Thus, one of the fundamental criticisms of the strategy is that it is more about preparing Europe for competition from global power blocks than addressing uneven peripheral development within the EU. Krathe (2001) argued that the ESDP effectively turned a blind eye to the potential for increased competition between and within urban systems and that it failed to effectively address the tension between competitive and cohesion.

Linked to this, Albrechts (2001) pointed out that the ESDP is firmly located in a top-down policy formulation model and that its construction as a technocratic process is at odds with democratic discourses which might articulate different spatial formations referenced in historically and culturally embedded settlement patterns. Certainly, the Irish tradition of dispersed rural settlements seems at odds with the assumptions made by the Perspective about highly urbanized urban regions (Greer and Murray, 2003). But, this in turn raises questions about the capacity of the ESDP to be implemented giving its non-binding, 'influencing' status (Faludi, 1997). Faludi (2000) pointed out that the absence of maps makes it difficult to realize what the ESDP means in practice and argued that it might have been easier for the authors to find consensus around the text rather than a detailed working through of the spatial formations in schematic formats. Ultimately, the success of the ESDP would be evidenced in the way in which member states have drawn on the ESDP to formulate national and regional strategies (Newman and Thornley, 1996). Certainly, Herrschel and Newman (2002) argue that the RDS in Northern Ireland can be located within the ESDP and the principles of balanced spatial development. The remainder of the chapter tests that assertion and the logic of ESDP principles at the sub-regional scale.

The NSS and the RDS

The NSS and the RDS were prepared separately but there were close links at senior levels in both civil services, especially around cross-border planning and integration. A Discussion Paper was prepared by the Department of the Environment (Northern Ireland) in 1997 and this was subjected to a wide-ranging consultation process led by a consortium of the two Universities in the region (McEldowney and Sterrett, 2001). *Shaping Our Future* was published as a draft plan and subjected to an *Examination in Public* led by a 3-person independent panel. The final strategy was published in 2001 as the Regional Strategic Framework for Northern Ireland to 2025. At the outset the strategy notes that:

> The RDS is consistent with the integrated approach of the European Spatial Development Perspective (ESDP), which is an important policy framework for member states within the European Union (EU). Although non-binding, it informs the preparation of regional spatial strategies by seeking to secure balanced and sustainable development in the interests of economic and social cohesion across the EU (DRD, 2001a, p.6).

Evidence of the ESDP imprint was seen in a number of ways including the development of balanced and polycentric urban systems based on hubs and clusters, key and link transport corridors and main regional gateways of ports and airports. One of the key strategic objectives was:

> To strengthen the role of Londonderry as the regional city and transport hub of the North-West, offering key infrastructure and services in administration, education, health, energy, industry, commerce, shopping, cultural and tourism amenities; and reinforcing the complementary employment and service roles of Limavady and Strabane (DRD, 2001a, p.81).

McEldowney and Sterrett (2001), argued that one of the consistent themes to emerge from the consultation process was that of regional cohesion and that this had a significant impact on the guiding principles in the RDS:

> The proposed Spatial Development Strategy, for example, illustrates the structure of connections between east and west and north and south as well as between urban and rural areas. This cohesion is further reinforced in the designation of seven large towns, outside of Belfast and Derry/Londonderry, as major service centres (McEldowney and Sterrett, 2001, p.44).

Neill and Gordon (2001), also pointed out that regional politicians exercised their voice through the newly established Northern Ireland Assembly and development interests in regional towns also helped to shift emphasis on to centres outside the two main cities. Similarly, Greer and Murray (2003) argued that the final strategy contained a more substantive debate about rural issues than that included in the initial discussion paper and highlighted the role of well-organized NGO networks in raising the distinctive rural personality of the region as a mainstream planning issue. Whilst the ESDP might have provided a useful conceptual language to explain the overall shape of the RDS, its actual content was strongly influenced by the civic and political exposure to which the early drafts received.

Similarly, McDonagh (2003), pointed out that the NSS drew less on trans-European planning principles and more on local clientism and technically produced notions of regionalism within Ireland. The NSS runs from 2002 to 2020 and again was subjected to a wide public consultation and advice from a panel of international experts. The strategy recognized the priority to enhance the competitiveness of Dublin but highlighted the need to decentralize services, facilities and jobs from the Eastern seaboard in order to develop a balanced spatial economy. Conceptually, the plan drew on the ESDP and specifically upon Danish experience which "included a key role for urban centres at strategic locations acting as national 'locomotives' of regional growth – embracing a positive partnership between town and country, which recognizes the strengths of both cities and diversified rural districts" (DELG, 2003, p.146).

Much of the language in the Strategy was shared with the RDS as a national spatial balance was to be achieved by strong *gateways* in nationally significant centres, *hubs* in smaller towns that support the capabilities of the gateways to other areas and county towns that capitalize on local roles but which are linked to the roles of the gateways and development hubs. Rural areas are to benefit from enhanced local employment opportunities and from the development of their resource potential (DELG, 2003, p.39). The strategy goes on to develop more detailed planning frameworks in 8 Regional Authority areas of which the *Border Region* stretching from Donegal to Louth, is one. The contested nature of the border, currency and tax variations and its precarious economic position making it a particularly interesting place to explore the logic of supra-scale European planning ideology (Murtagh, 2002).

> There is a strong dynamic at present in the relationship between Letterkenny and Derry. Shaping Our Future … identifies Derry as a major regional centre for the North-West, including Donegal. The development of the Letterkenny/Derry as a linked gateway will enhance this relationship and strengthen the North-West. Letterkenny will be further developed in association with Derry in a way that ensures both continue to be effectively linked, have complementary strengths and, in essence work together as a gateway for the North-West (DELG, 2003, p.46).

Yet the evidence for this observation is not strong. Letterkenny had a population of 11,996 in 1996 (DELG, 2003, p.144) whilst Derry/Londonderry city had a population of 85,300 in 1998 (DRD, 2001b, p.53) so at the outset the sheer scale of the relationship is an uneven one. The concept of linked gateways along a notional economic corridor has important appeal for local politicians and business interests but it is not clear what is the nature, source and content of the 'dynamic' referred to in the NSS. Moreover, it is not obvious how these connections would be made in regional or local planning, through economic development strategies or in structural arrangements to develop cross-border administrative, civic or political cooperation. McDonagh (2003) was especially critical of the strategy as it failed to recognize the inherent potential of regions based on participative democracy and decentralized control relying instead on artificially produced but administratively convenient spatial disaggregation of the national territory. Certainly, border communities share common problems in their dislocating fiscal, political and administrative arrangements. However, whether a common border definition is suitable for planning in the North-West periphery, or in disadvantaged rural communities in Fermanagh and Leitrim, (as well as the high growth Dublin-Belfast corridor), is questionable. For McDonagh the political clientism of 'giving something to everyone', rather than a genuine attempt to restructure the greater Dublin congestion, explains the distribution of gateways and hubs and the shape of sub-regional planning units within the state. He pointed out that the *National Development Plan* controls budgetary expenditure for major infrastructure provision including transport and housing and came before the publication of the NSS and that the National Rail Strategy was also agreed and published in advance of the physical plan.

Case-Study: North-West Cross Border Area

Van den Berg (2001) provides a useful empirical framework for evaluating the robustness of cluster-specific conditions in the North-West. In particular, he asserts that a combination of hard and soft assets are required for synergistic growth. Drawing on his framework, this section looks at three specific sub-regional issues:

* Economic and labour market structures;
* Fixed infrastructure; and
* Governance and education.

Economic and labour market structures

Figure 13.1 below examines the labour market structure of the District Council areas in the North-West (Derry, Strabane and Limavady District Councils) although it is not possible to directly correlate these with Donegal due to differences in the classificatory systems used. The analysis uses Labour Force Survey data from 2001 and shows that there is a strong comparison between the profiles of the areas analysed. For example, correlation analysis revealed coefficients of 0.925 and 0.861 between (a) Derry and Strabane and (b) Limavady and Strabane respectively. Where data are comparable it also shows a remarkable overlap between Donegal and the North-West Region. For example, 23 per cent of the labour force worked in manufacturing in Donegal compared with 21 per cent in Derry and 26 per cent in Limavady. This symmetry suggests that in the North-West at least, there is little differentiation in the functions of the main settlements in the region.

Part of the explanation for this is the lack of cluster engines in the local economy. 'Spiders', 'flagships' and 'engines' are terms used to describe those services or industries that can ignite and sustain clustering in the urban region (Van den Berg, 2001). Even a simple audit of potential cluster engines in Table 13.1 reveals weak evidence of a sub-regional dynamic. The textile industry was the mainstay of the local economy but has suffered badly in the global restructuring and competition from low priced labour markets in the Third World. Much of the traditional skills base has been displaced by systems manufacturing. The research and educational capacity that supported the sector has been lost, especially at University level (DLSP, 2002).

The electronics sector is weak outside Derry District and even here there are concerns about the extent to which this is supported by region-specific R and D facilities and services (DLSP, 2002). Research by the City Council also suggested that there are few 'traded interdependencies' between firms and sectors within or between main settlements. The table below shows that many are branch plants of parent companies in the US or Europe and they neither collaborate nor compete in local market conditions, except for skilled labour (DCC, 1999).

Fixed infrastructure

An overriding concern for the North-West region is the poor condition of infrastructure, especially for road and rail travel. The region's airport is deficit funded by the City Council at £1m per annum and continues to be a contentious issue in the local press and politics (O'Neill, 2002). The table below shows that it is in a weak position relative to other regional airports and that Donegal Airport at Carrickfinn clearly displaces a proportion of business especially with direct flights to Glasgow where there are strong ties due to inter-generational immigration. Here again, there is evidence of competition, (not collaboration), between local authorities in the region. This in turn is not likely to either assemble or crucially sustain the balance of infrastructure needed for regional development.

Table 13.3 looks at the use of airports by manufacturing businesses in the Irish Cross-Border region. It suggests that 8.1 per cent of businesses in the Republic of Ireland and 10.2 per cent of concerns in Northern Ireland use the City of Derry airport although significantly fewer rely on the city's port at 2.4 per cent and 4.4 per cent respectively. The data shows that the border economy still looks to large-scale infrastructure in the metropolitan eastern seaboard for commercial traffic.

Table 13.1 Major Employers in the North-West and Potential Cluster Sectors (continued on next page)

Area	Textiles	Chem./Pharm.	Electronics	Engineering	Services
Derry Twelve foreign owned businesses on the IDBR in the Derry City Council area.	Lee Apparel (USA) Desmond & Sons Fruit of the Loom (USA)	Du Pont (USA) Northbrook	Stream International Seagate Technology (USA) Raytheon Systems (USA) Singularity Norbrook Technologies	Precision Engineering E&I Engineering Allgo Engineering	***
Strabane One foreign owned business on the IDBR in Strabane District Council area.	Octopus Sportswear Herdsmans ***	***	***	***	Ulster Bank

	Desmond & Sons		HUCO Lightronic (Germany)		
Limavady Three foreign owned businesses are on the IDBR in the Limavady Borough Council area	Courtaulds Lingerie	***		***	***
Donegal Twenty-five foreign owned businesses are situated within the Donegal County boundary.	UNIFI (USA) Fruit of the Loom Ltd. Magee & Co. Ltd.	Donegal Healthcare Abbot Ireland Pacificare International	Seagate Technology (USA) Interventional Technologies	Bonnar Engineering	Prumerica Systems (USA) Various Financial Services

Source: *VOSS Information System, DCDB*

Table 13.2 Passenger Movements by Main Airports and Airports in North-West Region Area

Airport	1996	1997
Dublin	9,091,296	10,333,202
Belfast International	2,351,000	2,459,344
Shannon	1,740,650	1,822,427
Belfast City	1,361,000	1,280,000
Cork	1,124,320	1,196,261
Connaught Regional Airport	161,432	172,290
Sligo	26,500	28,350
Donegal Airport – Carrickfin	14,049	21,681

Source: *Coopers Lybrand/Indecon, 1997*

The delicate position of major fixed infrastructure in the North-West is further exacerbated by the poor road and rail connections. The railway is poorly used, the rolling stock old and the track bed in urgent need of renewal. Road widening schemes and bypasses have helped to ease specific bottlenecks but have not significantly reduced journey times to Belfast (DLSP, 2002). Moreover, the fibre optic network capacity is poorly used and stops on the Northern side of the border. This relates to van Geenhuizen and Rieveld's (2002) notion of *border-barrier effects* where territorial partition prevents effective natural integration of services and facilities.

North Donegal is also poorly serviced by high voltage electricity cabling mainly because of environmental objections to pylons rather than capacity problems in the Irish grid. The potential to address this supply from the Northern side has been discussed but has not emerged in any meaningful cross-border project.

Governance

The problems of internal and external hard infrastructure are matched by poor governance connections in the North-West. Part of the explanation is the weak status of local government in both jurisdictions. The North Cross Border Group has attempted to link cross-sectoral interests on both sides of the border especially around the delivery of the EU INTERREG III Community Initiative Programme.

Table 13.3   Comparative Analysis of Usage of Ports and Airports by Manufacturers in ICBAN/NWRCBG Area

Facility	Republic of Ireland per cent	Northern Ireland per cent
Belfast City Airport	20.2	44.5
Belfast International Airport	36.3	68.6
Belfast Port	21.0	46.7
Larne Port	45.2	51.1
Derry Port	2.4	4.4
Enniskillen Airport	0.0	0.7
Derry City Airport	8.1	10.2
Dublin Airport	65.3	14.6
Dublin Port	55.6	2.2
Dun Laoghaire Port	20.2	2.9
Rosslare Port	8.9	0.7
Cork Port	0.8	0.0
Sligo Airport	8.9	-
Carrickfin Airport	6.5	0.0
Galway	0.8	1.5
Shannon	3.2	-
Connaught Airport	3.2	-

Source: *Coopers Lybrand/Indecon (1997)*

The Group has also made progress in determining strategic priorities and lobbying for improvements on the main road linking Donegal to Dublin, part of which runs through Northern Ireland. However, the weaknesses of local government and strong centralisation in both the Republic of Ireland and in Northern Ireland has produced an array of new governance structures in the form of partnerships for the delivery of a plethora of European and mainstream government arrangements. Certainly, a healthy civil society is evidence of the *institutional thickness* relevant to local development but in the North-West the overload of structures has created a confusing and competitive governance map. In Healey's (2002) terms it is often difficult to locate the key sites of decision-making, which is especially confusing for inward investors and developers. In Northern Ireland, Central Government Departments and Agencies are responsible for planning urban regeneration and economic development, whilst on both sides of the border, local authorities have attempted to develop independent economic and business support functions. Local Strategy Partnerships have been established to deliver the EU PEACE II Programme yet separate structures have been set up to implement LEADER + and INTERREG III between 2000 and 2006.

Table 13.4 Educational Provision in the North-West Cross Border Region (continued on next page)

Town	Name of Institution	Main Courses Available	Student No.s: 2000 - 2001	Quality Assessment
Derry	University of Ulster, Magee College	• Information Technology • Eng. & Built Env. • Social Sciences • Business & Mgt. • Life & Health Sciences	2,756	HEFCE
	North-West Institute of Further and Higher Education	• Computing • Mechanical, Electronic & Civil Engineering	23,695	BCS, CITB, City & Guilds, EDEXCEL, ITC, IATI, IEHO, etc…
Strabane	North-West Institute of Further and Higher Education	• Science • Building Studies • Administration & Management Studies • Tourism & Hospitality	(Students attend the NWIFHE both in Derry & Strabane)	
Limavady	Limavady College of Further & Higher Education	• Leisure Management • Information Technology	Unavailable	***
Donegal	Letterkenny Institute of Technology	• Computing & Data Comm. • Applied Computing • Mech. Engineering • Industrial Design	1951	***

Killybegs Tourism College	• Professional Cookery • Hospitality Skills • Tourism Skills	291	National Tourism Certification Board
National Fishery College	• Marine Engineering • Commercial Fishing • Navigation • Boat Handling	488	Bord Iascaigh Mhara certified

Source: DCDB and respective websites

Education policy provides evidence of the weak strategic approach to sub-regional scale thinking and service provision. In 1998/99, Derry had 6,834 University and higher education student places but this compared unfavourably to other regional towns such as Galway (12,749), Limerick (12,710) and Cork (17,033) (DCC, 1999). The table below shows that there is a high degree of overlap between the courses offered at higher educational establishments and that the University of Ulster and the Letterkenny Institute of Technology have not developed the complementarities that could build a hierarchical, differentiated and interconnected strategy for the wider region. Yet it has been recognized in the development literature that the knowledge economy is vital in securing suitable growth and promote the distinctive qualities of the North-West in particular. Competitiveness rather than collaboration hallmarks service delivery and the search for students in an increasingly contested business market.

Implications for the North-South Growth Corridor

The ESDP has had important rhetorical appeal for national planners in Ireland but it is questionable whether it is the intellectual or conceptual source of either the NSS or the RDS. It is also questionable whether it makes sense to the strategic planning of the North-West cross-border region specifically. The reality is that the North-West is a weak peripheral area with a deficit infrastructure and a competitive rather than a collaborative approach to sub-regional development. The notion of polycentric development, which is a feature of both national strategies, is barely recognisable in the North-West. There is little differentiation or interdependence between settlements, expensive fixed infrastructure has been difficult to sustain and collaborative planning on a cross-border basis in the maintenance of regional assets such as airports, power and education has been slow to emerge.

This raises the potential of Derry city as a *space of* regionalism where peoples everyday 'life-worlds' can help to shape their use of place and the meaning they attach to wider concept of regionalism in the North-West. Paris and Robson (2002) showed that the greater Derry housing market has spread across the border into Donegal. Despite currency and fiscal variations, Donegal is now part of the suburbanisation of the city. Retailers have responded flexibly to the dual economy for some time and currently make arrangements for payments to be made in either Sterling or Euros. Given public expenditure constraints, the reality is that the infrastructure deficit will be most effectively addressed in the short term at least by concentrating resources on the rationalisation of facilities that strengthen the capacity of Derry to operate as a *sub*-regional city. For that to happen, there needs to be political consensus about the appropriate scale for regional planning. A cross-border plan that sees Derry at the heart of the North-West of Ireland would help to re-orientate regional planning in both jurisdictions. In particular, the artificial construction of the border region in the NSS would be challenged by a city region plan, which would in turn recognize the comparative limits of Strabane and

Limavady and the fragility of a development corridor between Derry and Letterkenny.

However, it would also challenge the status of the North-West within border spatial dynamics in Northern Ireland specifically. The regions economy is increasingly shaped by the dynamics of the Belfast Metropolitan Area and there is little point in seeing Derry as its settlement equivalent in the North-West. Huggins's (2003) *Competitive Index* showed that the West of Northern Ireland was ranked 138th out of 149 United Kingdom regions and Peter Hall made the point about national growth patterns when he stated that:

> The basic geography of Northern Ireland suggests strongly that there is in reality only one city region for planning purposes. Of course, Londonderry is a distinct centre in its own right; but it does not command a region sufficiently large to act as a logical planning unit (Hall, 1999, p.76).

Certainly, Derry/Londonderry has the scale and capacity to develop economic opportunity, jobs and services in its own right, but spatial planning priorities must prioritize its strategic connection to Belfast. The logic of a major airport located so closely to the region's main international airport, needs consideration. There is a need to recognize its real economic baseline as a platform for local development. Here, the ESDP and the way in which it is interpreted in cross-border region has only partial relevance and would seem more appropriate to advanced high-growth urban agglomerations than to Europe's uncertain periphery. The need to make sense of places of regionalism from the perspective of people who use and construct them is still relevant in the context of European enlargement and policy standardisation.

The danger is that imported concepts such as development corridors might be transplanted onto territories where they may not be at the best basis for regional analysis and policy development. The Derry/Letterkenny corridor is primarily a container where activities happen rather than a dynamic interactive economic space on which substantive economic development can be created. A more appropriate audit of the qualities of regions centred on notions of collaborative planning involving the key stakeholders in the urban region might offer a better starting point for the North-West.

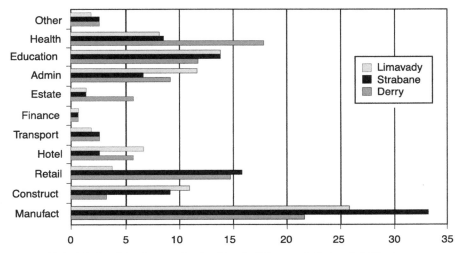

Figure 13.1   Major Employers in the North-West and Potential Clusters Sectors

References

Albrechts, L. (2001), In Pursuit of New Approaches to Strategic Spatial Planning. A European Perspective *International Planning Studies* 6(3), pp.293–310.

Anderson, J. and O'Dowd, L. (1999), Contested Borders: Globalization and Ethnonational Conflict in Ireland, *Regional Studies* 33(7), pp. 681–696.

Atkinson, B. (2001), The Emerging 'Urban Agenda' and the European Spatial Development Perspective: Towards an EU Urban Policy? *European Planning Studies* 9(3), pp.385–406.

Coopers and Lybrand/Indecom (1997), *The Economy of the Border Region,* Unpublished.

Copus, A.K., (2001), From Core-periphery to Polycentric Development: Concepts of Spatial and Aspatial Periphery, *European Planning Studies* 9(4), pp.539-552.

Davies, L. (1998), The ESDP and the UK, *Town and Country Planning: March issue* pp.64–66.

Department for Regional Development (2001a), *Shaping Our Future, The Regional Development Strategy for Northern Ireland 2025* (Belfast, DRD).

———, (2001b), *Shaping Our Future, The Family of Settlements Report* (Belfast, DRD).

Department for the Environment and Local Government (2002), *The National Spatial Strategy 2002–2020* (Dublin, The Stationary Office).

Derry City Council (DCC) (1999), *One Integrated Economic Development Strategy* (Derry/Londonderry, DCC).

Derry Local Strategy Partnership (DLSP) (2002), *Interim Integrated Local Strategy, Derry/Londonderry* (DLSP).

EcEldowney, M. and Sterrett, K. (2001), Shaping a regional vision: the case of Northern Ireland, *Local Economy* 16(1), pp.38–49.

European Commission (1999), ESDP-European Spatial Development Perspective (Brussels, CEC).

Faludi, A. (2000), The European Spatial Development Perspective – What next?. *European Planning Studies* 8(2), pp.237–250.

————, (2001), The Application of the European Spatial Development Perspective : Evidence from the North-West Metropolitan Area, *European Planning Studies* 9(5), pp.663–675.

Greer, M. and Murray, M. (2003), *Rural Planning and Development in Northern Ireland* (Dublin, IPA).

Groth, N.B. (2000), Urban systems between policy and geography, *Regional Studies* 34(6), pp.571–580.

Hall, P. (1999), The future planning of city regions, in F. Gaffiken and M. Morrissey (eds), *City Visions: Imaging Place, Enfranchising People* pp.61–78 (London, Pluto).

Healey, P. (2002), On creating the city as a collective resource, *Urban Studies* 39(10), pp.1777–1792.

Herrschel, T. and Newman, P. (2002), *Governance of Europe's City Regions: Planning, politics and policy* (London, Routledge).

Huggins, R. (2003), Creating a UK competitiveness index: regional and local benchmarking, *Regional Studies* 37(1), pp.89–96.

Jenks, M., Burton, E., Williams, K. (1996) (eds), *The Compact City – A Sustainable Urban Form?* (E & FN Spon, Oxford).

Jones, M. and Maclead, G. (2003), New regional spaces, new spaces of regionalism: territory, consciousness and the English question, *Paper resented to the Regional Studies Association Conference, Reinventing Regions in the Global Economy Conference, Pisa, 12th–15th April.*

Kloosterman R.C. and Musterd, S. (2001), The Polycentric Urban Region: Towards a Research Agenda, *Urban Studies* 38(4), pp.623–633.

Krätke, S. (2001), Strengthening the Polycentric Urban System in Europe: Conclusions from the ESDP, *European Planning Studies* 9(1), pp.106–116.

McDonagh, J. (2003), A national spatial strategy for Ireland, *Paper resented to the Regional Studies Association Conference, Reinventing Regions in the Global*

Murtagh, B. (2001), The URBAN Community Initiative in Northern Ireland, *Policy and Politics* Vol.29, No.4, pp.431–46.

————, (2002), *The Politics of Territory* (London, Palgrave).

Murtagh, B. and McKay, S. (2003), Evaluating the social effects of the EU URBAN Community Initiative Programme, *European Planning Studies* Vol.11, No.2, pp.193–212.

Neill, W. and Gordon, M. (2001), Shaping Our Future? The Regional Strategic Framework for Northern Ireland, *Planning Theory and Practice* 12(1), pp.31–52.

Newman, P. and Thornley, A. (1996), *Urban Planning in Europe – International Competition, National Systems and Planning Projects* (Routledge, London).

O'Neill, C. (2002), Financial turbulence still gives a bumpy ride, *Belfast Telegraph,* 16th December 2003, p.13.

Paris, C. and Robson, T. (2002), *Cross Border Housing in Ireland* (Belfast, NIHE).

Richardson, T. and Jensen, B. (2000), Discourses of mobility and polycentric development: A contested view of European spatial planning. *European Planning Studies* 8(4), pp.501–520.

Shaw, D. and Nadin, V. (1996), Spatial planning and territorial change in Europe, Paper presented to the European and Regional Studies Conference, Exeter (UK, April 1996).

Van Den Berg, L., Braun, E. and Van Winden, W. (2001), Growth Clusters in European Cities: An Integral Approach, *Urban Studies* 37(2), pp.1121–1138.

Van GeeNnhuizen, M. and Rietveld, P. (2002), Development of Border Regions: Have sea border regions maintained advantages over land border regions, in Y. Higano, P. Nijkamp, J. Poot and W. van Wyk *The Region in the New Economy* (Aldershot: Ashgate Publishing).

Vickerman, R. (2000), Going trans-European: planning and financing transport networks for Europe by M. Turro, Oxford, Elsevier Science, *Journal of Transport Geography* 8(4), pp.312–313.

Williams, R.H., (1996), European Union Spatial Policy and Planning (London: Paul Chapman Publishing Ltd.).

Chapter 14

Local Authorities and Managing Cross Border Projects

Derek Birrell

University of Ulster

Introduction

In this chapter I am drawing mainly on a research project undertaken in 2001 on cross border co-operation between local authorities funded by the Centre for Cross Border Studies (Birrell and Hayes, 2001). This project had focused on the characteristics of cross border co-operation and had included material on the management of cross border co-operation and I will return to that shortly.

Cross border co-operation in local government has increased substantially in the last 20 years. Before 1985 co-operation was largely limited to a number of activities which arose out of geographical necessity, for example, the Erne catchment areas scheme or some local networking in the immediate border areas. Tannam (1999) describes the range of factors limiting cross border co-operation from the 1960s until the mid 1980s under the concept of 'bounded rationality'. The subsequent major impetus for the growth of co-operation came from two sources, the political salience of co-operation following a series of political and constitutional initiatives, ranging from the Anglo-Irish Agreement of 1985 to the Good Friday Agreement of 1998 and secondly the implementation of a range of EU initiatives, from the Intereg programme of 1990 to the EU Special Support Programme for Peace and Reconciliation after 1995. A further more practical developmental factor was the emergence of facilitating mechanisms mainly in the form of NGOs to foster and support cross border co-operation in local government, for example, the Local Authority Linkages Programme of Co-operation Ireland.

Structure and Functions

Cross border co-operation has to be set in the context of some significant differences between the two jurisdictions in terms of structure and functions and forms of governance. The Local Government system in Northern Ireland consists of a single tier of 26 district councils, seven of which have boundaries with the

South. The Republic of Ireland has a multi-tier system of local government with 29 county councils, five county boroughs, 54 borough and urban districts and 26 town commissions. Historically prior to local government reorganisation in 1972 Northern Ireland had a rather similar tiered structure (Birrell and Hayes, 1999). The local government system in the Republic has remained rather resistant to proposals for major change (Carroll, 2000). Obviously some difficulties can arise in matching the multi-tier system in the South with a single tier system in the North.

Northern Ireland's district councils have a limited range of functions and lack some of the functions which remain the responsibility of local government in the Republic of Ireland, particularly housing, planning and roads. The main direct functions of Northern Ireland's district councils are leisure services, community services, building control, environmental health refuse collection, tourism, parks and cemeteries, harbours community relations and aspects of economic development. Local councils in the Republic are mainly responsible for local roads, housing, planning, environmental regulation, water services, waste management, urban renewal, traffic management, building control, fire services, public libraries, arts and culture, parks and recreation. They do not have the same responsibilities as councils in the North for economic development, tourism and community services. While county councils and county boroughs have a full range of responsibilities the urban authorities, the borough councils and the urban districts have a more limited range of functions. In both jurisdictions there has been some increase in recent years in functional responsibilities. In the South legislative change has given a general competence to local authorities to improve the social and economic development of their areas and this has been used to increase involvement in tourist-related activities, the environment and industrial development. In the North powers have expanded in the areas of community services, community relations, waste management emergency planning and perhaps most significantly in economic development.

Characteristics of Cross Border Co-operation

The study identified the following characteristics of cross border co-operation in local government:

- It was mainly EU funding driven and project driven and consequently operated outside mainstream funding. EU funding requirements have determined the nature and scope of the co-operation with EU requirements setting guidelines for the subject matter of projects, the management of projects and the monitoring of projects.
- Overall there has been a focus on the area of economic development. Within this certain themes have dominated related to SME development, ICT projects, e-business and the promotion of inward investment. Although it has been

suggested (Tannam op.cit., p.153) that economic co-operation is primarily a response to political rather than economic concerns elected politicians from all parties can agree more readily on practical economic action to improve living standards.

- The importance of the role of facilitating/promotional bodies and intermediary bodies in the development process. This is a well established model in Ireland through the cross border facility work of such bodies as Co-operation Ireland, Northern Ireland Voluntary Trust, Area Development Management Ltd and Combat Poverty Agency (ADM/CPA, 1999). The role of Co-operation Ireland's Local Authority Linkages Programme has been crucial in the initiation of many cross border contacts.

- There are relatively few large-scale cross border projects or enterprises involving local authorities and consequently management activity is on a small scale. Major projects are limited in number and many links are limited in their development so that most local authorities have not experienced major cross border engagement.

- Perhaps not unexpectantly cross border co-operation is concentrated on the border areas. Unsurprisingly there are very few linkages with councils in the South and West and some attempted collaborations had failed largely because of the distance included. Perhaps surprisingly there was very little cross border activity involving the seven urban district councils and two borough councils.

- It is, however, worth noting that 25 out of the 26 district councils in Northern Ireland reported participation in cross border collaborative ventures.

Types of Linkages

The study identified five major types of linkages involving local authorities in cross border co-operation.

a) One-to-One Linkages

This is the simplest form of development and contact and such linkages between two local authorities are fairly extensive. Many of these linkages have been facilitated by the Local Authority Linkages Programme which helps identify compatible local authorities, provides start-up funding and developmental guidance. These linkages tended to be focused on a rather limited range of activities involving visits and exchanges of information relating to economic tourist and cultural projects. Relatively few had developed to actual cross border working. Some examples were Armagh/Kilkenny with a small business initiative involving the craft industry and Fermanagh/Lisburn with a waste management project.

There were a number of one-to-one linkages outside the ambit of the Linkages Programme. Again few had progressed beyond visits and exchange of information. Typical was a Derry City Council-Limerick County Borough link related to traffic management. Newry Council and Dundalk Urban District Council had developed links on a range of economic and cultural activities and had emerged as a strong lobbying group on road improvement issues. Armagh-Sligo County Council had developed a one-to-one economic linkage to more wide-ranging co-operation. Another form of one-to-one linkage that has a high public profile in twinning Ball (1992) reported that 60 per cent of local authorities in Britain were involved in twinning arrangements with local authorities in Europe but the total number of cross border twinning arrangements was six. Twinning is based on a formal agreement but mainly relates to culture, sporting and civic activities.

b) Local Government Cross Border Networks

This is the oldest and most developed model of cross border co-operation with three networks of local councils stretching along the whole border, the East Border Region Committee, the Irish Central Border Area Network and the North-West Region Cross Border Group. Two of the networks were established in 1975/6. You will see from the table that some councils in the networks have no boundary adjacent to the Border and while some view this as upsetting the cross border ethos somewhat the inclusion of more district councils had produced more balanced networks in terms of political composition and had provided a larger population basis. The objectives set by the networks are very much geared to the strategic development of the infrastructure of their regions mainly embracing economic investment, rural regeneration, tourism, community economic development, environmental regeneration and transportation. The North-West region network has been responsible for a very high profile project, the Lough Foyle Car Ferry. The networks also have operated as a strong credible lobby group on behalf of cross border work. Again access to EU funding provided the key to significant development and helped build the capacity and confidence of the networks (Greer, 2000). For Intereg 3 the three groups have, in the last year, produced a Border Corridor strategy covering Integrated Area Development Strategies.

The successful Border Corridor proposals embrace three measures: business and economic development; the knowledge economy and human resource and skill development. The three networks will play a significant role in the administration of Intereg III monies.

c) Linkages Between Councils and Other Agencies

Given the mismatch of functions between local authorities a council sometimes has to enter into collaboration with a non-council body across the border if they wish to pursue a joint venture. This would apply in the area of housing where in the South the local authority is the responsible authority but in the North it is the Housing Executive. Examples of such co-operation include a Louth Local Authorities-NIHE Newry link which involved staff exchanges and joint research into homelessness while a similar Leitrim County Council-NIHE link focused on housing needs in rural area.

Other examples can be found relating to roads, libraries, fire services but the most significant examples of this type of linkage relate to economic development. In the Republic of Ireland County Enterprise Boards have existed since 1993, consisting of representatives of local authorities, employers, trade unions and state agencies. Their main activity is to give support to new and existing businesses. They are not responsible to County councils but to the Department of Enterprise, Trade and Employment in Dublin. Tradenet is a project to give companies, mainly from the Belfast-Dublin corridor, the opportunity to meet like-minded businesses across the border using the internet. This is probably the most comprehensive business development project involving local authorities. However, while nine councils from Northern Ireland are involved it is not the county councils from the South but seven County Enterprise Boards who form the linkage. A similar situation exists with County Tourism Committees and more recently with County Development Boards in the South with a remit for the economic, social and cultural development of their areas.

d) **Partnerships Involving Local Authorities**

Outside the cross border networks the most developed examples of local authority linkages take the form of partnerships involving a grouping of agencies. Both jurisdictions in Ireland have seen the emergence of new forms of governance, mainly types of quangos often in place of or instead of local government. A study in the Republic of Ireland (Adshead and Quinn, 1998) sees the Irish government's formal incorporation into the policy process of new agencies as challenging the traditional structure of subnational (local) government. Walsh et al. (1998) identified partnerships in Ireland as a formal organisational framework for policy making and implementation which mobilizes a coalition of a range of partners. Hughes et al. (1998) has described the growth of partnerships in Northern Ireland, particularly prompted by EU initiatives.

There are examples of quite developed cross border partnerships involving local authorities with a range of voluntary, community and other statutory bodies. Some of these linkages began as links between local authorities but in order to develop further it was necessary to establish links with other related agencies and this reflects the limitations of the functions of local government. The Blackwater Scheme originally involved three councils, Dungannon, Armagh and Monaghan County Council in a rural redevelopment project of the river Blackwater catchment area. The Blackwater scheme has grown through entering partnerships with community groups and one project Plato Blackwater has substantial private company involvement. The Omagh-Sligo Partnership was also originally a linkage between two local authorities but it was recognized that a partnership with other economic development agencies was necessary to take the linkage forward. The partnership now includes Sligo County Enterprise Board, Sligo and Omagh Chambers of Commerce, Omagh Enterprise Company and the Sligo and Omagh leader companies. Other examples are the Newry-Dundalk Business Linkage Programme, The Lakeland Partnership for Innovation and the Omagh-Monaghan Digital Corridor. There are also a number of Tourism partnership, for example, the Cavan-Enniskillen Tourism initiative and the North-West Passage which was a consortium of four district councils and three regional tourism organisations in the South (O'Maolain, 2000).

e) **Transnational Local Authority Linkages**
A number of linkages took place in the context of a wider European partnership of councils. Examples are the Edge Cities Project as a partnership of six local authorities in the edge of capital cities which included Fingal County Council and North Down District Council. The Four Cities Project links Dublin, Belfast, Liverpool and Brussels through an EU Intereg funded initiative. The BRAKS project involved Armagh, Kilkenny and cities in Bulgaria, Hungary and Romania as part of the EU Ouverture programme in promoting small firm development and an enterprise culture. Such transnational projects tend to have very specific objectives and require substantial administrative input from the lead partner. The number of such transnational links involving councils from North and South is not large but they have some attraction in areas where there may still be unionist political concerns about single links.

Managing Cross Border Projects

An examination of existing management arrangements suggested the following typology or classification but this has to be considered in the context of the limited nature of collaboration.

a) **Councillor Dominated Formal Management Committees**
The traditional local government committee structure tends to dominate larger linkages with a management structure composed of councillors along with senior official and project manager in attendance. The clearest examples are the Cross Border Networks and such linkages as the Blackwater Scheme and Dundalk-Newry. While the networks report to the full council they are to quite an extent autonomous and some linkages have been established as separate legal activities to facilitate speedy decision-making.

b) **The Partnership Model**
When linkages take the form of wider partnerships it is normal to have a management committee which represents the major partners, for example, the Sligo-Omagh partnership had five councillors from each council but

representatives from ten other partners. There has been a move towards the partnership model (Greer, 2001) as part of a general trend in local governance. Requirements of Intereg III have required the Cross Border Networks to expand their management committees to include economic and social partners. It can be argued that the achievement of having elected councillors sitting and working together across the border should not be lost in the creation of larger more inclusive committees.

c) Official Led Management Group

A number of projects reported a management group or committee consisting only of officials. Smaller projects and council-agency/quango linkages are likely to have small management committees which exclude councillors. The Tradenet project has a management committee of local economic development officers. The rationale for such groups lay in terms of specialist knowledge and everyday work, although such groups are accountable to each council involved.

d) Project Managers

The most effective and popular model for running cross border projects was the appointment of a dedicated project manager to manage the day-to-day running of the project. This was seen as the key to a successful project and had value in terms of the development of specialist expertise, building up networking, co-ordinating across the border and adapting to the sensitive aspects of cross border working. Special funding or secondment normally supports project managers. These managers tended to be employed on a short term ad-hoc basis and some lacked organisational support. There were few examples of a specialist cross border development officer working for a council or between councils with a remit to develop new projects. County Leitrim did have a special projects officer to further cross border contacts. The alternative model of project management was a shared manager, where the responsibility for project management rested with an officer who had other responsibilities, in the North usually an economic development officer or a community services or tourism officer, and in the South usually a development officer or sometimes a recreation officer. There was wide agreement that a range of management skills were peculiar to cross border work, flexibility to work across jurisdictions, sensitivity to the political and reconciliation dimensions, ability to relate to councillors and patience with gradual progress.

e) Cross Border Development Units

There were few examples of cross border development units whether in individual councils or in collaborative projects. Even the cross border networks have a fairly minimal management structure with a project manager and some clerical/secretarial assistance. The new Intereg 3 developments will lead to an enhanced management team. The Sligo-Omagh partnership was of interest as an attempt was made to produce a cross border development unit with a special project's officer and a research officer.

Guidance to Management

There has been very little analysis or discussion of the most effective form of management for cross border projects in local government. The respective central Government Departments with responsibility for local government have to my knowledge published or circulated no advice or guidance on cross border collaboration. Nor are there many opportunities for officers, managers or members of management committees to meet to share experiences, expertise or problems. Stutt, writing in 1997 pointed to difficulties arising from the absence of locally based and managed organisations working on a cross border basis in the border regions. The issue of the management of cross border projects more generally has recently attracted the attention of the Northern Ireland Affairs Committee of the House of Commons as part of their investigation and report into the Peace II programme. This report (House of Commons, 2003) noted that the managing authority for the Peace II programme was the new cross border Implementation Body, the Special European Union Programme Body. The Select Committee noted difficulties (p.43) in running programmes which provide a radical customized bottom-up approach and which is simultaneously a top down structural funds programme. It called up on the Minister of Finance to take urgent personal management charge of the Peace Programme although in practice it could be viewed as a responsibility of the North-South Ministerial Council.

There is actually in place a mechanism for the dissemination of European practice in cross border co-operation LACE-TAP (Linkage Assistance and Co-operation for the European Border Regions – Technical Assistance and Promotion) was established by the Association of European Border Regions as the observatory for cross border co-operation. LACE-TAP has 12 offices throughout Europe and an office for the Ireland/Northern Ireland Border region has been set up in Monaghan which disseminates information and organizes seminars and study visits. The European Commission through the LACE-TAP has published a Practical Guide to Cross Border Co-operation involving local authorities (European Commission, 1997). This and subsequent documentation show that the Irish experience is not dissimilar to European experience in terms of initial development based on individual initiatives, identifying potential, working to develop objectives and implement a project or in terms of project content with schemes in transport, environment, tourism and SMEs. Christiansen (1999) argues that many cross border endeavours in the rest of Europe, like Ireland are low-key. However, there is often more emphasis in LACE-TAP publications on the establishment of structures with technical/administrative, financial and decision-making capacities. Examples can be found of very large projects with advanced structures more akin to forms of regional government and administration such as EUREGIO with an independent legal status and its own authority and staff with high level political representation or PANIMA on the German-French Border which comprises representatives of the regional government with a cross border secretariat. Shelbeck (2001) suggests that in contrast to these formal regional structures, local government co-operation arises more spontaneously.

Loughlin (2000) sees forms of 'network governance' as providing the necessary institutional design for cross border collaboration based on more open, horizontal and flexible administrative and management practices and arrangements rather than traditional, hierarchial, vertical and closed structures.

Barriers to Co-operation

Cross border co-operation and its development has also to be seen in the context of overcoming barriers to co-operation. Local government co-operation differs from most other sectors of co-operation in that it is highly politicized through the predominant role played by local politicians. Cross border co-operation is still a sensitive political issue among many councillors who represent unionist parties. O'Dowd and Corrigan (1995) showed that practical economic co-operation was acceptable to most unionist councillors but support was divided for development into other areas. There still appears to be a lack of political will in councils outside the border areas to give much importance to cross border co-operation and nationalist councillors dominate in border areas. The study found some examples of political difficulty but every cross border management committee identified included councillors from unionist parties and some councillors did refer to a major attitudinal change to cross border activity. The position of councillors from the South is somewhat different in that they tend to be very positive towards cross border co-operation but it is not of major importance to them.

The degree of cross border co-operation not surprisingly reduces with distance from the border for reasons of geography and politics. It is more difficult to identify common interests in areas away from the border. One nationalist council in North Antrim reported difficulty in sustaining linkages although some councils located further from the border do have links and the distance factor becomes less significant in the context of wider links with councils other countries.

I have already referred to the mismatch of council functions as inhibiting cross border co-operation and this was widely acknowledged as a barrier. The major problems are the Northern council's lack of responsibility for housing, planning, roads and fire services and for Southern councils lack of responsibility for economic development, community services and tourism. The areas where a local authority can work directly with a local authority across the border are quite limited.

Although there has been substantial funding from the EU, the issue of adequate and sustained funding presents difficulties. Basically local authorities throughout Ireland are not funded by the respective central governments for cross border working. Central authorities in Dublin and Belfast may not be entirely aware of the scope and nature of cross border co-operation and the need for adequate financing may not be recognized given the availability of EU funds. A further obstacle identified was a lack of communication between councils across the border even at the level of Chief Executive and County Manager. Councils, staff and politicians generally do not have detailed knowledge of how local government works in the other jurisdiction. There are also significant differences in the operation of councils. County managers in the South have more powers than chief executives in the North. There may also be differences in the category or grade or profession of officials who take on responsibilities for cross border working. Local authorities are also often implementing nationally set social and public policies and there are significant policy and legislative differences in areas such as housing, planning and waste management.

Other barriers which inhibit co-operation relate more to all forms of cross border working, e.g., differences in employment law, recognition of professional qualifications, differences in health and safety measures and in tax and social security (PriceWaterhouseCoopers, 2001).

Conclusions

Despite the range of functional, structural, political and management difficulties cross border co-operation involving local authorities has been of significance in the border areas. The three local authority networks have provided a degree of strategic vision for economic and infrastructural developments along the border. The practical achievements are most clearly to be found in the promotion of ICT, SMEs, community enterprises, tourism, environmental and cultural activities. A major achievement has also been the establishment of working relationships across the border although in terms of the whole scenario of local government activity cross border co-operation is still a small element. Cross border co-operation is not a statutory responsibility of local authorities. The North-South Ministerial Council and the Implementation bodies have sought to encourage co-operation in areas of local government services, an approach based on, an approach one commentator has described as 'establishing patterns of contacts between elites' (Coakley, 2001) but such an approach may not be as effective as a bottom-up approach. While this paper has discussed the structural factors influencing the development of cross border co-operation it is worth noting that a number of items have forced their way on to the cross border agenda involving local authorities either directly, in partnership or in a lobbying role, in such areas as waste management, environmental awareness, roads and emergency services. The key structural problems remain the mismatch of functions, the limitations on functions and lack of mainstream finance plus political volatility. The potential for more effective cross border co-operation would be enhanced by more funding, more specialist project management and more focused administrative arrangements.

References

Adshead, M. and Quinn, B. (1998), *The Move From Government to Governance: Irish Development Policy's Paradigm Shift*, Policy and Politics 26.2, 209–226.

Ball, M. (1992), *Twinning and the Enabling Authority, Local Government Studies* 18.3, pp.226–39.

Birrell, D. and Hayes, A. (1999), *The Local Government System in Northern Ireland*, Institute of Public Administration (Dublin).

———, (2001), *Cross Border Co-operation in Local Government. Centre for Cross Border Studies* (Armagh).

Carroll, D. (2000), Local Authorities, *More than Service Providers* (Institute of Public Administration Dublin).

Christiansen, T. (1999), '*The Bigger Picture' No Frontiers North South Integration in Ireland Democratic Dialogue* (Belfast).

Coakley, J. (2001), North-South Co-ordination in Wilson, R. (ed.), *A Guide to The Northern Ireland Assembly* (Stationery Office, Belfast).

Co-operation Ireland/ADM/CPA (1999), *Border Crossings, Lessons from the Peace Programme* (Belfast).

European Commission (1997), *Practical Guide to Cross Border Co-operation* (Brussels).

Greer, J. (2000), *Local Authority Cross Border Networks: Lessons in Partnership and North-South Co-operation in Ireland* 48.1, pp.52–68 (Aldershot: Administration).

———. (2001), *Partnership Governance in Northern Ireland: Improving Performance* (Aldershot: Ashgate Publishing).

House of Commons (2003), *Peace II Northern Ireland* Affairs Committee Volume 1 (Stationery Office, London).

Hughes, J., Knox, C. Murray, M. and Greer, J. (1998), *Partnership Governance in Northern Ireland* (Oaktree Press, Dublin).

Loughlin, J. (2000), *The Cross Border Challenges and Opportunities Posed by the Transformation of European Governance.* Conference Paper (QUB).

O'Dowd, L. and Corrigan, T. (1995), *Buffer Zone or Bridge: Local Responses to Cross Border Economic Co-operation in the Irish Border Region* 42.4, pp.335–351 (Administration).

O'Maolain, C. (2000), *North-South Co-operation in Tourism* (Centre for Cross Border Studies, Armagh).

PriceWaterhouseCoopers (2001), *Study of Obstacles to Mobility* (North/South Ministerial Council, Armagh).

Shelbeck, W. (2001), EUREGIO, *Pioneer in the Practice of European Cross Border Co-operation* 49.2, pp.35–47(Administration).

Stutt, C. (1997), *Cross Border and North-South Co-operation,* in Review of Northern Ireland Administrative Arrangements (Belfast).

Tannam, E. (1999), *Cross Border Co-operation in the Republic of Ireland and Northern Ireland* (Macmillan, Basingstoke/St.Martins, New York).

Walsh, J., Craig, S. and McCafferty, D. (1998), *Local Partnerships for Social Inclusion* (Oaktree, Dublin).

Chapter 15

Towards an Hypothetical Regional Plan for the Dublin-Belfast Corridor

John Yarwood
Former Director, Urban Institute, Ireland

Introduction

Whilst we were preparing the conference on the 'Dublin-Belfast Corridor 2025', it became evident that there was no clear, common understanding of what such a corridor would constitute on the ground. I do not refer here to its economic function or other abstract attributes and aspects, but rather to its concrete configuration. The organising group therefore felt that we should prepare a hypothetical 'design' of a physical type, in order to communicate a general vision and allow it to be tested in discussion. This chapter describes such a plan.

To prepare a competent, authoritative plan would be a major undertaking, of course, and we were in no position to do that. We did feel, however, that it would be both possible and helpful to evoke a general picture illustrative of key principles. We also felt that only by looking at the totality of the corridor would it be possible to manage its emergence. A rational corridor plan could not emerge from a set of local plans, such as those mentioned by McEldowney and O'Connell, being "glued together", (which is what tends to have happened hitherto.) On the contrary, the overarching corridor concept would provide the framework from which the set of local plans should be developed.

We set up a series of design brainstorming sessions, often called 'charettes', which were held in UCD and Queens University Belfast. Members[1] mostly knew the physical region very well, and we used coloured pens and large sheets of tracing paper over large scale base maps. These were then developed into

---

[1]   The participants in the charettes included Bill Morrison, (Professor at the University of Ulster and former Belfast City Architect and Planning Officer), Dr William Hynes, (Dept. of Regional and Urban Planning at UCD), Malachy McEldowney, (Professor of Environmental Planning at Queen's University Belfast, Sean O'Laoire, (Consultant with Murray O'Laoire, Dublin), and two of his staff, plus Henk van der Kamp, (Acting Head of Urban Planning Dept at Dublin Institute of Technology), and John Yarwood, (Director of the Urban Institure Ireland, UCD).

electronic presentation maps for the conference, but here we show the hand-drawn graphics: *Figure 15.1, Legend for Corridor Plan Drawings. Figure 15.2 Dublin-Belfast Corridor Plan: All Sections. Figure 15.3, Dublin-Belfast Corridor Plan: Southern Section. 15.4, Dublin-Belfast Corridor Plan: Central Section. Figure 15.5, Dublin-Belfast Corridor Plan: Northern Section.*

The first part of this chapter begins by postulating four general physical characteristics of a corridor, with the principles underlying them. The second part applies these characteristics to the specific Dublin-Belfast case, and presents a hypothetical layout. Lastly we discuss several issues or dilemmas connected with implementation of the corridor.

To begin with however, we revisit the question of whether the corridor exists at all. Whereas almost everyone talks confidently as if it does exist, (probably because it seems so logical that people assume it must or, at least, should do so) such evidence as we have casts doubt on its actual existence. The main commuting linkages from Dublin are westwards into Kildare, rather than northwards towards Belfast. It also seems that the urban growth in towns outside the metropolitan area is relatively small, and provides no evidence of major economic development, and that Dublin is a primate city, or to put it differently, the region is not polycentric. In Chapter 9 van Egeraat and Sokol come to similar conclusions, based on the low connectivities of towns outside Dublin. Finally, in Chapter 12 Chris Paris demonstrates that both cities are growing roughly evenly in several directions, and that the supposed corridor arises only because the two commuting hinterlands are beginning to coalesce.

It does seem that the growth of Dublin at least is driven by the search for readily available housing land more than employment land and that many location decision makers looking for business sites feel that only the metropolis is sufficiently well connected to merit their attention. This results in the creation of dormitory towns, with employment in growth sectors being quite highly focused in the metropolitan area, with much long-distance commuting and congestion at central points as a result. The emergence of corridors in this situation is just the creation of dormitory 'strips' along main radials. It is not a polycentric phenomenon, which would imply that the main settlements should attract employment in ratio with residences.

But this will not readily happen unless the regional planners can create a level of connectedness and accessibility which allows other nodal points to compete in these terms with the metropolitan nodes in the view of business. Another key factor in location choice for business will be access to markets, meaning the size of markets (for labour, skills, property, customers and suppliers) as well the various travel costs. However, for housing (in the case of Ireland), many purchasers welcome a certain sense of remoteness and ruralism.

The corridor into Kildare, for example, may work well for dormitory purposes, but business is looking for other attributes. The destination beyond Kildare is Galway and it is relatively small as well as a long way away. A Dublin-Galway axis would not help much to create a bigger or more accessible market for those locating along such an axis. Other examples are in principle the same, except for the Dublin-Belfast case. The linearity of a corridor form may carry certain advantages arising from its geometry, provided it is not too long or attenuated, whereas a 'spider' form could be less efficient in promoting connectivity and minimising journey costs.

My opinion is that only the Dublin-Belfast corridor could work as an economic growth engine for this island, because it can bring a relatively large population within a zone of relatively low travel cost and is 'wired' into several ports, airports and universities, (as well as established clusters). There is no alternative with the same scale or assets. But why then is it not emerging already, even though many people have talked as if it were?

The reason may be that such a phenomenon needs strong leadership from the state level if it is to overcome the inertia of the natural conservatism of the business community. Whereas, the householder may willingly seek isolation, the businessperson wants the reassurance of being part of a clearly emerging trend. He or she rarely seizes the initiative ahead of the generality, because they need many other parts of the 'jigsaw' to be reasonably assured.

Some other authors in this book have written as if the two governments had already wholeheartedly espoused the corridor project, but my impression is that we have not yet reached that point. Certainly it is fashionable to speak as if we had, but no-one has yet commissioned a planning study on the topic, and only a group of academics would be sufficiently brave or foolish to stick their necks out. There is some opposition certainly, caused by the fear of weakening the potential of the remoter parts of the island, although Cussen and Hetherington addressed this in their chapter. But in any event, this book ends with an attempt to outline the sort of physical plan which one might expect to emerge from a planning study of the traditional sort, in the hope that it might cause readers to coalesce around a shared image, and stimulate further progress.

Four General Characteristics of the Corridor

Multi-Modal Movement Spine

Our design workshops postulated four elements of a multi-modal movement spine, roughly in parallel, and linked together at nodal points referred to as 'interchanges'. These elements are described below.

- **High Speed Train, (HST).** This service would stop infrequently, and might either have a new, separate right of way or share that of the stopping service, depending upon detailed study. It would connect from Central Dublin (Docklands) to Larne via a station west of Dublin Airport, Drogheda-Navan, Dundalk-Newry, and Central Belfast.

- **Local Stopping Rail.** This would be based on the existing line, with frequent stops. The branch to Navan would be reopened.
- **High Speed Road and Fast Bus.** This would be the motorway in the Republic, becoming a dual-carriageway north of the Border. Spur roads connecting to local towns would be infrequent.
- **District or Principal Road and Local Bus.** This road would parallel the High Speed Road, and would provide frequent exits to access local developments.

The point of a multi-modal arrangement is to allow travellers to optimize the best attributes of each mode, and to make it relatively easy to combine different modes in the same journey.

There would be several types of interchange. Rail-rail interchange would allow travellers to move from a slow train to a fast train, by crossing a platform, and the timetables would minimize waiting times. Road-rail interchange would be facilitated by car parks at stations. High speed rail access would entail multi-storey car parks above stations. Road-road interchange would occur at the spurs from high speed roads. Freight terminals should be planned at a few key places where main employment centres are located.

Buses would be highly coordinated with both road and rail. Their special attribute is flexibility, of course. Within the corridor, residents or workers in small towns, villages and rural areas would travel by bus or car to rail stations. The aim in urbanized areas should be to achieve an attractive standard of walking distance and frequency for buses. Bus priority measures will be needed in historic towns.

Integration of Land Use and Activity Pattern with Movement Interchanges

In general, such interchanges will become the points of highest accessibility (or 'location potential') if the planning is done with skill. The location and density of activity should therefore be closely coordinated with the movement system. Useful data exists which relates the patronage levels of public transport to variables such as walking distance to a station or stop, frequency of service, connectivity by these services to other destinations, the various convenience and comfort factors, including the availability of information, and so on. Coordinated planning should optimise public transport patronage.

There might be major business parks clustered around the main interchanges. The minor type of interchange should have minor business parks and high density housing around them. Similarly, local centres, schools and medium density housing should focus upon local interchange types. It will be necessary to allow an integrated movement system design to direct the land use allocations, density regulations and architectural layout. Detailed design is required, particularly of footpaths and shelters since pedestrian movement is an important component of the strategy. Prosser and I discuss this topic in Chapter 8 and mention some Irish cases, including the Cork Area Strategic Plan, (CASP), which exemplifies some important points.[2]

Such coordination on the ground is most likely to be implemented if the identified land is pro-actively 'delivered', as Scott, Redmond and Moore discuss in Chapter 10. This could be done by public acquisition, or by public-private partnership action. For example, investment in rail, road and site servicing projects could be cross-financed by private firms from the enhanced value of nearby land.

Also, land delivery may not be successful in promoting development of the right type in the right place if no effort is made it is to stop development in the wrong place, (which means its inaccessibility to a public transport spine). The planning authorities should limit more strictly than hitherto the creation of ultra low density housing in rural areas or open country, since this is likely to boost car dependency and so undermine the strategy outlined here. The undisciplined scattering of development of any type is a bad thing, particularly in the context of corridor development. Indeed, the corridor could do a lot of harm in the long term if control of development were weak, because the enhanced efficiency of movement and increased accessibility would then lead to an even broader spatial spread of development, leading to an ever increasing demand for movement, and creating ever-increasing congestion via a positive feedback loop.

We should not speak of a movement corridor simply, but perhaps of the *Integrated Movement and Activity Corridor.*

Retaining Community Identity, Accommodating Development to Landscape Context and avoiding 'Sprawl'

As one drives or walks around the territory within the latent corridor, one is struck by the insensitivity of much recent development from an aesthetic standpoint. The scale is not the issue, but rather the rupture between the suburban style or the repetitive, mass form of the new in relation to the richness and *sui generis* idiosyncrasy of the old, as well as the rupture between the crass assertiveness of the new and the inflected subtleties of the contextual landscape. Phil Geoghegan makes these points in Chapter 11.

The risk is that a hundred mile strategic diagram might be transformed from paper directly into local action on the ground, without an intervening stage of mediation, able to recognize the *genus loci,* which is to say, the trees and hedgerows, streams, walls, vistas, topography and rich heritage unique to each of a thousand different places. Important are the settlement boundaries or edges, so that

---

[2]   See Cork County Council and Cork Corporation 2000. The plan envisaged a rail-based corridor development between Midleton and Blarney, in which urban growth was clustered around a series of stations. The consultants, Atkins Ireland, undertook some detailed studies to estimate patronage levels, but they have not been published. The Suburban Rail Study, prepared by Ove Arup and Partners, concluded that the Cork rail spine was viable and recommended that it receive government funding.

areas of distinct identity do not co-allesce. The view from the surrounding landscape of each development should be designed in a crisp and elegant way, so that each place 'sits' harmoniously, with a definite boundary and a becoming modesty. The Irish local planning system does not do this job very well, and one recoils with horror to think what might happen if the implementation system for the corridor broke down in detail.

The risk is the emergence of suburban *sprawl* along a hundred miles, in which local uniqueness was seriously compromised. The concept must recognize this not only at an aesthetic level, but equally in terms of local economy, society and cultural activity.

Each town or subregion within the corridor should be supported in the development of its own unique activity and identity, because it is ultimately from the interaction of these distinct but diverse elements in space that the mega-city region would derives its quality.

Helping a Polycentric Settlement Structure to Emerge

A corridor is simply a linear polycentric mega-city region. There are other types of structure, of course, but in all cases, certain questions have to be answered about its rationale. There are three basic points to make here. They concern first, the compactness of the urban form; second, the internal balance between activity types or land uses within each urban centre, thirdly, the size, number and distribution of distinct urbanized centres.

The first point is that each important urban centre should be fairly compact. By this term we mean that it should have a definite boundary, and within that a reasonably high density. This is the opposite of urban 'sprawl'. First, a sprawling form will fail to generate adequate patronage levels for public transport. Also, physical and social infrastructure service provision will be uneconomic, with regrettable consequences for pollution of groundwater as well as social sustainability. Secondly, there will be aesthetic consequences. The rural areas of the corridor will be increasingly suburbanized, and the character of the landscape will be compromised.

The next point concerns 'self containment', which means that most people living in a town should also work in the same place. As Chapter 5 shows, the Dublin hinterland counties have about half the resident population commuting elsewhere, (mainly to Dublin itself) for employment, whilst less than two thirds of the work force of Dublin actually lives there. Currently the Dublin area is not polycentric, but, (to simplify), comprises a single city surrounded by dormitory towns, and the entirety is thought to be unsustainable for this reason, (amongst others). The solution in principle, would involve the creation of far more jobs in urban centres currently with low ratios of jobs to resident workers. It would also be advisable to facilitate the relocation of residents when they move to a job in a different town, by (for example) abolishing stamp duty.

The third point concerns the question of whether a small number of large growth centres is preferable to a large number of small growth centres, and how in either case the location pattern of centres should be structured. Both the National Spatial Strategy and the Regional Planning Guidelines for the Greater Dublin Area, (discussed in Chapters 3 to 6) postulate a 'Settlement Hierarchy', which defines a typology of settlement functions and sizes. The 'Gateway' function envisages a highly self-sufficient town with a self-sustaining economic dynamic, capable of servicing a region. This is thought to require a population of 40 to 60,000 people. The 'Major Growth Town' would be dependant for some services on an adjacent city, whilst being above the critical mass necessary for a diverse and dynamic local economy. This is not likely to work if smaller than 15,000 people, and would then be likely to become a dormitory for the city. Below this population, the town would be best regarded as a rural or subregional service centre. The hierarchical concept helps (a) to obtain a spatial spread of service and so maximize the accessibility of a dispersed population to urban services, whilst also (b) allowing maximum concentration and the achievement of critical mass at certain focal points, (which is required to establish service viability). The task is to balance the objectives of accessibility/spread and critical mass/quality, which are potentially in contradiction.

I am postulating that Newry-Dundalk, located at the mid-point of the corridor, has the potential to become the second-tier city of the corridor. Intuitively, I think this will become the third largest city on the island (after Belfast and Dublin) at some point in the new century. I think that the third-tier cities will arise between Newry-Dundalk and (a) Belfast and (b) Dublin at the points with important interchanges.

The pro-active facilitation of such a pattern will help avoid the tendency for the corridor to become an elongated suburb of Dublin in the south and Belfast in the north. Then the intended corridor would become merely a 'tunnel'. This appears to be the current trend, and Chapter 5 shows that Drogheda and other towns around Dublin have low self-containment and major levels of out-commuting. In other words, they are dormitory ex-urbs parasitic upon Dublin. This would imply high levels of inter-urban commuting, and success in developing efficient linkages would not have the effect of enhancing a polycentric region, but on the contrary, would lead to ever-increasing and ultimately unsustainable travel demand.

Report on the Corridor Plan

Greater Dublin Area

We have incorporated the Greater Dublin Area Regional Planning Guidelines into our corridor plan. This is discussed in Chapter 6, but we briefly recapitulate it again here, for the sake of completeness. Five 'satellite' towns are proposed, namely Drogheda, Navan, Maynooth, Naas-Newbridge and Wicklow. They would experience major managed growth. The 'jobs ratio' would rise substantially from 0.5 or 0.6 to 0.7 or 0.8, or, in other words, the development in these towns would be markedly jobs-led in future.

The towns would be linked together by a road, which has already been the subject of study. It is referred to as 'DOOR', or the Dublin Outer Orbital Route.[4] The five towns already lie on the main radial roads out of Dublin leading to the other key cities and regions of Ireland. There are railway lines roughly parallel to the radial roads. The satellites thus would lie at the intersections of the radial and the orbital routes.

There is an outer ring of eight towns which lie on another orbital route, further out than DOOR. The towns are, (from north to south) Dundalk, Ardee, Kells, Mullingar, Tullamore, Portlaoise, Carlow and Enniscorthy. They are already connected orbitally by a route, (comprising the N52 and the N80). The National Roads Authority has included in its long-range strategic programme the upgrading of this route. The radial railway lines, which connect to the inner five satellites from Dublin, travel further outwards, to the outer ring of eight towns, (and ultimately travel to the other cities of Ireland on the west and south coasts (such as Sligo, Galway, Limerick, Cork, Waterford, and Rosslare).

Refer to the plans shown in Chapter 6 illustrating the Regional Planning Guidelines. To sum up, the future regional structure of Greater Dublin resembles a half wheel, with Dublin at the hub, radial rail/road spokes and three concentric, orbital rims, (namely the M50 Ring Road; the DOOR and the N52/N80 orbital beyond that). The strategy outlined in Chapter 6 also indicates the settlements and the investment nodes for employment parks should all fall within development corridors, around the various multi-modal movement channels, and specifically should be clustered closely around the major interchanges.

This chapter goes beyond the Regional Planning Guidelines in some respects, however. There is an unresolved debate about Dublin port, which is adjacent to major city-centre urban regeneration zones. A long tunnel, now under construction, connects the port to the northern fringes of the city and thence to the M1, the Belfast motorway. This may be technically sound in a narrow sense, but it is open to several policy objections nonetheless. The port capacity is currently too limited, and the matter requires ongoing consideration. The relocation of the port has been debated, involving a site at Loughshinny, a village on the coast a short distance beyond the outer suburbs to the north. In our hypothetical plan, we show the port at Loughshinny, in order to test its role in the corridor as a whole.

The hypothesis envisages the construction of a rail tunnel from Heuston station to Connelly station, which would allow the various radial railway routes to be connected, so that services could connect across the city and allow through working, so integrating public transport for the entire city-region and beyond. The

---

tunnel project received in principle approval from the government over a year ago. From Connelly station, lines could be extended into the docklands area. If the docks had by then been relocated to Loughshinny, a huge area at the heart of the city would become available for development. This area would contain both Ireland's main railway terminal and its main ferry port. The land lies immediately adjacent to the countries' financial services centre. The centre of Dublin has serious traffic congestion, but the road tunnel would pass below the city and link a major docklands regeneration into the Belfast motorway and the corridor towns. This would create a lower level of congestion and high accessibility, which together with excellent public transport services would be able to support high densities of development. The High Speed Train (HST) terminal would also be there, with the first stop at Dublin International Airport.

Turning now to the railway and the airport, the hypothesis is that the airport terminal, (much expanded as has been proposed), is rebuilt at the western end of the runways. (The present terminal is at the eastern end). The present plan is to connect the airport to Dublin by a light rail link into the city, but this fails to recognize the opportunity to integrate the airport into the corridor as a whole. Taking a more visionary point of view, this hypothesis envisages an HST line connecting the proposed Dublin Docklands terminal via an upgraded Maynooth line to the western side of the airport, and thence along the entire corridor via Drogheda/Navan, Newry/Dundalk, Central Belfast and finally Larne, with its short ferry crossing to Scotland.

Is it possible to imagine that by 2050, engineering techniques might make it feasible to enable the train to pass by tunnel or bridge from Larne to Scotland, so that one could get on the sleeper in Dublin and wake up in Glasgow, Edinburgh, Manchester or Lille. Perhaps this goes too far, but the real point here is that with no 'corridor thinking', we tend to see decision areas in isolation. The question is posed as 'how can we connect Dublin Airport to Dublin city centre?' A better question might be 'how can the airport play the strongest role in developing a mega-city region for Ireland?'

Central Section of the Corridor

The central section is illustrated in Figure 16.2 Hypothetical Corridor Plan: Central Section.

Navan and Drogheda
Drogheda has little expansion potential in a eastwards direction, due to the steep sided river valley where the small port facility is located. To the west, north and south, the M1 motorway by-pass provides access potential. Here, however, particular attention would have to be paid to the impact on the Boyne Valley. The town is already planned to expand north and south in the County Development Plan, and here we have envisaged a loop road that serves both north and south expansion land, connecting them together with a bridge crossing the river on the

east side of town. Both ends of the loop road would connect into the existing M1 motorway. From the southernmost intersection, the Dublin Outer Orbital Route (DOOR) would begin. It would travel westwards to a point south of Navan, and then swing south to Maynooth and thence Naas.

The HST line, which we discussed above, would travel from Dublin northwards, parallel to the N2 road past Ashbourne to a point just south of Navan, and then turn east as far as the west side of Drogheda, where it would cross the existing Drogheda-Navan rail branch line, approaching the town on its west side. From here it would travel northwards parallel to the new M1 motorway, in the direction of Belfast. In this vicinity, (west of Drogheda), there would be a major multi-purpose investment node, clustered around an important modal interchange. It would be, in effect, an urban expansion westwards of Drogheda (as the town currently exists), and would be connected to it by local distributor roads. There would be another, (perhaps smaller), investment node south of Navan, served by the HST line, the Navan branch line and the DOOR.

The government already commissioned Ove Arup and Partners to consider the proposal to reopen the (existing but discontinued) Navan branch line that connects into the main Dublin-Belfast line at Drogheda. They found that it would not be viable. From my experience with the Cork-Midleton branch line, which was approved in the same study, I suspect that the Navan project failed because the proposal did not include sufficient development close to stations. Here, therefore, we envisage historic and new stations being opened with village growth clustered around stations, as well as the two investment nodes served by stations. Of course, development with no attractive station access possibilities might not be viewed favourably.

The existing main line between Dublin and Drogheda would also access the new Dublin port envisaged at Loughshinny. The line would have to be slightly diverted, and here we propose an investment zone associated with the port. This would be immediately adjacent to the M1 Dublin-Belfast motorway. A new railway station and freight depot would be located at the port. This line would also have more housing development clustered around historic or new stations, in order to ensure that 5,000 persons live within walking distance of each station.

The main landscape factors are, firstly, the coastal strip, with beaches, lagoons, low cliffs, ornithological sites, pleasant historic villages and historic fortifications, and secondly, the Boyne Valley, which is an area of great natural beauty, historic and numerous archaeological sites. Considerable study would be needed to allow the strategic planning ideas to be turned into a serious project.

Newry/Dundalk
The idea of a twin mini-metropolis here has been much discussed in the recent past. The hypothesis is that the two towns should be developed as an integrated 'linear cluster city'. The towns are separated by a ten-mile belt of hills, characterized by landscape of natural beauty, as well as a serious insecurity problem in the recent past. However, the topographic difficulties for development

can be exaggerated, and there are large areas of relatively flat land. The most practical approach to planning may be a string of development zones, tied together by a local movement spine, rather like a string of beads.

This town has the potential for major growth beyond that of any other centre in the corridor. It appears to be the 'hinge' of the corridor as a whole. Travelling from Dublin towards Derry and the north west of the island, one would use the M1 to Dundalk and turn left. Travelling from Belfast towards Galway, Limerick and the south-west of the island, one would use the corridor south to Dundalk and turn right. Furthermore, the outermost orbital route around Greater Dublin connects back into the north-south corridor spine at Dundalk.

Dundalk is also at the mid-point of the corridor, and is by far the most self-contained urban centre, or to put it another way, it has a low proportion of both in-commuting and out-commuting, as Chapter 5 makes clear. This means it lies beyond the reach of Dublin, and probably Belfast likewise, with the potential to be an autonomous and self-sustaining growth engine. This is the best place to create really major growth, because it would avoid the risk of becoming a suburban extension of either city. The combined population of the immediate subregion is already approaching 100,000, and it is plausible to contemplate its rapid growth, reaching 200,000 by the middle of the present century.

One gains the impression that local political and business leaders are tantalized by the potential for integrating the economies of the two places. It may be a little frightening in its radical flavour, but time passes, and people will grow quite quickly comfortable with the logic of the proposition. In recent years there are signs of growing prosperity, confidence and local pride. Cross border cooperation and institution-building are proceeding apace, as Birrell makes clear in Chapter 14.

We turn next to consider some hypothetical ideas for a physical plan. The existing railway would have new and existing stations used to move people locally within the new city and external destinations in the corridor. The HST line would share the same right of way between Dunleer, south of Dundalk, and the northern edge of Newry. From here a new HST track would parallel the A1 as far as Lisburn at the southern fringe of the Belfast Metropolitan Area. It would pass Banbridge, but a station there would probably be too frequently spaced to be practical. The existing line from Newry via Portadown and Lurgan would be retained and function as a local service. The HST line would have a single station for both Newry and Dundalk located half way between them.

The current proposals of the government of Northern Ireland envisage a dual carriageway below motorway standard connecting the M1 in the Republic at the border to Belfast, bypassing Newry, Banbridge and Dromore. In this proposal, it would be paralleled by the HST route mentioned above. The local trains would share a platform with it at this station, with coordinated timetables and through baggage handling services.

The existing Dundalk town would be expanded on its west side as far as the M1 motorway, but not beyond it. A separate cluster of development would lie south of here, expanding Blackrock westwards to the motorway. Quality of ground and flood risk limits the scope for expansion north and east. However, a multi-use investment node is envisaged on the north, with a freight depot, having road and rail access, as well as a function servicing the nearby port at Greenore, (and connecting via a river bridge to the port at Warrenpoint).

Development north of here would include two key elements. Opportunities for shared north/south projects would be developed, such as (a) an all-island joint government centre, with presence of international institutions as well; a north/south 'multiversity' or academic institution, and an all-Ireland stadium or sports complex, and (b) a leisure-oriented zone, including country clubs, countryside resort complexes, and a rural villa or second home cluster at very low densities. Thirty years ago, the government of the Republic commissioned such a design for a Government Centre in Dundalk, but the emerging 'Troubles' put a stop to progress.

The wider area had a higher degree of political independence in the Middle Ages than it has more recently had, being sandwiched between two great lordships, so that the past contains some interesting echoes of what might emerge in the future.

Newry itself would be expanded primarily on its northern side and its north west side in the direction of Bessbrook. The topography around the town is rather difficult, in contrast to Dundalk, which although close by, has extensive flat land.

Northern Section of the Corridor: Belfast Metropolitan Area and Larne

The new HST route would enter central Belfast from the southern suburbs via a tunnel to a central interchange, and travel thence via Newtownabbey and Ballynure to Larne and the ferry to Scotland. However, Belfast as a metropolitan area has a rather dispersed structure, with many areas quite poorly connected to the core. This gives rise to the question as to how they can be integrated most effectively into the corridor. During our charettes on the corridor, we addressed this important question, and we concluded that the most convincing and appealing idea was, (what we called) the *'Figure of Eight'*. This idea envisaged two road/rail loops structuring west Belfast and east Belfast, with the HST station at the cross-over point. This would deliver travellers from the various dispersed nodes to the spine of the corridor.

The eastern loop within the 'Figure of Eight' would connect the Centre-City Airport-Carnduff-Bangor-Newtownards-Comber-Carryduff-Centre. Part of this rail line exists already from the centre to Bangor. The proposal is to extend the line so as to access the various centres to the south-east of Carnduff and Bangor, and return the loop back to the starting point: (in other words to the centre). This investment would make best sense if the stations had infill development around them so as to maximize their patronage. The western loop within the Figure of Eight would connect the Centre-Lisburn-Glenavy-International Airport-Antrim-Centre. All of this line exists already, although some links have been closed to traffic. Upgrading would be needed. In this case also, the rail loop would have new stations around which development would be clustered.

It was also envisaged that the Figure of Eight be reinforced by road projects. On the east side, the various towns would be accessed by a new road which would leave the motorway spine of the corridor near Lisburn and travel along the east edge of the urban area to Bangor, where it would connect into the A2, so as to form an eastern loop. On the west side, the corridor spine road from Newry and Banbridge would cross the M2 to the airport, and thence across the M1 to Ballyclare and thence to Larne. The M1 and the M2 both lead to Belfast centre, and so this creates a loop system roughly parallel to the western rail loop.

The road/rail Figure of Eight would intersect with the corridor spine at the Central Belfast corridor interchange. It would be connected by a short rail link to the City Airport and the Ferry Terminal, which are located close by. This point of high accessibility would be the stimulus for a major urban regeneration project at Belfast docklands, somewhat similar to the idea described earlier for Dublin.

Within this system, the opportunity would arise to create several intermodal interchanges, between local rail, HST routes and major roads. These interchanges would be closely integrated with urban expansion sites and new investment nodes. The greatest such opportunity would obviously be at Belfast Docklands, where density could be very high, but other nodes should be studied, particularly where rail intersects with the M1, M2 and the spinal road, such as Antrim, Glenavy and Hillsborough. Finally, such a node arises at Larne port, where the HST line intersects with the corridor spine road and the existing Belfast-Larne commuter line.

Comments of Implementation

Anyone with practical experience of implementation of such strategies, and experience of Ireland as a whole, is bound at this point to express serious concerns about these propositions. They are likely to say that, although the technical studies might be done perfectly well, and they might confirm the feasibility and even the desirability of the plan, nevertheless, in reality, implementation might prove to be impossibly difficult. There are several arguments to support such an argument, but two in particular merit mention here.

The first argument is, (if we can express this in negative terms), that Irish political attitudes tend to the fundamentally parochial, or, (to look at it in a more positive vein), we tend to carry subsidiarity as far as we possibly can. The greater the cooperative vision entailed by the scale of the idea, the less likely is it that the necessary teamwork could arise. I attended many local political meetings about the Greater Dublin Area Regional Planning Guidelines in 2003/04, and before that about the Cork Area Strategic Plan. I was powerfully struck by the initial lack of interest in overarching concepts, and the intense focus upon the effects on small places and small groups, particularly if they are rurally rooted. The possible benefits or losses arising from large strategies upon small places were of little or no interest if this entailed collaboration with other places or groups, or seemed likely to involve the exercise of interdisciplinary thinking or centralized power. Talk of synergy led nowhere in the short run and the belief seemed to be that the whole adds up to not one jot more than the sum of the parts. If this is true for plans connecting adjacent counties, then we should imagine the difficulties across the border.

The other argument is to do with finance. The concept of cost-recovery is not popular at the grass roots, and this conditions the terms of political debate. The sort of ideas outlined here do cost someone a lot of money, and however favourable the economic or financial return may be, they can only be financed if the beneficiaries and consumers agree to pay for some portion of benefits or consumption, and also the enhancement of asset values attributed to the investment is, in sufficient part, recovered from the owners of the assets. The 2000 Planning and Development Act established the basis for this recovery of enhanced values , although it has been utilized but seldom. The value of land, (especially in the middle of the corridor,) may rise massively if the total concept is espoused officially, if the infrastructure is created, the land disposed of and the permissions are granted in a timely and orderly manner. The expectation is that this action and investment, (and the consequent rises in asset value), are a 'gift' from society to beneficiaries. Any attempt at cost recovery tends to be experienced as oppressive, and an attack on the rights of the owner. The general result is a failure to invest in public goods, and if this were the case here, then there would be a risk that such a project would turn out to be quite negative in its impacts.

The best approach to such dilemmas might, in the author's opinion, be to foster demand from the bottom up, since implementation by fiat from the top down might fly in the face of local mentalities. After the conference in Newry of September 2003 on the theme of the corridor, which was extremely well received and extensively reported in the media, there was some demand from senior and middle-ranking government officials for an informal cross-border 'policy community' to be created, with the aim of continuing the debate, and starting to develop and deepen the proposition of the corridor. This did not go ahead, and most of us agreed that, upon reflection, it would be an empty talking shop. In other words, there is still a leadership vacuum, and no-one has the brass neck or confidence in their authority to wave the corridor flag (as it were).

The author must therefore leave this question in the air, without any crisp answer. Some things are clear, at least. A corridor will be implemented in Ireland only with strong, albeit informal, cross-party political leadership from the top down, allied to a grass-roots support movement, probably led by the business community, coming together through a forum of a voluntaristic, non-governmental type, which would start by commissioning a visionary study, deeper and richer than anything we have been able to produce in this book.

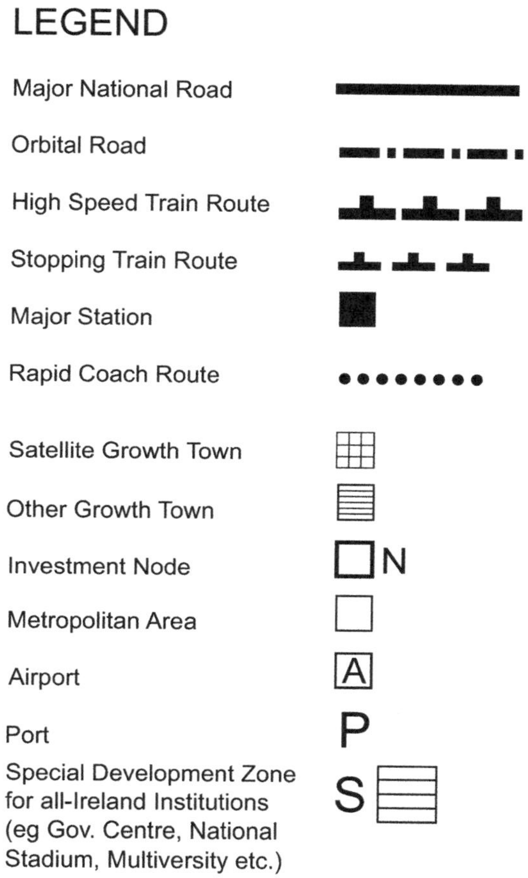

LEGEND

Major National Road	▬▬▬▬▬
Orbital Road	▬ ▪ ▬ ▪ ▬ ▪
High Speed Train Route	⟂ ⟂ ⟂
Stopping Train Route	⟂ ⟂ ⟂
Major Station	◼
Rapid Coach Route	••••••••
Satellite Growth Town	⊞
Other Growth Town	▤
Investment Node	□ N
Metropolitan Area	□
Airport	Ⓐ
Port	P
Special Development Zone for all-Ireland Institutions (eg Gov. Centre, National Stadium, Multiversity etc.)	S ▤

Figure 15.1   Legend for Corridor Plan Drawings

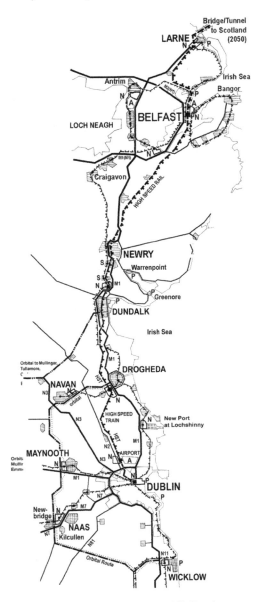

Figure 15.2   Dublin-Belfast Corridor Plan: All Sections

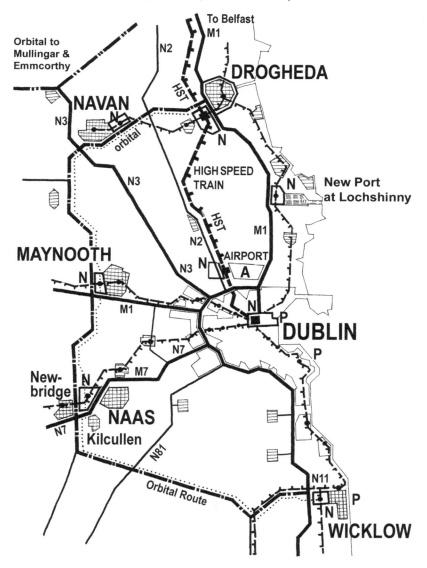

Figure 15.3   Dublin-Belfast Corridor Plan: Southern Section

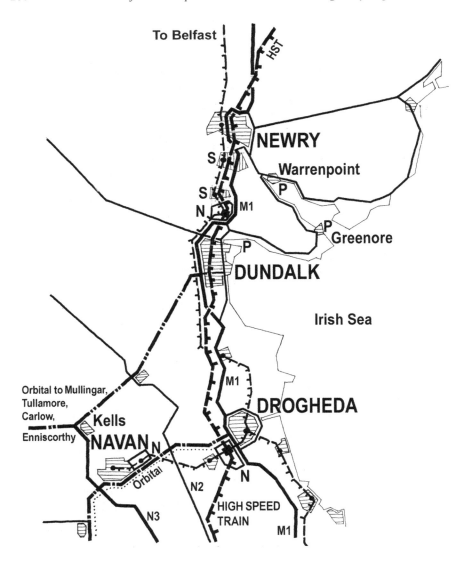

Figure 15.4   Dublin-Belfast Corridor Plan: Central Section

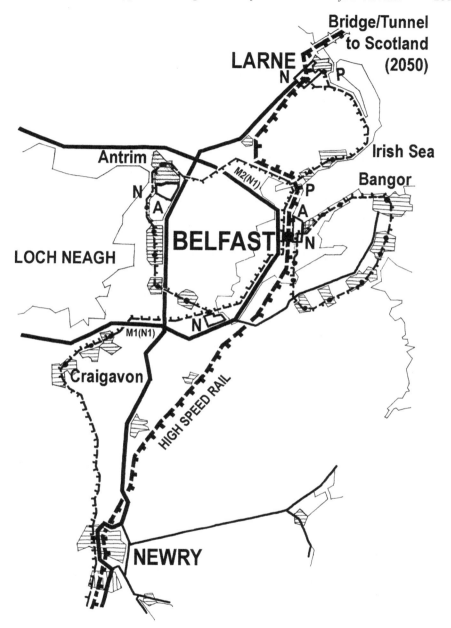

Figure 15.5   Dublin-Belfast Corridor Plan: Northern Section

Index

For Product Safety Concerns and Information please contact our EU representative GPSR@taylorandfrancis.com Taylor & Francis Verlag GmbH, Kaufingerstraße 24, 80331 München, Germany

Batch number: 08153795

Printed by Printforce, the Netherlands